The
Hell-Fire
Friars

Other titles by Gerald Suster also published by
Robson Books

*Champions of the Ring: The Lives and
Times of Boxing's Heavyweight Heroes*

*Generals: The Best and Worst
Military Commanders*

The Hell-Fire Friars

Gerald Suster

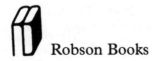

Robson Books

First published in Great Britain in 2000 by Robson Books,
10 Blenheim Court, Brewery Road, London N7 9NT

A member of the Chrysalis Group plc

British Library Cataloguing in Publication Data
A catalogue record for this title is available from the British
Library

ISBN 1 86105 345 2

Typeset by FiSH Books, London
Printed and bound in Great Britain by Creative Print &
Design (Wales), Ebbw Vale

Contents

Introduction 1

1 Sir Francis Dashwood (1708–81) 14

2 John Montagu, Earl of Sandwich (1718–92) 28

3 The Political, Religious and Sexual Context 35

4 The Influence 46

5 The Monks of Medmenham 61

6 William Hogarth 92

7 Medmenham Abbey 97

8 The Boot and the Petticoat 108

9 'That Devil Wilkes' 115

10 Mean and Vicious 122

11 West Wycombe 128

12 The Pagan Influence 134

13 Tantra 144

14 A Magical Mystery Tour 148

15 Freemasonry and Rosicrucianism 158

16 The Return of Wilkes 170

17 Doings of Dashwood   177

18 Weird Scenes Inside the Gold Mine   183

19 Twin-Sexed   189

20 A Freeman   191

21 The Franklin–Dashwood Book of Common Prayer   197

22 The Diplomacy of Franklin and Dashwood   202

23 'Liberty!'   208

24 John Wilkes: Pillar of the Establishment   212

25 The Survivors   217

26 Dashwood's Daughter   226

27 Pale Imitations   229

Conclusions   234

Appendix   239

Select Bibliography   242

Index   244

Introduction

Sex, politics and religion are probably the most interesting topics in life, other than art and science. Small wonder, then, that these three leading subjects were barred from discussion in Victorian gentlemen's clubs; and smaller wonder that they were the principal subjects of discussion in the gentlemen's clubs of the eighteenth century, particularly in that notable grouping commonly known as 'The Hell-Fire Club'. The popular scenario?

The Hell-Fire Club gloated over a naked virgin spreadeagled upon their altar. Sir Francis Dashwood drank greedily from a human skull, filled with the blood of freshly slaughtered human babies. His deputy, the Earl of Sandwich, blabbered barbarous incantations to Satan as his associates plotted to take over the government. John Wilkes MP, enemy of Sandwich and future Lord Mayor of London, suddenly released the baboon earlier presented to the Club by the Governor of Bengal, Sir Henry Vansittart. This baboon pounced upon Sandwich, who thought it was the Devil and who screamed for the mercy of Jesus...

This is an amusing story and given the comedy, perhaps it is a pity that it never took place. The truth is much more interesting than this silly legend. We are embarking upon a study which will raise questions about fact, myth and legend, about fiction, and about the nature of history. For instance, members of the alleged

1

'Hell-Fire Club' never used this ascription, calling themselves 'The Monks of Medmenham' or 'The Knights' or 'The Friars of St Francis of Wycombe'. Nevertheless, this grouping had an extraordinary effect upon affairs of the mid-eighteenth century. Part of the fascination of this scrutiny is that the many accounts vary vastly. Our enquiry becomes a quest after the elusive nature of truth itself.

'The Hell-Fire Friars', as their enemies termed them, were accused by many throughout the centuries, of orgies and Devil worship. Although they numbered many of the country's leading luminaries among their adherents, it seems that they never bothered to refute such crass allegations. As Bertrand Russell would later ask: 'Why get upset when silly people say silly things?' No one denies that there was a grouping of individuals around Sir Francis Dashwood, that they met at Medmenham Abbey on the Thames and at his nearby estate at West Wycombe, that this grouping lasted for twenty to thirty years and that, wittingly or unwittingly, there were serious political consequences. It has been alleged that members of the group dominated the government of Great Britain from 1762 to 1763 with the regime that the London mob derisively scorned as 'The Boot and the Petticoat'. It has been claimed that the internal quarrels of the Friars, most notably that between Sandwich and Wilkes, sparked off the rise of democracy in England. It has even been said that the Club was linked to other esoteric cabals in America, France and Germany, all of them professing a hidden wisdom and practising curious religious rites. There is finally the claim that when this grouping was dislodged from government officially, it went underground and proceeded to exercise strong unofficial influence.

Certainly a legend was launched. How much of it is true? 'What is Truth?' asked Pontius Pilate – but one is still waiting for an answer. The principal problem is that all who have studied this matter differ so widely in their conclusions. Established facts, once proven beyond reasonable doubt, form the basis of all historical work. Yet as Professor E.H. Carr has shown in his outstanding book, *What Is History?*, the art of the historian does not consist merely of relating the facts, since everything that has ever happened is a fact. It consists of *selecting* the facts which, consciously or unconsciously, the historian thinks to be significant in the ideological context of the time.

The historian emphasises the facts considered to be important from the perspective embraced, and neglects others. To some, the Knapton portrait of Sir Francis Dashwood is pregnant with significance of his beliefs but to others, it is a mere frivolity. It is impossible to find *objective* history.

In endeavouring to discern the truth about the Friars one encounters formidable difficulties. The first consists of the lack of documentary evidence. It is said that the steward, Paul Whitehead, spent the three days before his death painstakingly burning all papers. If he did, one wonders why. If he didn't, one wonders why it was said. There must have been *some* papers that no longer exist. If Whitehead didn't burn them, who did? No one even pretends to know. Just a few pages from Medmenham Abbey's cellar-books have survived, mere fragments dating from 1760 and now preserved at West Wycombe. These record bottles of wine issued to members under pseudonyms for their 'private devotions'. The names can be worked out without particular difficulty but all that is proved for certain is that ten men assumed false names and drank wine at Medmenham Abbey.

'Of the dozen and a half Franciscans who can tentatively be identified, only four put anything on record about the frolics of Medmenham: Dr Bates, John Wilkes, Charles Churchill and John Hall Stevenson,' Eric Towers writes in his scholarly study, *Dashwood: The Man and the Myth*. He adds: 'There is reason to doubt the truthfulness of all four.' Dr Benjamin Bates knew Dashwood as a friend for about twenty-five years. After the latter's death, he indignantly denied all accusations, declaring that the association consisted of genial gentlemen and insisting that it 'was most unjustly stigmatised by some of the scandalous and sarcastic fabrications of its contemporaries'. Possibly; though a cynic might agree with the comment Mandy Rice-Davies would make in court in two centuries' time and apply it to the testimony of Dr Bates:

'Well, he would, wouldn't he?'

John Wilkes stated that there was more to the activities at Medmenham than plenty of wine and a good, hearty dinner. There was fornication too. 'Among the amusement,' Wilkes continues, 'they had sometimes a mock celebration of the more ridiculous rites of the foreign religious orders, of the Church of Rome, of the Franciscans in particular...' Yet Wilkes states that he was never admitted to the chapter-room where these strange rites took place. His words were also written after a savage quarrel with the Friars. This conflict was so bitter that it nearly cost Wilkes his life, his livelihood and his liberty. Even so, there is no reason to doubt Wilkes's account of Dashwood's architecture and landscape gardening.

Charles Churchill, the poet, was a good friend to Wilkes and supported him during the latter's vicious quarrel with the Earl of Sandwich. This led Churchill to pen some biting satires. He had the intuition of a strong and genuine poet, he had eyes to see and ears to hear, but he was guessing from a hostile perspective, for in common with Wilkes, he never entered the chapter-room where the religious rites were celebrated.

John Hall Stevenson, graduate of Jesus College, Cambridge and friend of the author of *Tristram Shandy*, Laurence Sterne, met Dashwood via Wilkes. In consequence he took his Skelton Castle, near Middlesbrough, and remade it into Crazy Castle Hall as a venue for his own club, the Demoniacks. His book *Crazy Tales* was published in three volumes, including *The Confession of Sir F— of Medmenham and of the Lady Mary His Wife*. Of course, Lady Mary wasn't Dashwood's wife – it was Lady Sarah – but Stevenson tended to use the phrase 'Lady Mary' to denote lascivious aristocratic ladies. The tone of this piece, eventually published in 1795, varies from the satirical to the scurrilous to the simply silly.

During the eighteenth century, others less well connected contributed to the mythology of the Friars' activities. In 1765 Charles Johnstone published the third volume of his novel, *Chrysal: Or the Adventures of a Guinea*, which was written solely to make money but upon which so many writers on the Club have depended. The narrator is a guinea which passes from hand to hand, being possessed for a time in the palm of a character who is recognisably the Earl of Sandwich. Dashwood and John Wilkes can also be clearly recognised in this narrative, although Johnstone is wrong about every verifiable fact of Dashwood's life. Eric Towers is correct in calling him 'a timid pornographer'. The activities at Medmenham Abbey are described in a manner intended to be breathlessly lurid. Here we find the tale of Wilkes releasing a baboon as Sandwich invoked Satan: this was flagrantly plagiarised from Ned Ward's *The Secret History of Clubs* (1709). Unfortunately, *Chrysal* founded a legend of black magic and satanism.

More was to come from Sir Nathaniel Wraxall, whose *Historical Memoirs* were published in 1815. Wraxall tried to give the impression of being an insider even though he had never been remotely connected with the Dashwood circle. This did not stop him from writing:

> Rites of a nature so subversive of all decency, and calculated by an imitation of the ceremonies and mysteries of the Roman Catholic Church to render religion itself an object of contumely, were there celebrated, as cannot be reflected on without astonishment and reprobation. Sir Francis himself sometimes officiated as high priest, habited in the dress of a Franciscan monk, engaged in pouring a libation from a communion cup to the mysterious object of their homage.

'Who is this rascal?' George Selwyn asked when Wraxall entered White's: and Selwyn knew Dashwood well. So did Lord Monboddo, who called him 'The purest ourang-outang in Great Britain'. As the *Edinburgh Review* declared: 'Here *lies* Sir Nathaniel Wraxall'.

The New Foundling Hospital for Wits, 1771, edited by J. Almon, is no more than a book of jottings and jokes which on occasion employs techniques of juxtaposition and collage. The balance of evidence points to Wilkes and Churchill as the authors. One finds a few clues there, as one does in the writings of Horace Walpole, who knew of the Club and its members without being one himself and who commented acidly on the resulting activities in his many letters. One uncontested member, George Bubb Dodington MP, later Lord Melcombe, makes a number of enigmatic and intriguing references to the matter in his *Diaries*.

Trawling the nineteenth century leaves one no wiser and no better informed. The mid-Victorian era saw the publication of *The History and Topography of Buckinghamshire* by James Joseph Sheahan. By his own admission, Sheahan followed Johnstone's *Chrysal* and so stated that 'the mysterious ceremonies appear to have been something approaching to Devil-worship and a mockery of the rites of religion, with every worst form of debauchery'. Henry Spencer Ashbee, the noted connoisseur of erotic literature, had a more balanced attitude in his notes on the Wilkes/Potter *Essay On Woman*:

> [Dashwood's] ... profligate morals are not less denoted by another painting still preserved. In this he allowed himself to be delineated in the habit of a Franciscan friar, and upon his knees, but with the Venus de Medici before him as the object of his adoration. He was in truth and almost professedly what is termed a man of pleasure; an associate of Wilkes and Lord Sandwich; a partaker in the orgies of Medmenham Abbey.

At least there is no satanism here; but there is no extra information either.

Unfortunately, standards slipped lamentably in the entry for the customarily laudable and reliable *Dictionary of National Biography*. The standards of the *DNB* are usually strict and properly thorough and this was normally the case when Sir Leslie Stephen, father of Virginia Woolf, managed its entries. One wonders how he could allow the inclusion of the entry on Dashwood by one Arthur Frederick Pollard, who declared that the Friars 'amused themselves with obscene parodies of the rites of Rome. Dashwood acted as Grand-master of the order and used a communion cup to pour out libations to heathen deities, even administering the sacrament to a baboon.' This myth of drunken and sinister orgies was further popularised by a brief mention in Jerome K. Jerome's delightful comic novel, *Three Men in a Boat*.

The twentieth century witnessed a surprising number of endeavours to understand a complex series of fascinating issues. *The Lives of the Rakes* by E. Beresford Chancellor was published in six volumes between 1924 and 1925. This is an amiable work by an affable amateur. Chancellor tells good stories and skilfully brings his characters to life. Reading his books is rather like having a bottle of vintage port with a charming old gentleman from a bygone era. He dismisses the testimony of Walpole: 'I am always inclined to doubt Walpole, especially when he becomes alliterative.' He makes precious little distinction between fact, fiction, myth, legend, rumour and hearsay: it's just one good, hearty clubman's story after another. He relies too much on Johnstone's *Chrysal*. He discerns no political significance in the Friars at all, writing: '...the impious imitation of religious observances was the motive of its inception'. Chancellor makes Bubb Dodington the fool of the book and insults this noted political fixer quite mercilessly as a useless clown. Then he proceeds to praise Dodington's fellow MP, George Selwyn, as one of the finest ornaments of his age in spite of his predilections for necrophilia and gloating over public executions, habits which are excused as mere minor eccentricities. Chancellor states of Dashwood: '[he] possessed at least a warm heart and had the courage to champion the despised and oppressed'.

From Chancellor's charming portrayal of jolly japists performing corking wheezes and wizard pranks accompanied by precious little else of lasting interest, one turns to *Witchcraft and Black Magic* by Montague Summers, published in 1926, and finds a sinister conspiracy of evil satanists. Summers was a curious pervert who stoutly defended the hideous tortures of the Inquisition in rolling cadences of resonating prose and who could discern witchcraft and black magic at a barn dance. His view of the matter was dismally predictable: 'The tale of profligacy might be told but the tale of satanism must not be so much as whispered, cost what it may...but it is also certain that among the vile there were viler still, the elect, or in plain words, satanists, devoted to the worship of the fiend.'

In 1939 Ronald Fuller came forward with *Hell-Fire Francis*. 'The spectacle of a crowd of exhibitionists and perverts building altars to their own obsessions is not an edifying one,' he wrote, '...Yet it is the historian's business to explore not only the highways, but the back-streets and the slums...However repellent and depraved they may have been, the activities of the Friars of Medmenham occupy an obscure niche in our history.' That said, Fuller found Dashwood and his associates to be little more than dissipated, lunatic orgiasts.

Rather more scholarly work appeared from America in 1942. This was *The Clubs of the Georgian Rakes* by Louis C. Jones, who adopted an agnostic perspective and who summarised the state of research without committing himself on either political or religious issues. In his tentative opinion, it is difficult to discover the nature of the Friars' religion and he finds it likely that they were simply enjoying a roistering and rumbustious revel. Jones argues that although there was much in common among the members politically, there is no evidence of an organised political movement. However, he makes it surprisingly evident that his study of Dashwood has led him to applaud the man.

The Satanic Mass by H.T.F. Rhodes was published in 1954. This interesting work also relied too much upon Johnstone's *Chrysal*. Although Rhodes praises Dashwood's 'sincere reverence for the arts', he also makes of him a satanist and 'a man who did nothing scandalous by halves...Buried under many layers of sexual and bacchanalian rubbish was the two-faced god with emphasis upon the "satanistic".' Raymond Postgate would have none of this nonsense in *That Devil Wilkes* (1956). This determinedly rationalist study dismissed the notion that there was anything more to the Dashwood circle than debauchery, degeneracy and dissipation. 'As foolish looking as Dashwood's own round face', he writes of the members, who apparently endured 'neither gifts of mind nor, except perhaps in one direction, gifts of body... Dashwood's greatest practical joke was the Order of Medmenham Monks itself.' Postgate's verdict is that if any religious element existed at all, it was merely a mockery of Catholicism by lapsed and drunken Protestants.

The Hell-Fire Club by Donald McCormick (pseudonym of Richard Deacon) endeavoured to explore the matter further in 1958. Regrettably it included unconvincing fictitious conversations in a misguided endeavour to lend life to the matter. However, McCormick did not condemn his subjects, whom he saw as being straight rakes as he formed his own unique judgement: 'But, capricious, wayward, wanton and madcap as the Medmenhamites may have been, they are something more than an excuse for nostalgic yearning for more spacious days. There are certain facts about the decline and fall of rakemanship which explain in part at least the political and social sins of omission which have besotted British life for more than a century.'

A rather different point of view was advanced by Dan P. Mannix in his *The Hell-Fire Club* (1961). This most entertaining book discloses that the Friars were debauched and evil satanists who wanted to run the country for foul and fell purposes. The point was pursued further by Eric Maple in *The Dark World of Witches* (1962). 'The infamous Hell-Fire Club at West Wycombe organised black masses which were celebrated over the bodies of nude girls... one lamp standard consisted of a huge artificial bat complete with an erect penis... Beautiful women, quite naked beneath the robes of nuns they wore, submitted joyously to the caresses of the wild gang, which also practised incest as a sideline.' Anyone in search of pornography will be disappointed by Burgo Partridge's *A History of Orgies* (1966): 'It was he (Dashwood) who officiated at the sinister preparatory ceremonies in the chapel, who administered a perverted sacrament to the Medmenham baboon, who initiated new brothers into the order, who offered libations to the Devil.' Any seeker after new information will be disappointed too. This is yet another rehash of some old potatoes.

We receive a very different perspective from Dr Betty Kemp,

Fellow of St Hugh's College, Oxford, in her *Sir Francis Dashwood: An Eighteenth Century Independent* (1967). This is a meticulously researched analysis of Dashwood's political career put properly into its eighteenth-century context. Although the political research of Dr Kemp puts one in debt to her, she entirely ignores all religious matters. As far as the Friars are concerned, Dr Kemp argues that myth, legend and malicious gossip should be dismissed as unworthy of even a cursory examination. She portrays Dashwood as a pleasant, dull, worthy and well-intentioned man who liked to host pastoral picnics and jolly boating parties for his friends and neighbours. This portrayal does not quite fit with Dr Kemp's verdict on Sir Francis: 'In private life Dashwood was a man of intelligence, discrimination and some originality. Honest, courageous, fearless, steady, are phrases used by contemporaries to describe his political conduct; phrases like – careless of popularity, quick and generous, ready patron of new ideas – are contemporary comments on his character.'

Do What You Will: A History of Anti-Morality (1974) by Geoffrey Ashe, late Senior Scholar of Trinity College, Cambridge, sees Dashwood as a political visionary, discerns a political movement based upon Bolingbroke's *The Patriot King* and perceives the Friars to be wild rakes devoid of serious religious purpose, though part of a continuous hedonistic philosophy. Ashe also gives the enquirer an entirely new perspective on Bubb Dodington, whom Chancellor had damned as a useless clown, by praising him as an astute, sensible, humane and civilised politician.

A new approach was proposed in 1977 by Jesse Lasky Jnr and Pat Silver in their essay, 'Hell-Fire Dashwood', published in *Men of Mystery*, edited by Colin Wilson. Here they urged a study of the architecture, from which they drew controversial conclusions. In their view, Dashwood was restoring pagan worship. Professor Jeffrey Russell, of the University of California, would not agree. According to his *History of Witchcraft, Sorcerers, Heretics and Pagans* (1980):

Sir Francis Dashwood presided over the Hell-Fire Club, which boasted a number of distinguished and liberated spirits, including Benjamin Franklin. The club met in natural caves in Buckinghamshire to enjoy food, drink, gaming and sex. As in the old tradition, they met underground, at night, secretly, and practised something like orgies. But they did so in jesting parody. They enjoyed their reputation as rakehells, but none of them believed in either hell or the Devil and their salutations to Satan were wholly jocular . . .

One wonders precisely what Professor Russell means by 'the old tradition'; one wonders too how one might practise 'something like orgies' as opposed to orgies.

Dashwood: The Man and the Myth by Eric Towers appeared in 1986. Lt-Col. Towers was a late Scholar of Jesus College, Cambridge and his work has made life easier for subsequent researchers. He is clearly sympathetic to Dashwood and is sound on political analysis. He tackles accusations of satanism and black magic and dissects them into torn tissues of untruths.

'My interpretation of the caves remains as stated,' he wrote to me, 'that they were used as a Dionysian oracular temple, based upon Dashwood's reading of the relevant chapters of Rabelais. And they must be seen in conjunction with the golden ball on the church tower up above – an anticipation of Nietzsche's Apollo-Dionysus view of human nature and the purpose of religion.'

In his otherwise outstanding book, Towers does not examine the architecture of Medmenham and the caves of West Wycombe so as to establish beyond all reasonable doubt the central thrust of an eminently sane argument. Nevertheless, any historian owes a debt to his work, best repaid by exploring the issues further.

Sir Francis Dashwood, the present baronet, published *The Dashwoods of West Wycombe* in 1987. As one would expect, he is sound on family history and notable in arguing the case for his ancestor's positive political contribution. However, religious matters are rather brushed aside and the Friars are presented as 'Knights', enjoying a genial and civilised evening's entertainment.

The view of the orthodox historian is that Dashwood headed a club of rakes dedicated to little more than having a good time. So far, so innocent. This shallow view conspicuously fails to discern the facts. Dashwood spent a fortune on the architecture and ornamentation of Medmenham Abbey; a fortune on the curious church he built at West Wycombe Park; an even greater fortune on an intricate maze of caves with an artificial river roughly fifty-six yards away from the church; yet more on erecting a hexagonal mausoleum next to the church, allegedly to honour the club steward, Paul Whitehead; and much more on extending the exterior and decorating the interior of West Wycombe House.

If a man spends such vast sums of money on architectural extravagances, it can be argued that he is mad, or else a rich spoiled brat squandering his patrimony upon follies. Neither of these 'explanations' is convincing. No one doubts that Dashwood liked to carouse with his companions and that he liked to womanise but nobody other than biographer Ronald Fuller has ever doubted his sanity. Much of the time he was a plain-spoken English country squire who always said what he thought without any fear of the consequences. Moreover, whilst a rich brat might like to erect follies, if there is nothing more to it than that, these will be devoid of purpose. Even if there is some momentary inspiration, this won't last, as the Friars did, for roughly thirty years.

The purpose of this work is to seek answers to questions of abiding interest. Who exactly were these people grouped around Sir Francis Dashwood? For what values, if any, did the man stand? What was the precise nature of the Friars' religious activities? Were there any political beliefs held in common? If so, what did they do about them? What were their social mores and sexual customs? Were these, by any chance, part of Dashwood's religion? Did he have a religion or was he just a rake? Who was a member of his alleged inner circle and who was acquainted with his outer circle? Did they have esoteric or political links with the American and French revolutionaries? What were they actually like as people? What effect did their lives have upon their space and time and what are the effects upon us here and now?

It can safely be stated that Sir Francis Dashwood had little interest in satanism. He was far too intelligent a man to be concerned with anything so puerile. However, he was clearly a gentleman with an impassioned interest in religious matters. Although sceptical by temperament and harbouring a hatred of hypocrisy, he desired the divine nevertheless and celebrated it dramatically wherever he found it. Prudes and prigs deplored his actions and slandered his name. He shrugged his shoulders and carried on doing what he believed to be right. It can truly be said that they don't make them like him any more. If only they did!

1

Sir Francis Dashwood (1708–81)

It would be hard to find a more interesting man, exemplifying every paradox of his century, than Sir Francis Dashwood. 'He had the staying powers of a stallion and the impetuosity of a bull . . . he fornicated his way across Europe,' Horace Walpole observed, and added: 'He was seldom sober but always charmingly tolerant and frank.' Apparently Sir Francis 'far exceeded in licentiousness anything exhibited since the days of Charles II . . . there was not a vice for practising for which he did not make provision', according to an anonymous source. 'He was the only one to show real gifts of imagination and true mental abilities,' John Wilkes nevertheless wrote long after his expulsion from Dashwood's club. The ladies seemed to like him. 'Sir Francis Dashwood stuck by us all night and is a very entertaining man,' Mrs Pendarres informs Mrs Dawes in Mrs Delaney's *Autobiography* concerning a ball given by Frederick, Prince of Wales. Two centuries later, the Reverend Montague Summers would brand Dashwood a 'satanist' and H.T.F. Rhodes would call him 'a dissipated ecclesiastic'.

It is not an easy task to understand this extraordinary man. André Gide and Norman Mailer both gave us guiding words of wisdom when Gide said: 'Please do not understand me too quickly'; Mailer later added: 'Please don't understand anybody too quickly.' Obviously there are clues to comprehension in the ancestry. Dashwood's grandfather, Alderman George, had steadily built up a family business by trading with China, India and the Levant. Dashwood's uncle Samuel had made the first large-scale English purchase of Bengal raw silk in 1685. In 1700 the *Dashwood* frigate of 375 tons sailed to Amony, China with £40,000 worth of gold bullion and wool. It returned with exquisite Chinese porcelain: a profit was made on that voyage.

The Dashwoods were a worthy old Dorset family with an eye for opportunities in business. By 1700 they had £10,000, roughly £500,000 in today's terms, invested with the East India Company, enabling them to import spices and silks. More silk, more porcelain and tea too were imported from China. The Dashwoods followed a golden rule of trade in buying commodities cheaply and selling them expensively. Dashwood's father Francis became the Member of Parliament for the pocket borough of Winchelsea and was created a baronet by Queen Anne in 1707.

There is a painting of Sir Francis Dashwood senior at the ancestral home of West Wycombe House and it depicts a shrewd man pondering his past, present and future business dealings. Certainly he celebrated many forms of fecundity, for he married four times. Mary Jennings, the daughter of a business colleague, was his first wife and she bore him two daughters, Mary and Susannah, both of whom married into the country gentry. After her death, Dashwood senior moved from trade to the aristocracy in securing his next marital alliance with Lady Mary Fane, daughter of the fourth Earl of Westmorland. She was the mother of our subject, and of a daughter, Rachel, but she in turn died in 1710. The third wife was Mary King, niece of Dr John King, former rector of West Wycombe and then a master at Charterhouse School. This marriage was undeniably fertile, for there were two sons, John and Charles, and two daughters, Henrietta and Maria. Mary King died and her widower then married Lady Elizabeth Windsor, daughter of the Earl of Plymouth, but died without further issue in 1724. He is buried next to his first three wives in the family vault at West Wycombe church.

According to legend, the new baronet rejoiced when his father died and drank his cellar dry. He could equally well have been drowning that night in his own filial grief. He had been only two years of age when his mother had died and now his father was gone when he was sixteen. Fortunately his maternal uncle, John Fane, later Earl of Westmorland, became his guardian and took to the wilful, high-spirited boy, then at Charterhouse School. He acceded to his ward's request for private tutoring and when Dashwood reached the age of eighteen, the guardian allowed him to undertake the Grand Tour. The future Earl of Westmorland would always be a valuable and influential benefactor and ally of Dashwood and even though the latter did not need it, would remember him generously in his will. Dashwood would state: 'I am so affectionately attached to Lord Westmorland by the indissoluble ties of gratitude and friendship that without his approbation and concurrence I never could so much as seem to forget my duty towards him.'

His father's legacy to the young Dashwood gave him four thousand acres of prime land in Buckinghamshire and money sufficient to gratify every possible whim. His wealth and social position gave him the opportunity to do whatever he liked and he did. One pities the anonymous tutor who accompanied Dashwood on his travels for legend has it that the tutor was a pious Catholic and his charge delighted in shocking him. 'Taste the sweets of all things,' Dashwood declared as he embraced French and fencing in Paris. He drank deeply, fornicated fully and bought books. An inventory of his library discloses that he purchased the complete works of Racine, Corneille, Molière – and the works of the man who would inspire him most, François Rabelais.

His despairing tutor tried to convert him to Roman Catholicism by taking him to the Sistine Chapel in 1728, where he urged the virtues of penitence and exhorted Dashwood to emulate the example of the monks who were publicly flagellating themselves. Dashwood noticed that the monks' whips were softly innocuous and was disgusted by the hypocrisy. He responded by entering the Chapel on Good Friday, disguised in a long cloak from which he produced a bullwhip to lash the penitents with vengeful savagery. '*Il diavolo! Il diavolo!*' they screeched as they ran. Unfortunately this practical joke aroused the ire of the Inquisition and would have caused a serious diplomatic incident had Dashwood and his excruciatingly embarrassed tutor lacked the wisdom to leave town.

Sir Francis had not yet done with jests that baited the Catholic Church. According to the present baronet, his ancestor disguised himself as the sick and absent Cardinal Ottoboni so as to attend the funeral of Pope Clement XII in 1730, and a spectator is quoted as saying: 'Never in my life have I witnessed anything so mad and so original.' Dashwood continued on his way to Venice, then the principal trading centre of occult books, in December 1730, as a letter from Colonel Burgis, the British Resident, testifies. He visited Padua, Florence and Naples, falling in love with the splendours and beauties of both classical civilisation and the Italian Palladian architecture based upon it. This style had been devised by Andrea Palladio, born Andrea di Pietro, and this influential seed would in time burst into full fruit at West Wycombe. Dashwood also met the Milanese painter, Giuseppe Borgnis, whose brush would grace the interiors of West Wycombe House.

Dashwood's enraptured enthusiasm for Italy and its arts led him to become a founder member of the Society of Dilettanti. This was established in 1732 and by 1736 there were forty members gathering for dinners. They met at the Bedford Head, then the Fountain in the Strand and then the Star & Garter in Pall Mall. 'The nominal qualification is having been in Italy; and the real one, having been drunk,' Horace Walpole wrote acidly, probably angered by his lack of membership. Members' portraits were at that time painted by George Knapton and in later years the Society would donate to the newly established Royal Academy of Art, founded by Sir Joshua Reynolds, and would also give grants to selected students for travel to Italy. This society still exists today, still practises a curious initiation ceremony concocted by Dashwood and celebrated a jubilee in 1983.

Dashwood pressed on with his reckless explorations of experience. In 1733 he sailed with Lord Forbes to St Petersburg, where he disguised himself as King Charles XII of Sweden and was presented at court, enjoying during his recorded fortnight an affair with the Tsarina, Anna. That is the account of the *Dictionary of National Biography* although Eric Towers doubts its veracity. About two years later, the young baronet visited Greece to imbibe more classical culture and, no doubt, many other things too. From there he proceeded to Turkey, doubtless bearing in mind the commercial connections of his family with the Levant. It is not known whether or not he would have agreed with a later visitor to that country, Lord Byron: 'In England the vices in fashion are whoring and drinking, in Turkey, sodomy and smoking.' This journey inspired Dashwood to found the Divan Club, along with Lords Sandwich and Duncannon, for those who wished to celebrate Turkish culture. The club was duly inaugurated at the Thatched Tavern, St James's Street, in January 1744 but unfortunately expired with only three members present in May 1746.

Dashwood was definitely a clubbable man who enjoyed the energies of elitism. His wealth and social position gave him entry to White's Club in 1743. His interest in science made him a Fellow of the Royal Society in 1746. Three years later he was given an honorary Doctorate of Law at Oxford University. He used his position to get to know the leading men and women of his era.

Italy and its influence remained at the forefront of Dashwood's activities. Returning there in 1739, he spent most of his time in Florence, and encountered Horace Walpole and Lady Mary Wortley Montagu, England's leading feminist intellectual, one year later. After a visit to Venice once again in 1741, he returned to England and chose to enter politics, all the while also planning other wild and extravagant schemes, and passionately pursuing multifarious interests. On the 5 May 1741, he was elected MP for New Romney. In 1747 he was re-elected. He became the MP for Weymouth and Melcombe Regis in 1761 and was re-elected in 1762. His blunt speaking, without care or concern for peer pressure, sometimes caused a stir in Parliament for he impressed some and appalled others. Horace Walpole accused him of posing as Mark Antony in deliberately cultivating a roughness of speech and his unparliamentary language did on occasion shock some of his more timid colleagues. In fact, this wasn't a pose: the headstrong Dashwood was a gentleman who liked to use plain language and who did not suffer fools gladly. In 1763 he was elevated to the House of Lords as Lord Le Despenser, the premier baron of England. He gave his country forty years of untiring parliamentary service.

His career in the House of Commons was distinguished by a cavalier disregard of both public and private opinion. He was in a unique position of being able to say or do whatever he thought fit without fear of reprisal. He did not appear to care how unpopular he might become, providing that he was acting in accordance with his own esoteric code of honour. In 1755 he upset the government by opposing the hiring of Russian and Hessian mercenaries to fight in British colonial wars. His view was that the troops should be British or else we shouldn't be at war at all. In 1757 he made himself doubly unpopular by his courageous defence of Admiral Byng.

During the course of the Seven Years War between the nations of Europe, Admiral Byng had been ordered to sail upon and storm Minorca, then held by the French. Unfortunately, British naval intelligence had vastly underestimated French naval and military force in the region and Byng found his squadron to be hopelessly outnumbered. He therefore ordered a quiet retreat in good order and no British sailors or ships were lost. The Admiralty responded by giving Byng a court martial for cowardice in the face of the enemy and sentenced him to death. Dashwood led the fight in the Commons over this flagrant miscarriage of justice. It did no good. Admiral Byng was shot on the deck of his own ship, '*pour encourager les autres*', as Voltaire observed. Dashwood's subsequent stout defence of the rights of the American colonists trebled his unpopularity in certain circles.

He was independent of both Crown and Party, as Dr Betty Kemp has exhaustively demonstrated. He made his political views clear enough with *An Address to the Gentlemen, Clergy and Freeholders of... Great Britain* (1747).

'Man has a natural right to be free... by Freedom is not nor can be meant that every Individual should act as he lists, and according as he is swayed by his own Passions, Vices or Infirmities: but Freedom is a Right every Man has to *do what he will* with his own...' (Italics mine.) Here we see Dashwood at the age of thirty-nine resolving that there is a series of distinctions between whim, want and the power of will. Too idealistic? Hardly. He put his will into practical action, being an active member of parliamentary committees responsible for the repair and building of roads and bridges, the establishment of toll-booths for roads throughout the kingdom and the detailed and dull but essential matters of drainage and coastal navigation. He was responsible for having a new road built from High Wycombe to West Wycombe, thus giving needed and appreciated employment to able-bodied men in his constituency; and he did this at his own expense.

Some of his proposals were thought to be mad at the time but anticipated future developments. Dashwood proposed that the seven-year term of Parliament should be reduced to one year or at most three. The Parliament Act of 1911 finally cut the length to five. He opposed the notion of a standing army and urged that it should be replaced by a militia similar to the Territorial Army of today. The Militia Bill, which he had introduced in 1745, finally had its major proposals legislatively enshrined by the Militia Act of 1757, which created a Home Guard of 32,000 men. Dashwood, as Lord Lieutenant of the county, was made colonel of the Bucks Militia in 1759, appointed John Wilkes as his lieutenant-colonel in an action devoid of snobbery and gave part-time employment to 360 men.

The open flaunting of his independence did not prevent Dashwood from holding offices of state from 1761 to 1781. His enemies have accused him of plotting for the establishment of the so-called 'Hell-Fire Ministry' of 1762–3 under Lord Bute. Certainly the members of this government and its supporters in Parliament had much in common. This matter will be explored more thoroughly in its proper place. It is unfortunate that Dashwood was given the job of Chancellor of the Exchequer, for he openly confessed his inability to do sums in excess of five figures. Dan P. Mannix has a sinister Dashwood proudly boasting: 'I'll be the worst Chancellor that England ever had.' One leaves such a dubious distinction to those closer to our own time whilst observing that this is not quite what Dashwood said. His words were: 'The boys will point at me in the street and say: "There goes the worst Chancellor that England ever had".' John Wilkes remarked that he 'couldn't even add up a tavern bill'.

In fact his tenure as Chancellor was not quite as bad as legend has it. Dashwood was charged by Bute with the onerous duty of raising taxes in order to pay for the Seven Years War. Dashwood consequently introduced a cider tax. The principle of this tax was sufficiently sensible as to be used by subsequent governments in amended form, but it became deeply unpopular on account of the powers it gave to Customs & Excise officers to raid private houses on suspicion that they might be harbouring illicit stills. This unpopularity contributed substantially to the fall of Bute's ministry.

Dashwood was given a sinecure as Keeper of the Wardrobe from 1763 to 1765 and returned to active government service between 1766 and 1781 as joint Postmaster-General. Here he executed his duties with distinction, facilitating inexpensive written communication. A six-day post between England and Ireland was established in 1767. A reform of letter collection from London receiving houses was implemented in 1769. Dashwood set up the Penny Post Office in Dublin in 1773, thus pioneering the establishment of the English penny post by Sir Rowland Hill in the 1840s. His curious and inventive mind also led him to investigate transport in a search for a more efficient method than 'the post boy on horseback'. The first mail coaches finally took to the roads in 1784, three years after Dashwood's death.

'He has reorganised the postal services of England,' his friend Benjamin Franklin wrote, 'and provided something like a national postal service.' Franklin must also have appreciated Dashwood's

Plan of Reconciliation (1770), proposed to avert impending war between Great Britain and the restless American colonies. Common sense did not prevail and the consequence was a stupid war.

So far, Dashwood sounds like a worthy Tory squire of his time, with a mite of perception, a sense of humour, immaculate integrity and a wild streak but nothing more, other than a conspicuous dedication to unexciting public service and a propensity and large appetite for the principal pleasures of his era. After all, he was known to socialise contentedly with many who did not share his political views in the many taverns which he entered and in the wide variety of clubs to which he belonged. As a drinking-club song of the day has it:

> We have no idle prating
> Of either Whig or Tory;
> But each agrees
> To live at ease
> And sing or tell a story.
>
> We're always men of pleasure,
> Despising pride and party;
> While knaves and fools
> Prescribe us rules,
> We are sincere and hearty.

Was there much to the man other than this? His marriage was completely conventional. The bride was Lady Sarah Ellys, widow of a country gentleman, Sir Richard Ellys, and she married the bridegroom on 11 December 1745. Horace Walpole called her 'a poor, forlorn Presbyterian prude'. Eric Towers is scornful of this description. 'Forlorn she may have been during her widowhood, but once married to so ebullient a man as Dashwood, there was neither reason nor opportunity for Presbyterian prudery.' On the face of it, one sees a customary dynastic marriage of the time, contracted for commercial reasons. The dowry of Lady Sarah included a house in Hanover Square and Place House in Ealing.

All accounts state that Dashwood was unfailingly kind to his wife though he continued to womanise relentlessly. She does not appear to have involved herself with the Friars. The marriage lasted contentedly enough for twenty-three years until the death by natural causes of Lady Sarah in 1769.

Marriage did not prevent Dashwood from returning to his beloved Italy without his wife in 1752, for a mystery tour. No one knows precisely where he went. Venice has been proposed. It was the European centre of esoteric studies. Certainly Dashwood's private library discloses books about magick, bought in Venice, but the date of the purchase is unclear. Another possibility is Naples. He had first been there in 1738 to view the initial excavations at Herculaneum (Pompeii) and some assert that he returned to view the arts of the brothel in the 'House of Mysteries' ten years later. Perhaps he visited both Venice and Naples. In any event, his travels resulted in notable contributions to British culture. *Antiquities of Athens* by James Stuart and Nicholas Revett, a friend of Dashwood, was published in 1762 by the Dilettante Society. This prompted a fashionable frenzy for 'Grecian Gusto' and led eventually to the English acquisition of the Elgin Marbles. Revett then led Richard Chandler and William Pars on an expedition to Asia Minor in 1764–6, publishing the results as *Ionian Antiquities*. Sir Francis Dashwood as Baron Le Despenser, presented the first two copies of this book to the King and Queen in 1770.

Politics, travel, marriage and antiquarianism were not sufficient to accommodate Dashwood's gargantuan appetite. Architecture was another of his true loves, inspiring him to order, between 1739 and 1771, a succession of experiments and improvements at West Wycombe. After his mysterious Italian journey of 1752, Dashwood returned to lease Medmenham Abbey, six miles from West Wycombe and on the Thames near Henley. This was given architectural additions according to his deepest desires and its motto, inscribed in stone, was taken from Rabelais: 'FAY CE QUE VOUDRAS'.

Attention was paid to the art of landscape gardening. John

Wilkes, MP and future Lord Mayor of London, went to visit Dashwood in order to resolve a quarrel, subsequently describing the delectable view from the golden globe erected by his host atop the church of St Lawrence at West Wycombe. Wilkes gazed down upon a gorgeous garden, fashioned in the form of a naked female. This must have put him in a receptive state of mind for his host's 'wise reasons and dazzling offers'.

The library of Dashwood displays the liberality of his culture. One notices that what is probably the first copy of the *Kama Sutra* brought into England was given and inscribed to Dashwood by Sir Henry Vansittart, a Friar of St Francis and an enlightened Governor of Bengal. This is a manual of Hindu Tantric techniques of sexual love and in it Vansittart has written: 'To the Founder'. Dashwood specifically left it in his will to his esoterically inclined illegitimate daughter, Rachel Fanny Antonina.

It is obvious that as a man, Dashwood was clearly broad-minded, cultured, courageous, good-hearted and good-humoured, as even his foes allowed. The conduct of his political life was on some occasions inept but it was never dishonourable. He always had the courage of his convictions, supported by a broad perspective based on his many travels, his wide reading and his social intercourse with so very many sorts of human beings. He was gracious and genial to his friends and although he hit hard, he was chivalrous to his enemies. When fancy took him, he was a wild rake although he faithfully performed all his family obligations. Internally he was governed by his own sense of honour and no one could force him to compromise. There is an anecdote which displays Dashwood's character; the event took place in the House of Lords on 7 April 1778.

William Pitt the Elder, former Prime Minister and now Earl of Chatham, launched a savage attack upon Dashwood, awakening the House with scathing sarcastic witticisms and the thundering oratory which had once fired a nation. In the midst of his peroration he unfortunately suffered a seizure and collapsed. Dashwood was among the first to rush to Pitt's assistance.

This was an undeniably Christian action and Dashwood would

later contribute to Christianity further by revising the Book of Common Prayer in partnership with Benjamin Franklin. This is still used in most American Episcopalian churches, though the credit is always given to Franklin and never to Dashwood. Some have seen in his contribution the repentance of a rake who knew that death was fast approaching but there is no evidence for this at all. Dashwood simply wanted common prayer for the common people and desired to make the services shorter. The nature of elitist prayers for an elite is of course a principal subject of this work.

Many writers have studied Dashwood: few have understood him. Painters have attacked the subject too. The Divan Club portrait shows a jovial and bibulous man with expanding jowls, dressed in Turkish costume: a brooch symbolising the sun crests his turban; his left hand is uplifted to display five fingers and his right is poised with a glass of wine so as to toast 'The Harem'. Another shows him in late middle age as a much more thoughtful man, with his chin in his hand and his thumb raised to indicate his throat, as he ponders his failure as Chancellor of the Exchequer and his elevation to the peerage. Nathaniel Dance painted him in the first flourish of youth as a Franciscan monk. Carpentiers portrayed him as Pope Pontius VII and toasting a statue of Venus. This image was repeated and embellished by William Hogarth, then done by Knapton in 1742.

It is not easy to assemble all the various pieces adding up to the jigsaw puzzle that is Sir Francis Dashwood; and there is another dimension yet. In spite of his membership of White's, the Dilettante, the Divan, the Commons, Oxford University and the Sublime Society of Beefsteaks, Dashwood was determined to found yet another club. He wished to gather around himself the foremost people of his time capable of sharing and enjoying the sexual, political and religious vision his travels and experiences had developed. In popular parlance, this venture became known as 'the Hell-Fire Club' and was roundly abused, though its adherents referred to it as 'The Monks of Medmenham' or 'The Knights' or 'The Friars of St Francis of Wycombe'.

At a date given differently by every historian who asserts it,

Dashwood and the Earl of Sandwich founded this new club. Legend has it that this took place in a tavern at some time after 1755. Which tavern? Accounts vary once again but the name 'George' the King – does not. The George & Vulture in the City has been plausibly proposed. It was there that Philip, Duke of Wharton, set up the original Hell-Fire Club in the 1720s. It has also been argued that the venue was the George Inn, Borough High Street, Southwark, a pub promoted by some as the Tabard where Chaucer's *The Canterbury Tales* begins, but unquestionably the tavern celebrated by Charles Dickens in *Little Dorrit*. Sir Francis Dashwood, the present baronet, states that whilst one cannot be sure of the precise place, the Club 'probably started in the 1740s . . . flourished until 1763 . . . did not die out until 1774 or even later . . . '

The purpose was to add an element of religion to cultured dissipation and civilised debauchery. In later years, Sir William Stanhope would write to Dashwood, excusing himself from attendance but asking that the brethren 'may have my prayers, particularly in that part of the Litany when I pray the Lord *to strengthen them that do stand*'. The emphasis upon this phrase was added by the present baronet. One might well wonder: what did they stand for? Carpentiers, Hogarth and Knapton have all given us essentially the same visual image. We see a man who embodies the masculine worshipping the feminine, enshrining the initial polarity and subsequent union of the male and the female in a blazing stream of pure energy that is the sacred essence of religion itself.

John Wilkes wrote of Dashwood's 'Libations to Bona Dea'. Dashwood's devotions vouchsafed him a vision of life and he endeavoured to translate it practically into ritualistic, architectural, political and clubbable terms. He wanted peace and prosperity for one and all and his bluff country manners gave him the common touch; but he also wanted an exquisitely enjoyable club for a cultured elite, determined both by birth and by merit, for essentially he appreciated excellence.

The Friars assembled around Dashwood and those acquainted with them, possessed a common philosophy of sex, politics and religion. By 1762 they were dominating the government of Great Britain. Our contemporary chaos theory of physics states that any system will always contain within itself a factor infinite and unknown which will bring about its breakdown. This is precisely what happened here and the random factor was John Wilkes.

Dashwood, premier baron of England, never thought that his endeavour to engineer an elite would result in an infamous legend and the irresistible rise of democracy.

2

John Montagu, Earl of Sandwich (1718–92)

Sir Francis Dashwood was a warm, genial man, albeit one with a hot temper; Sandwich was cold. Nevertheless, the two men were good friends. One can imagine them visiting a sleazy tavern together for the purposes of getting drunk and picking up tarts. Dashwood would no doubt talk genially to the people while a silent Sandwich wondered why his friend was bandying words with peasants.

Many disliked John Montagu and wrote or spoke scathing words about the man. Horace Walpole detested him, writing: 'It is uncommon for a heart to be so tainted so young... there is an inveteracy, a darkness, a design and cunning in his character which stamp him as a very unamiable young man.' Sandwich has been quoted as saying: 'The corruption of innocence is in itself my end.' Lord Chesterfield called his life 'one uniform, unblushing course of debauchery and dissipation'. That noted authority, Anon, damns him still further: 'Seldom has a man held so many offices and accomplished so little... he walked as if he were trying to go down both sides of the street at once... mean to his mistresses and treacherous to his friends... no man ever carried the art of seduction to so enormous a height... he can never lose the smell of brimstone... as mischievous as a monkey and as lecherous as a goat... the most universally disliked man in England.'

So far, he sounds rather interesting and it is hardly surprising that Dashwood wanted to meet him. John Wilkes would later call Sandwich 'the most abandoned man of his age' in his *Letter to the Electors of Aylesbury*. Charles Churchill assailed Sandwich with uncharacteristically clumsy verse:

> Search East, search Hell, the Devil cannot find
> An agent like Lothario to his mind.

The London mob hated Sandwich for attacking their champions of democracy, Wilkes and Churchill. It was the apparent sexual hypocrisy of Sandwich that was railed against by the mob and for once Horace Walpole found himself in agreement with the common people. 'Sandwich has outsandwiched himself,' he wrote to George Montagu on 20 November 1763. 'He has impeached Wilkes for a blasphemous poem, and has been expelled for blasphemy himself by The Beefsteak Club.'

'That Jemmy Twitcher would 'peach me, I own surprised me', was the line in John Gay's *The Beggar's Opera* which obviously referred to Sandwich. Gay's work was sensationally successful, and the mob took to calling Sandwich 'Jemmy Twitcher'. The Earl's behaviour could be too excessive even for his friend Dashwood. 'I never expected to hear the Devil preaching,' Dashwood sighed as Sandwich tried to impeach Wilkes.

Few later historians have a good word to say for Sandwich. H.T.F. Rhodes comments on 'that corpse-like face with its expression of a slow arrogance'. E. Beresford Chancellor called Montagu's speaking 'awkward, loose and detached – as awkward as his attitudes, as detached as his thoughts and as loose as his morals'. One edition of the *Encyclopaedia Britannica* called his regime at the Admiralty 'unique for incapacity'. The *Dictionary of National Biography* declares his naval administration to have been 'disastrous'.

There are 'Two sides to a Sandwich', as Linda Colley declared in her perceptive *Observer* review of *The Insatiable Earl: A Life of John Montagu, Fourth Earl of Sandwich* (1993) by N.A.M. Rodger. One should look at the facts. The Montagus were not an

especially wealthy family and relied on favours from the court.
They served the Stuarts then switched their allegiance to the
Hanoverians. John, the great-grandson of Rochester, poet and
rake in the reign of King Charles II, was educated at Eton and
Trinity College, Cambridge, succeeding to the earldom in 1729.
He went on the Grand Tour, visiting France, Italy, Sicily, the
Greek islands, Turkey and Egypt, then returned to England in
1739 and entered politics. In 1744 the First Lord of the
Admiralty, the Duke of Bedford, gave him the office of Junior
Lord in Pelham's ministry. Although Sandwich was a notorious
alcoholic, compulsive womaniser and addict of the gaming tables,
he fast earned a reputation as a workaholic too. Throughout his
life he would display the addictive behaviour and stubborn
courage of a frail male who has lost his father in infancy.
Throughout his life, his health was poor.

His frailty was demonstrated in his response to the Jacobite
rebellion of 1745. He sank into nervous depression, probably
because he was unable to clarify where his own family's loyalties
stood between the conflicting Houses of Hanover and Stuart. The
Hanoverians and their many supporters defeated the Stuart
uprising and the neutral Sandwich was made Plenipotentiary to
the States of Holland in 1746. In 1748 he attended the Congress
of Aix-la-Chapelle, which ended the War of the Austrian
Succession, though the general consensus is that he was not a
particularly tactful diplomat. Nevertheless, he was made First
Lord of the Admiralty at a remarkably young age and took to the
work with outstanding public spirit and energetic thoroughness.
He lost no time in exposing the corruption and inefficiency of the
dockyards. This aroused the hostility of vested interests, his
enemies intrigued against him and on 12 June 1751, he was
dismissed by King George II.

Sandwich rebounded in 1755 as Vice-Treasurer, Receiver-
General and Paymaster of Ireland, then regained his position at
the Admiralty in 1763. The ministry fell but he bounced back
again as Secretary of State for the Southern Department (Foreign
Affairs) two years later in addition to sharing the post of joint

Postmaster-General with Dashwood from 1760 to 1770. In 1770–1 he was Secretary of State for the Northern Department, he was made a general of the Army in the following year and from 1771 to 1782, he was back in his favoured position as First Lord of the Admiralty.

The detailed examination of N.A.M. Rodger, supported by all available evidence, gives the lie both *Encyclopaedia Britannica* and the *Dictionary of National Biography* regarding the conduct of Sandwich as First Lord of the Admiralty. There he encouraged Captain Cook's voyages of exploration, which led to the discovery of Australia. The Sandwich Islands are named after him. His frequent visits to the naval dockyards led to an efficient improvement of storage facilities and a rebuilding of the fleet which had been left to rot during the 1760s. He delegated capably to men such as Charles Middleton and Hugh Palliser. Throughout his life he needed more money but no one could bribe him. He refused requests for patronage and was never personally corrupt. He bore his own unpopularity with a cold shrug of his shoulders and despised those who sought to cultivate popular favour.

If only the government had listened to the Admiralty under Sandwich! His insistence on the copper-bottoming of ships, for instance, led to a splendid British victory at the Battle of Saintes in 1782. Here, one year after his death, his strategy worked. In 1775, however, he had urged the immediate mobilisation of the navy for the upcoming conflict with the American States. The result of this war might well have been different had the advice of Sandwich been followed. As it fell out, Sandwich had to shoulder much of the blame for losing the American colonies.

In spite of his worthy endeavours at the Admiralty, he passed into popular legend as a figure of infamy. It is said that he hated to leave the gaming table and so simply ordered a servant to bring him 'a piece of beef wedged between two slices of bread'. On that day, the 'sandwich' was invented. The Victorians denounced him as an inveterate rake. One wonders how he managed to succeed so well with women. There was hardly a noted courtesan, including the beautiful Kitty Fisher, who did not welcome Sandwich to her boudoir. This was not merely a matter of money, for Sandwich had little to spread around and the top courtesans were in a position to pick and choose. His enemies have yet to explain why he was so popular among women.

The behaviour of Sandwich to Martha Ray also sheds interesting light upon his character. She was a working-class milliners' shopgirl. When Sandwich met her, he was old enough to be her father. He seduced her, then set her up in luxury. Tutors were employed to further her education and especially to advance her notable talents for music and singing, and these would make her celebrated in fashionable London, granting her fame in her own right. Meanwhile she continued as the mistress of Lord Sandwich and their relationship lasted for seventeen years. It was terminated by a tragedy.

A Lieutenant James Hackman fell in love with Martha Ray. She spurned his advances. He changed his career to become the Reverend James Hackman. She still refused his every overture On 7 April 1779 James Hackman killed Martha Ray. The weapon was a pistol. Afterwards Hackman tried to shoot himself and failed. Arresting officers found him trying to bash out his own brains with the butt of his pistol. He was tried, found guilty, sentenced to death and hanged. It is said that this is the only event of Lord Sandwich's life which caused him to break down and cry.

Sandwich found little consolation in the bosom of his own family. There was insanity within his own bloodline, his wife had gone mad and nearly all of his descendants had already died. One discerns the tensions tugging within the man on viewing James Northcote's portrait. Beneath the turban, the eyes gleam with cold steel, the nose denotes disdain for the plebeians, the mouth is sensuous though there is a determinedly fierce line by its right corner, the head is erect, the facial expression is arrogant and a skinny body wears a plenitude of puffed-out robes. One also notices his strong, jutting jaw.

In weighing up the evidence, one finds Sandwich to be very much a man of his family and of his time. Dashwood obviously liked him though temperamentally they were quite different. Dashwood possessed a tolerance which was lacking in Sandwich. Sandwich was a snob; Dashwood wasn't. Dashwood loved to fight but he never hit below the belt; the same cannot be said of Sandwich. Dashwood could forgive an attack upon his reputation whereas Sandwich relished a cold and cruel revenge. As will be shown, the quarrel between Sandwich and Wilkes tore apart the Club of Friars, constructed so painstakingly by Dashwood, and revealed an incompatible antagonism between elitism and democracy.

Whatever his many virtues, Sandwich could not bear Wilkes's arousal of the London mob in the cause of the common people. He felt that Wilkes had betrayed every value of the Friars of St Francis. This is why he felt no compunction in using grossly hypocritical tactics to impeach Wilkes. These may persuade one to despise him,yet Dashwood stood by his friend. Sandwich was an extremely sensitive man with gross appetites for drink, women, gambling and work, not to mention travel and the arts, and he lusted after religious truth.

More truth is conveyed by Hogarth's engraving, *Sir Francis Dashwood at his Devotions*, which inspired the Knapton portrait. A youthful, handsome Dashwood kneels in prayer, wearing the robe of a Franciscan friar. In the distance behind him, there is a gloomy Gothic landscape, a stormy sky and some strange buildings. His left hand is extended to touch his heart: the palm covers the anatomical position while the fingers locate a place of energy connected with the heart in the centre of the body. Both the Sufis and the Yogis see this as an essential source of human evolutionary energy; the Yogis call it a principal *chakra*, and their system of *chakras* corresponds with the Western notion of the endocrine glands.

The right hand of Sir Francis Dashwood is extended with thumb and first forefinger apart, thus making the sign known in circles of esotericists, occultists, magicians, Rosicrucians and witches as that of the horned god. As such he is displaying masculine energy and he is directing it towards the ankle of a naked and voluptuous figurine of a goddess, who reclines lasciviously upon the altar, apparently delighted with his devotions.

To Dashwood's left, death is symbolised by a Venetian carnival mask. In front of him, though behind the figurine of the goddess, there is an open book, though one cannot make out its nature. To his right, there is a cross hanging upside down from a string of pearls, in mockery of a rosary. The cross is of course a phallic symbol. It hangs over a shining dish or shield which symbolises the vagina and possibly the Holy Grail. Many delights spill out of this dish, including grapes, other fruits, seashells and more symbols of fecundity. One goblet is spilling flowers upon the floor. Another stands upright and bears a coronet. There is a halo to grace Dashwood's saintly expression.

Inserted within that halo and peering at the back of Dashwood's head, is a wicked portrayal of the beaky-nosed Earl of Sandwich.

3

The Political, Religious and Sexual Context

'It was the best of times, it was the worst of times,' Charles Dickens wrote about the eighteenth century in opening his novel *A Tale of Two Cities*, adding: 'It was the Age of Reason; it was the Age of Unreason. We had everything before us; we had nothing before us...' Dickens found paradox rather than platitude to be the key to the eighteenth century.

In 1688 there had been a momentous event in English history, subsequently described by the victors as 'the Glorious Revolution'. King James II of the Stuart house had in 1685 been bequeathed an ordered kingdom by his brother, King Charles II. He proceeded to upset not merely his enemies – which was only to be expected – but also all his friends and allies. The leading families of the nation found the King's conduct to be quite insufferable and decided to oust him peaceably. They invited his daughter, Mary, to become queen with her husband, William of Orange, as king. Having secured the backing of the Army under John Churchill, they simply wanted King James II to go away. James threw the Great Seal into the Thames and fled, all the while convinced that his enemies were pursuing him. In fact, their agents were ensuring his safe passage out of the country. Unfortunately, the sea captain of the ex-king's crossing to France saw through the latter's typically incompetent disguise and thought that he was doing his patriotic duty by bringing James back to England as a prisoner; so the revolutionaries had once again to arrange for his escape.

The ruling oligarchy then passed the Bill of Rights as William and Mary acceded to the throne. This bill had nothing at all to do with the rights of the ordinary subject. It simply limited the powers of the monarchy and increased the powers of the barons. After the death of Mary, followed by that of William, the oligarchy put Anne, another daughter of the exiled King James, upon the throne. In 1702 they passed the Act of Settlement, which made a puppet out of the monarch. He or she would have influence but was devoid of direct power.

During the reign of Queen Anne, the victorious Whigs battled and intrigued against the defiant Tories, many of whom still supported the Stuarts but who could not argue since the Queen was a Stuart. The problem was one of the succession, since all Anne's babies died and she failed to produce an heir. There was also a conflict of interests. The Whigs were landed magnates of largely liberal persuasion acting in concert with wealthy City merchants into whose families the daughters of the former often married. The Tories tended to be country squires of conservative views who favoured a restoration of the powers of the Crown. Queen Anne listened to her favourites, Lady Sarah Churchill and Mrs Abigail Masham, sometimes favouring one party and on occasion another.

The underrated Queen presided over a period of military glory, exemplified by Marlborough's victories over the troops of Louis XIV, of growing commercial prosperity and of quiet excellence in terms of literature: one thinks of Addison, Steele, Swift, Pope and Daniel Defoe. The architecture of the period has yet to be excelled for discreet elegance. When Queen Anne died in 1715, the ruling families brought over the Elector of Hanover and crowned him as King George I.

William Makepeace Thackeray, author of *Vanity Fair*, has written unforgettably scathing words about aristocratic grovelling to the Hanoverians in his *The Four Georges*. It suited the Whig magnates that King George I was a bore and a boor who couldn't speak English. A number of Tories had hoped in vain for the restoration of the Stuarts but a feeble Scottish rebellion under the Earl of Mar, badly conceived and maladroitly executed, was crushed rather easily. From that moment, the Whig oligarchy, consisting of a few hundred families, proceeded to run the country. They found their ideal leader in Sir Robert Walpole, generally acknowledged as England's first Prime Minister. This man was an exceptionally able individual. He had made a fortune from the notorious City swindle known as the 'South Sea Bubble' by getting out of it at precisely the right time, when the shares were peaking, then complacently contemplating the ruin of those who lacked both his acumen and his sources of information. He knew just how to manipulate the monarchs he served as First Lord of the Treasury. He favoured a policy of mercantile enterprise domestically and of peace in foreign affairs. The corruption of the time did not worry him: he frequently used its techniques himself in order to manage Parliament. 'Let sleeping dogs lie,' he murmured as his ministers lied, lied and lied again. His regime favoured established families and enterprising merchants with no ideology other than greed as the creed.

No one was sorry when that most unkingly king, George I, died. His son and heir, King George II, was equally undistinguished, making his principal contribution to national culture with the heavy sentence: 'I hate boets and bainters.' Walpole continued to be Prime Minister, and was a master of fixing votes in Parliament. At that time, the House of Lords controlled the majority of seats in the Commons. Only a minority of people had the vote at elections, voting was public and it was easy to bribe or intimidate electors. Any commoner sponsored by a lord would win a safe seat in Parliament and vote according to instructions. When stage plays satirised his rule, Walpole reintroduced censorship of the theatre, which would not be abolished until the 1960s. Nevertheless, England prospered peaceably under Walpole. By the standards of the time, the government was reasonably civilised, moderately effective and utterly unexciting. Such opposition as there was floundered in disarray.

As Sir Lewis Namier has demonstrated in his exhaustive studies of eighteenth-century politics, there was no ideological contest at all until the later years. One is surveying groupings of families and factions rather than contests of ideas. Then as now, politicians were solely interested in the spoils of office.

Some Tories still favoured a restoration of the Stuarts under Bonnie Prince Charlie, son of 'King James III', for they were unreconciled to the Hanoverian succession, which reigns over this nation to this day under the assumed name of Windsor. However, the 1745 rebellion of the Stuarts collapsed in a sad mixture of good intentions and incompetent generalship. Other Tories and some disaffected Whig radicals sought for some sort of ideological opposition based on the ideas set out in Henry St John, Viscount Bolingbroke's *Idea of a Patriot King*, published in 1749. Bolingbroke had negotiated the treaty that had ended the wars with France under Queen Anne in 1713. He had then endeavoured unsuccessfully to ensure a Stuart succession. The central proposal of his elegantly written book was that a wise, brave and intelligent king should break the oppressive power of the Whig magnates and govern strongly in favour of the arts, the sciences and the commercial welfare of the people.

Many Tory country squires had no interest in Bolingbroke's idealism. They simply resented the rule of Whig magnates and City merchants. They had no more interest in ideas and ideals than Sir Robert Walpole. They remembered, however, that the first Tudor king, Henry VII, had allied with the country gentlemen and appointed them as Justices of the Peace so as to break the power of the barons. Many were prepared for reasons of either sheer self-interest or mere gut instinct to back the notion of a 'patriot king' and, as it happened, there was a candidate in Frederick, Prince of Wales, who was an associate of the Dashwood circle. Some thought that this vain and handsome man could in time embody Bolingbroke's ideal and, as king of England, preside over an emergent version of a renewed Albion. There would be work and prosperity for the poor, increased enterprise for the merchants, a flourishing of arts and sciences and exquisite civilisation for an elite. Great Britain would hold aloft a torch of blazing human evolution.

This notion was supported by many of the Independents, such as Dashwood, who had traditional Tory instincts yet who owed allegiance neither to Crown nor to Party. The Tories had deplored the regime of Walpole. The Prime Minister's professional competence was not in question; his vision was, for as the Bible states: 'Where there is no vision, the people perish.' These men did not think that much good was being done to the nation by Whiggish oligarchical plundering and profiteering. It was Dr Johnson, a steadfast Tory, who declared to Boswell: 'Sir: the Devil made the first Whig.'

The Whigs merely laughed at such notions and carried on playing games of family and faction. Principles counted for nothing and office of state was all; ideas were merely a tiresome nuisance. King George II remained satisfied with his successive governments. When he was informed that a grouping had gathered around Prince Frederick, his son and heir, he simply dismissed the matter with a snort of: 'That booby.'

England was then a three-tier society. The aristocracy, gentry and nouveaux riches did virtually what they liked. As one lord declared languidly: 'These days a man can just about jog along at £40,000 a year.' The equivalent today would be an annual income of roughly £1.6 million. As always, the rich were careless of public opinion. 'Tomorrow, wind and weather permitting, I propose to be drunk,' another lord scribbled on a note to his butler, adding: 'Place a crate of sherry by my bedside and call me the day after tomorrow.'

The emerging middle classes deplored the degeneracy of those who believed themselves to be better. They were making money from merchandise and often married penniless daughters of the aristocracy, whose fathers had gambled away the family estates, thus rising to a position of influence via familial connection and money. Moreover, two revolutions were occurring which would bring them positive benefit: the agricultural and the industrial. New and more efficient methods of farming made many

agricultural labourers redundant. They could not restore their
fallen fortunes as of yore on common land, because common land
was being rapidly enclosed for private benefit by a series of Acts
of Parliament. Enclosure threw workers off the land and forced
them to look for work in the towns and cities, where new
inventions had led to a demand for low-waged industrial labour.
As the workers suffered, many middle-class men made a fortune
fast and began to agitate for greater influence in the politics of
their country.

This development created an underclass in the towns and
cities. Then as now, this underclass was utterly lawless. The most
draconian of punishments did not deter them from committing
atrocities of crime. There were areas in London where law and
order ceased to exist. Law enforcement officers, such as they
were, were publicly despised and frequently assaulted. In these
areas, life was nasty, brutish and short, as Hobbes had put it a
century earlier. To relieve the pain and tedium of their existence,
the poor flocked to watch bull-baiting, bear-baiting, cock-
fighting, public executions and prize-fighting with bare knuckles.

The London mob, who loved these contests, erupted out of
conditions of brutal poverty and squalor. Their children usually
went to work at the age of six. It was not unusual for a twelve-
year-old to finish a day's labour by taking a pint of gin at his local.
Alcoholism, violence, theft, rape and mugging were the rule in
most parts of London. It is all too easy to see the Georgian era
through rose-tinted spectacles that show us beautiful town
houses, squares, gardens, paintings, silver and exquisite side-
tables. One discerns elegance and clarity here, and quite enjoys
the picturesque images of gin palaces, drunken judges,
gentlemanly highwaymen, public hangings and pox-ridden
whores. The fact is that there was cultured life only for the
privileged few and for the rest, life was squalid. Crime increased
dramatically and the government responded with increasingly
savage measures; whilst the Church did nothing to ameliorate the
lot of the near-starving urban working class. The powers that were
responded to the wave of urban crime by passing increasingly

draconian measures. It was not uncommon for a child to be hanged for stealing a pocket handkerchief. These policies failed lamentably to deter crime and lawlessness.

The vast majority of the privileged few were incapable even of comprehending the phrase 'a social conscience'. It wasn't as if they particularly disliked the poor; they were just a tiresome nuisance. Certain areas of London were 'no go'; that was all right, they thought, for what sane man would want to go there? One is reminded of Voltaire's story of the peasant who implored the lord not to raise his rent. 'My lord, I must live,' the peasant begged. 'I fail to see why,' the lord replied.

For those lucky enough to be born into a tiny elite, however, life could be a joy. The gulf between rich and poor meant that just one guinea could purchase easy pleasures. This state of affairs has been summarised succinctly by Eric Towers:

> The prices and incomes . . . need to be multiplied by at least 40 to give a rough and ready guide to what they represent in today's money. An income of £500 a year enabled a family to live in genteel comfort, with servants and a carriage. A curate of the Church of England had to manage on £40 a year. More blessed by fortune, the Duke of Bedford had £5,000 a year from his London properties alone . . . A sustaining meal of roast or boiled meat or vegetables, followed by pudding, could be had for a shilling (5p) in London taverns . . . An intimate encounter with a reputable young lady of the profession in London cost a guinea, but less expensive facilities were readily available.

One is reminded of the famous sign outside one gin palace:

> Drunk for a penny.
> Dead drunk for tuppence.
> Clean straw for nothing.

Eighteenth-century England was a society utterly wearied by wars of religion and the vice of 'enthusiasm' was deplored. One can see why. The country had endured centuries of Roman Catholic oppression; a vengeful Catholicism without the pope under Henry VIII; vicious Protestant vandalism under Lord Protector Northumberland acting for Edward VI; then the fires of Smithfield where defiant Protestants were burned alive under the Catholic Queen Mary Tudor. This was followed by the allegedly moderate Settlement of Queen Elizabeth I. Here both Catholics and Puritans who could not conform to a compromise were persecuted by what G.K. Chesterton has termed: 'A government of torturers rendered ubiquitous by spies.'

The succeeding seventeenth century did little to further tolerance among the competing religious sects. King James I persecuted Catholics and so provoked the Gunpowder Plot. He persecuted Puritans and so caused inadvertently the sailing of the *Mayflower* to America. He also persecuted 'witches'. One can easily see why his great contemporary, King Henry IV of France, called this feeble scholar 'the wisest fool in Christendom'. King Charles I, James's son, supported the endeavours of that fussy and pedantic High Anglican, Archbishop Laud, to rule strictly on matters of Christian ritual and to govern the morals of an unwilling nation. Oliver Cromwell and the Puritan party had both king and archbishop executed but then proceeded to enforce countless petty moral regulations. The Restoration of King Charles II, a man with no interest in persecuting anyone for matters of belief, was greeted with a huge national sigh of relief. Extreme sectarians criticised both the liberality of his life and the plenitude of his mistresses whilst abusing him for tolerating any religion that was not a political threat.

Puritan and Catholic alike savaged this king's loose morals. The London mob disliked his liaison with a Catholic mistress, Louise de Querouaille, thought by many to be a pawn of King Louis XIV of France, and stoned her coach, only for another mistress, Nell Gwynne, to appear. 'Good people, desist,' the former Covent Garden orange seller implored these violent thugs; 'I am the English whore, not the French one.' The mob put down their stones and one is not surprised to learn that the dying words of

King Charles II were: 'Don't let poor Nelly starve.'

King Charles II did not want religion to be a political issue but it became so under his brother and successor, King James II, who was a Roman Catholic. A posturing poser, Titus Oates, caused riots by 'exposing' something he called 'the Popish Plot'. The King responded with ill-advised but savage penalties for dissent which contributed to his downfall. As England moved into the eighteenth century, there was a general recognition among the ruling families that there should be toleration in religious matters unless these threatened the political structure. This led to a somewhat bland notion of religion in the land. As Anthony Trollope would state one hundred years later: 'I like the Church of England, for it is the only institution which does not interfere with your politics or your religion.'

'Religion is the opium of the masses,' Karl Marx would declare at roughly the same time and the evidence of the eighteenth century bears out the testimony of both Trollope and Marx. Outside the growing cities, the small towns and villages were governed by the squire and the parson. It was the parson's job, in exchange for his living, to persuade the parish to acquiesce in the system as being part of the law of God. 'Render unto Caesar those things that are of Caesar: and unto God, those things that are of God', was a grossly overworked and misrepresented biblical text, used to justify that notorious hymn:

> The rich man in his castle,
> The poor man at his gate;
> God made them high and lowly
> And ordered their estate...

The poor were then ordered to join joyfully in a chorus:

> All things bright and beautiful,
> All creatures great and small:
> All things wise and wonderful;
> The Lord God made them all.

This added hypocritical insult to manifest injury. Religion became a matter of mere social conformity. One paid it mere lip service. This was exemplified by the sermon preached before King George I by the Bishop of Bangor, Benjamin Hoadly, in 1717. The Bishop argued that 'The Kingdom of Christ is not of this World.' Crown and Party responded by printing thousands of copies of his sermon. The Church of England justified not, as Milton wrote, 'the ways of God to man', but the ways of government to man.

The Church became a willing accomplice of the ruling oligarchy. There would no doubt be justice in the next world but there was no right to complain about injustice in this one. Religious dissidents would not be persecuted here and now; they would merely be ignored. The ceremonies of religion would be observed in a quiet and dull manner. Divine intoxication would be severely discouraged. There would be pleasant social rites instead. The parson became, of necessity, the ally of the squire. An intelligent man of religious persuasion could then get a decent living out of the Church of England, providing that he did not startle or arouse his parishioners into independent thought. The *Diary* of Parson Woodforde, for instance, is typical of the time. This kindly man rarely mentions his religion. Usually his record is of his gargantuan dinners; eating seems to have meant more to him than God.

It was certainly a relief to get away from those dreadful days of religious fanaticism and persecution but the result was a society which seemed to have no sense of religion at all. There was a variety of responses. Philip, Duke of Wharton, rejoiced in a mockery of Christianity, and founded the original 'Hell-Fire Club'. He would have agreed with Nietzsche that Christianity is 'the innermost stain, the one immortal blemish upon mankind'. After all, who could do other than loathe Christianity's deliberately organised torture and genocide of falsely accused 'witches' between the fifteenth and seventeenth centuries?

Mere mockery of this horrendous insult to the human race does not in itself constitute a religion. A more positive system came forth in the shape of Freemasonry, and Wharton became for a time its Grand Master. Freemasons accepted that there is indeed a Great Architect of the Universe and were content to invite Christians as members in order to educate them into principles of civilised toleration. Unsurprisingly, Freemasonry on the Continent was assaulted by the Spanish Inquisition and anathematised by the Pope.

A third sensibility was embraced by those who wanted life to mean more than merely 'birth, copulation and death' in the words of T.S. Eliot. Horace Walpole, son of the Whig Prime Minister, will serve as a curious example of this sensibility. He was a sceptic and an agnostic who felt that the three most honest words in the English language were: 'I don't know'. Even so, he felt within himself a hunger for something more than merely the cold and rational. He had Strawberry Hill built at Twickenham. Here he endeavoured to recreate a medieval castle as seen through eighteenth-century eyes.

The sensibility which inspired him to create this building also provoked him to pen *The Castle of Otranto*, the first Gothic novel (1765). Today it is hard to read this book without bursting into fits of mocking laughter or else flinging it away with impatience. Even so, this pioneering work founded the Gothic movement, with its love of gloomy landscapes, persecuted women and fatal men. The most notable exponent of Gothic romance was Ann Radcliffe, whose novel *The Mysteries of Udolpho*, along with *The Castle of Otranto*, created a literary tradition which still endures to this day. These seminal works were the foundation stones of supernatural horror in literature. Yet Walpole had no religious commitment to anything other than his own eccentric, aesthetic adventures. His comments on the Friars were rancid, probably because they did not make a member out of him.

There was a fourth sensibility. This consisted of an astonishing compound of literature, paganism, Templarism, Freemasonry, Rosicrucianism, Tantricism and general Renaissance influences. Dashwood was trying to syncretise a religion in an age where there was none.

4

The Influence

The essential characteristic of elitism is exclusivity. We should therefore not be surprised to find groupings forming exclusive clubs. These developed out of Elizabethan meetings of poets, scholars and politicians in taverns. 'In Good King Charles's Golden Days', as Bernard Shaw has it, the popularity of coffee and chocolate drinking led to the establishment of a number of houses open to the public and serving these beverages. In the late seventeenth century, when Dryden reigned as king of the coffee-house, there were noted establishments for poets, wits, Whigs and Tories, where news and gossip were exchanged and meetings were held. Some bright sparks devised the practice of 'clubbing' expenses. This often led to the hiring of a room, the election of a chairman, secretary and treasurer, a dues-paying membership and regular meetings at fixed dates.

Clubs were born out of these initially spontaneous gatherings. *The Secret History of Clubs* (1709) by Ned Ward lists thirty-one of them, including Bolingbroke's Saturday Club, the Tory October Club, the Hanover and the Green Ribbon. The Golden Fleece appears to have been merely frivolous. The Wet Paper was for those who desired the latest printed information. There was the Ugly and the Lying, presumably for the ugly and the lying; and the Ace of Clubs, which was so excessively exclusive that it expired within a year. The Beefsteak Club was founded in 1707 and resurrected in 1735 as the Sublime Society of Beefsteaks, which is still in existence today.

White's, Boodles, Pratt's, Brook's and other clubs which still endure were founded during this period. The purpose of founding a club is to assemble like-minded people, to ban bores and to close it to the general public.

Two clubs of the time which were in sharp contrast were the Mohocks and the Mollies. The Mohocks was for Hooray Henries who wished to prove their 'masculinity' by being violent thugs. They savaged with weapons elderly night-watchmen and anyone else who was outnumbered and helpless. They were disgusting, but not very different from our contemporary soccer hooligans in their Pringle cardigans. Meanwhile, the Mollies dressed up in women's clothes and cooed gently to one another.

Between these extremes, we find a clubman ably described by Geoffrey Ashe:

He is socially a gentleman and a womaniser... Comfortably off, fairly cultured, fairly well-read, he has absorbed a trendy optimism, and believes that Nature is on his side and he can do pretty much as he pleases. He dislikes the smug, philistine, corrupt Whig Establishment, and in that spirit may favour ill-defined schemes of opposition, even parlour Jacobitism. In that spirit also he is willing and even eager to shock. He flirts with blasphemy and magic. Yet he may still be glad to see the conventions upheld, as at the end of *Fanny Hill*, so that he can have pleasure in flouting them.

There was one club, however, which passed quite beyond the pale, so much so that on 28 April 1721, King George I issued an Order-in-Council against it. This Order was proposed by the Lord Chancellor, Baron Macclesfield. Its object was to suppress 'immorality and profaneness' and its victim was a grouping known as the Hell-Fire Club. This club met variously at Somerset House – for orgies, it was alleged – in Westminster and in Conduit Street near Hanover Square, Belgravia. The leader of these groupings was that extraordinary character, Philip, Duke of Wharton (1698–1731).

Wharton could have modelled for John Milton's Satan in *Paradise Lost*. '*Non serviam*' could aptly have been his motto. He was brilliant, erratic, underrated, dissipated and unreliable; ultimately he laid to waste his range of undeniable talents. Unlike Dashwood, he lacked the finances requisite for the realisation of his vision. By 1725 Wharton had debts of £70,000 and an income of just £1,200 a year.

Dean Swift liked Wharton and warned him against the vices of drink and financial extravagance, warnings which were in vain. Swift had nevertheless loathed Philip's father, Thomas, first Marquis of Wharton. This man had been noted mainly for writing the campaign song of the 'Glorious Revolution' of 1688, which ousted King James II of the Stuart family and replaced him with King William III of Orange, Holland.

'*Lillibulero bullen-a-la-leero-leero-leero*' had been the marching song of William's troops and was composed by Thomas working on a sound that effectively matches the heartbeat. Afterwards he boasted that he had sung King James out of three kingdoms. He also married the toast of the Kit-Kat Club, Lucy Loftus, who became the mother of his son. The godparents were King William III and the future Queen Anne. His son Philip was therefore perfectly positioned to make a major impact upon the nation.

He was given tutoring by Edward Young, a Fellow of All Souls, Oxford. His problem was that he could not conform. He married a woman of whom his father disapproved and defied all endeavours to have the marriage annulled by the Attorney-General, a friend of his father. The action failed and the father died a few weeks later; one suspects that Philip shed few tears. Going on the Grand Tour in 1716, he made contact in Paris with 'the Old Pretender', James Stuart, claimant of the Crown of England and Scotland and Wales and Ireland, and he accepted a 'Knighthood of the Garter' from him in 1726. Returning to Ireland, Wharton received further tutoring from Edward Young, whose reputation as a poet and scholar was increasing. Wharton did his tutor credit in the Irish House of Lords, stunning his peers with his clear, elegant and crisp speech accompanied by a sarcastic unveiling of common corruption. On his return to England he was created the nation's youngest non-royal Duke.

He then proceeded to outrage the very establishment that had favoured him. He went brawling in public. According to Ashe he upset the Musgrave family by taking 'the Luck of Eden Hall', their sacred chalice, throwing it up in the air and then missing his catch. So far, so bad. Yet he exposed the stock market swindle known as 'the South Sea Bubble' so fiercely and accurately that his opponent, Lord Stanhope, collapsed in the House with a cerebral haemorrhage. Wharton was a merciless and cynical critic of the government as he roared and roistered his way through the taverns and brothels of London.

Around 1720, he founded the Hell-Fire Club to mock and blaspheme the Christian religion and the society which supported it, attracting to its membership around forty 'persons of quality'. Unusually for the time, this grouping included women. The menus for their dinners were unusual too, for they included Holy Ghost Pie – an imitation Host flavoured with angelica root; Breast of Venus – poussin garnished with cherries so as to tip the breasts as nipples; and Devil's Loins accompanied by a beverage they called Hell-Fire Punch. As we have seen, this innocuous nonsense aroused the ire of the Lord Chancellor and the King. Wharton denied blasphemy in a speech he made in the House of Lords. Outside the House, he savaged the Lord Chancellor in satirical verse which implied that the latter was a rogue and criminal. He was right. Lord Macclesfield was subsequently convicted of corruption.

Wharton, a rebel at all times, was certainly no coward. He founded *The True Briton* journal, precursor of *The North Briton* of Wilkes and Churchill in years to come, which ran from 1723 to 1724, sold in thousands and upset the establishment. On the first page of the first issue, he declared for 'LIBERTY'. He also wrote: 'The two great Essentials, requisite for the well ordering of Society, are, To be allowed the full Extent of our Liberties, and To be protected in our respective Properties.'

The printer was Samuel Richardson, author of the century's

most influential novel, *Clarissa*. It can be argued that its villain,
Lovelace, was based upon Wharton. It can also be argued that his
sometime tutor, Edward Young, based the character of the infidel
Lorenzo in his hymn to immortality, *Night Thoughts*, on Wharton.
Wharton gave money to Young, even when he didn't have it to
spare, tried unsuccessfully to have Young elected as an MP and
gave him a human skull, fashioned as a candle-holder, in order to
inspire his poetry further. This laudable patronage of the arts did
not prevent Alexander Pope from verbal savagery at Wharton's
expense:

> Wharton, the scorn and wonder of our days
> Whose ruling passion was the lust of praise:
> Born with what'er could win it from the wise
> Women and fools must like him, or he dies:

And:

> A fool, with more of wit than half mankind;
> Too rash for thought, for action too refined...
> Ask you why Wharton broke through every rule?
> 'Twas all for fear the knaves should call him fool.

Of course, Pope was envious of Wharton's casual sexual success
with the delectable Lady Mary Montagu, whom the poet had
pestered in vain.

'Twenty very pretty fellows (the Duke of Wharton being
president and chief director),' Lady Mary wrote to her sister,
'have formed themselves into a committee of gallantry, who call
themselves "Schemers", and meet regularly three times a week to
consult on gallant schemes for the advancement and advantage of
that branch of happiness...These schemes,' she continued
excitedly, 'ought to be spread wherever men can sigh, or women
can wish.'

Perhaps unfortunately, these ingenious schemes were not
spread. Severe debts forced Wharton to flee the country. He

dazzled Vienna and then Madrid in 1725, annoying the British ambassador to Spain so much that London ordered his return: the Duke responded by throwing the order out of the window of his coach. When his wife died in 1726, he married an impoverished Irish maid of honour to the Spanish Queen. He proclaimed his conversion to Catholicism and the Jacobite cause, and denounced the Hanoverian monarchy for their trampling 'on the ancient nobility'. England responded with an indictment for high treason. Barred from his birthplace, Wharton drifted between France and Spain, delighting a few, amusing some and annoying many. His debauchery and dissipation continued undiminished. A fit struck him in May 1731 and he died without issue.

Nevertheless, he left two legends. One was the image of the satanic, defiant rake. The other was the tale of the Hell-Fire Club. Ireland took up this tale. Limerick saw the foundation of a Hell-Fire Club. The blasphemous 'Dublin Blasters', founded by self-professed satanist and painter Peter Lens, was reported to the Irish Parliament in 1737. Then Richard Parsons, first Earl of Rosse, and Colonel Jack St Leger, founded another Hell-Fire Club in Dublin. There they apparently toasted Satan with 'scaltheen' – hot whiskey and butter sprinkled with brimstone – and held orgies at Cork Hill's Eagle Tavern, at a lodge on Montpelier Hill and at Daly's Club on College Green.

Moreover, Wharton left a third legacy: Freemasonry. We shall be looking at this further in due course. For the present, let it suffice to state that the United Grand Lodge of England was founded in 1717 and Wharton was Grand Master 1722–3. He went on to found the first European Lodge in Madrid.

Rumour and hearsay followed Wharton long after his death. It was said that he had founded Dublin's Hell-Fire Club, the meetings of which were apparently chaired by 'a huge black cat'. By 1962, Eric Maple had 'a huge artificial bat complete with an erect penis', which he attributed to the Friars of St Francis. One is amused by his imagination but not impressed by his research. The claims become increasingly like a game of Chinese Whispers.

We should therefore look at the legends of the Hell-Fire Clubs with a healthy element of scepticism. Even so, there is evidence that Edinburgh witnessed pacts with the Devil at Halkerston's Wynd, Allan's Close, Carrider's Close, and Jack's Close, Canongate. John Kidgell, a dirty little man later used against Wilkes, was accused of Devil worship at Oxford University at a club which had prospered for decades, in an anonymous pamphlet issued in 1763. Meanwhile, according to Sir Arthur Quiller-Couch, the 'Appalling Club' was founded in 1738 at Jesus College, Cambridge, by the Hon. Alan Dermot. Legend has it that the seven founder members died one by one in increasingly horrible circumstances. Myth adds that their ghosts still shout and blaspheme in the college room they used at the top of Cow Lane staircase.

Myth and legend still surround the mysterious grouping at The George or The George & Vulture during the 1740s. Whichever inn it was, few doubt the eccentricity of the landlord. Apparently he bought 'a most notable and extraordinary cock vulture' at Peckham Fair, kept it in the yard and scared customers with tales of its supernatural powers, and it was added to the sign after his death. The cock is the principal symbol of Baphomet, the sexual deity the Knights Templar had been accused of worshipping when they were suppressed in the Middle Ages. Furthermore, according to Lasky and Silver, this bizarre landlord apparently lit his cellar with an 'Everlasting Rosicrucian lamp' in the ceiling. One rumour has it that this object came to grace Dashwood's West Wycombe caves but the visitor will not find it there now.

There are quite a few dubious stories about the Dashwood Club's time in a pub cellar. Ashe refers to 'a Black Mass, complete with a naked girl as altar, stretched out on a table in the bar', but wryly comments: 'presumably after closing time'. Thomas De Quincey mentions an anonymous lord who had a man run through with a kitchen spit in order to roast him alive; one is inclined to believe that the otherwise excellent De Quincey had had far too much opium and alcohol on the night he wrote that.

We will find sounder clues if we turn to William Hogarth. At some point between 1739 and 1745, he created that astonishing picture, *Charity in the Cellar*. Five men are boozing there. One is Dashwood. Another is Sandwich.

These two men had no need to form another club if the purpose was sociability and nothing more. There was White's, there was the Dilettante, there was the Divan, there was the Beefsteak, and so on and so forth. They were endeavouring to create something new. It would be a club, yes, and it would have all the benefits and characteristics of a roistering eighteenth-century club. However, there would be a religious vision. There would also be a political vision. And since a tavern cellar is hardly the ideal place for the realisation of these visions, there would be architecture, fusion and fixation at Medmenham Abbey and West Wycombe. It would incorporate a religious, political and sexual enchantment.

The eighteenth century was somewhat more liberated in its sexual attitudes than its ancestor, the seventeenth, or its descendant, the nineteenth. The Victorians condemned its morals as being lax. Lip service was paid to the strict sexual code of Christianity, and not much more. From time to time, there was a middle-class outcry against immorality and the authorities responded with a command to 'round up the usual suspects'. Prostitutes were in consequence arrested and sent to be flogged in Bridewell, where floggings were watched with satisfaction by Christians who had probably been their clients. Obviously this did no good and few really cared.

There is a certain animal impersonality about much eighteenth-century sexuality. We rarely find the Victorian notion of 'the purity of womanhood'. It was generally assumed that women were randy bitches. On account of this assumption, women enjoyed greater freedom than their granddaughters would. In the next century, old ladies would have to hide salacious novels under the sofa when demure young ladies entered the drawing room. In the eighteenth century, women of tart tongue, wit and intelligence were respected even if they were sometimes mocked as 'bluestockings'. Dr Johnson's celebrated comment on a woman preaching has often been misunderstood, for he was not referring to women of wit but to females devoid of humour: 'Sir, it is like a dog walking on its hind legs. It is not done well but one is amazed to see it done at all.'

The principal arena for the oppression of women was money. Once a woman married, she lost all rights to her money or her property, which passed into the hands of her husband. Small wonder, then, that many handsome and unscrupulous adventurers achieved their start in life and made their fortunes by charming and marrying a woman of means: Thackeray would portray this perfectly in his novel, *Barry Lyndon*. It took a century and the Married Women's Property Act to rectify this injustice.

Among the upper classes, most marriages were a dynastic arrangement. It was expected by the women that their husbands would frequently fornicate with other women; and many husbands allowed their wives the same freedom. One sees such an arrangement at the turn of the century when Sir William Hamilton turned a blind eye to the affair his wife Emma was enjoying with Nelson.

If a husband wasn't so tolerant, sexual life could be difficult for a woman. Under the law of the land, she could not divorce her husband for adultery, no matter how numerous the occasions, but he could divorce her for just one incident and keep all her property.

Among the working classes, many girls succumbed to the lure of prostitution. The price was cheap for any man of independent income but a girl could earn as much money from it in a day as she could from a month of legitimate sweated labour. If she attained a reputation as a minor courtesan and could set herself up in modest comfort, she could charge a guinea for an hour, roughly £50 in today's terms. The top courtesans earned far more and could pick and choose among the men to whom they distributed their favours.

Sometimes quarrels broke out between men over rivalries concerning the favours of a celebrated courtesan. This would lead to a duel, even though the custom had been declared illegal. One wonders what the lady thought as she watched this performance from her carriage. The etiquette was strict. One man would slap another's face with a glove and drop it on the floor. If the other man accepted this insult, he was permanently branded as a coward. If he took up the challenge, he had the choice of pistols or swords. Both men then named their seconds and met at dawn. Killing one's antagonist would probably lead to capital punishment, so it was very much a matter of satisfying honour. If swords had been chosen, the duellists were expected to fence well until first blood was drawn, at which point the seconds rushed forward to halt the contest and to persuade both men that honour had been satisfied. If pistols were the weapons, these were customarily discharged into the air – it was considered to be jolly bad form to shoot one's antagonist fatally – and again, the seconds rushed forward to assure the gentlemen that honour had been satisfied.

The burgeoning middle classes disliked duelling, casual sex, blood sports, indeed all the pleasures of the upper and working classes. It was among them that a re-emerging Christianity took a hold, most notably in the form of John Wesley's Methodism. This led to repeated calls for a reformation of morals. The ruling establishment responded by saying 'yes' and doing nothing.

One finds a fine portrayal of eighteenth-century sexual manners in *Fanny Hill* by John Cleland, which purports to be the autobiography of a prostitute. Subtitled *Memoirs of a Woman of Pleasure*, and written to stave off creditors, this was bought by an enterprising publisher for twenty guineas, then brought out in 1749, allegedly bringing £10,000 to its purchaser. Its explicit sexual descriptions caused an outcry among the clergy. The response of the establishment was typical of its time. After reprimanding the author before the Privy Council, they gave him a pension of £100 a year on condition that he wrote nothing more of that nature, and found him a job as an information officer.

To the many in this paradoxical century, sex was simply natural. To a few, it could be sacred.

Dashwood's inspiration was drawn from many sources including the Hell-Fire Club of Wharton and the eighteenth-century ideal of cultured clubbability: but we first find the notions of *Fay Ce Que Voudras* and of an Abbey of *Thelema* – Ancient Greek for 'Will' – in that extraordinary Renaissance work, *Gargantua and Pantagruel* by François Rabelais (1494–1553).

Starting out first as a Franciscan and then as a Benedictine monk, Rabelais subsequently abandoned monasteries to lead a stormy and controversial life in sharp contrast to the quiet of the cloister. He broke his vows by fathering a child in Lyons. He assailed monkish superstitions, declaring that monasteries were little other than protected enclaves of ignorance, bigotry, suppression and repression, serving no useful purpose either human or divine. He wandered around France earning his living as a physician, incurring the hostility of the Church but attracting the patronage of cultured men. The five volumes of *Gargantua and Pantagruel* are his principal legacy to posterity. It is generally accepted that Dashwood purchased this work in Paris during the course of his youthful Grand Tour.

There can be few works of Western literature that are more unusual or more outrageous. Even today, critics find it hard to make sense out of the material. Essentially, it hurls together every compound of verbal force and form in a manner that had never been done before and has never been done since. *Tristram Shandy* by Laurence Sterne and *Ulysses* by James Joyce are the only parallels.

The work begins as a fairy tale about giants written with excessive hyperbole, plunges into the grossest scatological obscenities and then suddenly proceeds to dazzle the intellect with its summaries of medieval learning, which is savagely satirised and unfavourably contrasted with the new knowledge of the Renaissance. From these sublimities of philosophical argument, it suddenly descends into sewers of anality, proceeds via vulgar marital comedy, then evokes folklore, myth and legend; then, after a lengthy, witty and humorous debate on marriage and the differences between men and women, it proceeds to parody tales of the quest for the Holy Grail in the 'Search for the Oracle of the Bottle'. When this Oracle is finally discovered, after descriptions of journeys which satirise travellers' tales and the works of fanciful geographers, it simply states: 'TRINC.'

Many have praised Rabelais as the supreme literary artist of his age; others find him unreadable. Probably one's best guide to this labyrinthine work is that unjustly neglected author Arthur Machen in his delicately argued work of literary criticism, *Hieroglyphics*. Machen opines that the difference between Literature and literature, between a work of art and a well-written political pamphlet, depends upon the presence of *ecstasy*, which he also calls 'wonder', 'rapture', 'awe' and 'a withdrawal from the common life'. Machen regards Rabelais as being one of the supreme exponents of the ecstasy revealed by the written word.

Three of the principal characters in the book are the giant, Pantagruel; Panurge, an enlivening rogue and rascal; and Friar John, a virile and active fighter. Machen urges the reader to see Pantagruel as the soul or unconscious of man, Panurge as the conscious mind, and Friar John as the body. Giving an analogy, he states that Pantagruel conceives the Great Work of literature, Panurge writes it and Friar John takes it to the printers. The giant Pantagruel who drinks in such copious quantities, is 'all athirst' for ecstasy, and the vine and his wine serve as hieroglyphics for that which is most sacred to the human spirit.

Dashwood may have missed the subtleties discerned by Machen a hundred and fifty years later; but ecstasy was what he wanted and he saw a way of obtaining it within the first volume of Rabelais, the history of Pantagruel's father, the giant Gargantua. When Friar John assists him by fighting bravely in a local war, Gargantua gives him an estate along the Loire, where John may realise his dream in founding the Abbey of Thélème, which will be the opposite of all others.

This Abbey is described in loving detail by Rabelais. The measurements are given with geometric exactitude and these tie in with Qabalah (see Chapter 14). It has six sides – the number Dashwood would use for his mausoleum at West Wycombe – with a round tower at each angle. There are six storeys with 'fine wide galleries, all painted with ancient feats of arms, histories and views of the world'. One section simply consists of six floors of books in Greek, Latin, Hebrew, French, Italian and Spanish – sadly, there is nothing there in English. Within, there are courts and fountains, roof gardens, art galleries, a theatre and a scented swimming bath. There are 9,332 rooms for the 'monks', and these have thick carpets in green and are adorned with tapestries, mirrors in golden frames and embroidered bedclothes. Other amenities include tennis courts, a maze, gardens, an orchard, a park, a wood and stables.

With the exception of the absence of books in English, it sounds like the best sort of luxury hotel. Who is considered worthy to enjoy its delights? Men must be good-looking or intelligent or delightful, preferably all three. Women must be beautiful, of comely build and with sweetness of nature. Anyone who doesn't like the Abbey is free to leave. As for the Rules:

> All their life was regulated not by laws, statutes or rules, but according to their free will and pleasure. They rose from bed when they pleased, and drank, ate, worked and slept when the fancy seized them. Nobody woke them; nobody compelled them either to eat or to drink, or to do anything else whatever... In their rules there was only one clause:

> *do what thou wilt.*

Small wonder that the mystic novelist John Cowper Powys celebrated Rabelais in the 1940s as the prophet of the future Age of Aquarius.

As Aleister Crowley, a twentieth-century proponent of 'Do what thou wilt', was frequently compelled to point out, this does not mean anything as trivial and vulgar as 'Do what you want.' In common with Crowley, Rabelais advocated self-regulation within the context of a sane and healthy society:

> People who are free, well-born, well-bred and easy in honest

company have a natural spur and instinct which drives them to virtuous deeds and deflects them from vice; and this they call honour... When these same men are depressed and enslaved by vile constraint and subjection, they use this noble quality which once impelled them freely towards virtue to throw off and break this yoke of slavery. For we always strive after things forbidden and covet what is denied us.

In *Gargantua and Pantagruel*, the Thelemites are encouraged to make money and marry, to develop every possible talent, to learn languages; to read, write, compose and play music; to wear fashionable clothes and anoint themselves with exquisite perfumes; to play competitive sports and games; and to communicate freely with one another. True, there is an element of elitism. The benefits of full membership flow only to magnanimous men who have embraced the New Learning of the Renaissance and to those 'flowers of all beauty... frank and fearless women'. Rabelais perceived them as being very much in accord with one another, rather than disputing during needless clashes of ego:

They most laudably rivalled one another in all of them doing what they saw pleased one. If some man or woman said, 'Let us drink', they all drank; if he or she said, 'Let us play', they all played; if it was 'Let us go and amuse ourselves in the fields', everyone went there.

Certainly the Thelemites live well. They have butlers, grooms, valets, chambermaids, chefs, barbers, perfumers, and 'goldsmiths, jewellers, embroiderers, tailors, wire-workers, velvet-weavers, tapestry makers and upholsterers; and there each man worked at his trade, and all of them for the aforesaid monks and nuns'. Others, however, are forbidden to enter the precincts of the Abbey: the old, the ugly, the diseased; and lawyers, money-lenders and those who are bad at heart. Over one gate, an inscription declares:

Enter not here, vile hypocrites and bigots,
Pious old apes, and puffed-up snivellers...

These aspirations were of course anathema to the Christian Church of that time and after. Rabelais made enemies wherever he or his works went.

His ideal of the Abbey of Thelema remained on paper until Sir Francis Dashwood said: 'Why not?'

5

The Monks of Medmenham

Sir Francis Dashwood pondered what to do with his time, his money and his energy. Having started on the transformation of the house and grounds at West Wycombe, having travelled widely and being a member of many exclusive clubs, he wanted to proceed further by realising a wider vision. The Monks were devoid of cheap and vulgar satanism for they were too cultured and intelligent to embrace so childish a superstition. Dashwood believed that the wise few could govern the ignorant many well, providing that these few were inspired by true religion.

The hypothesis is that this religion was essentially pagan in character. It was based upon the facts of nature, including worship of the male and female principles in life and their union – considered to be sacred rather than sinful. It included practices designed to advance human intelligence and evolution, influenced by occult works he had acquired in Venice: notably the works of Paracelsus, *The Isagoge* of the pseudonymous Artabel and *The Occult Philosophy of Cornelius Agrippa*. All this, he felt, should be done in exquisite surroundings, preceded and followed by fine wining and dining accompanied by sexual satisfaction. He sought an elite of peers and equals who would represent an aristocracy of the spirit, not mere material oligarchy, and thought that all would be best served if there were a 'patriot king' on the throne.

Looking out for the best and brightest of his time, Dashwood selected rakes rather than prudes. Drinkers and womanisers were men after his own heart. In those days and in those circles, you were either a three-bottle man or a four-bottle man; otherwise one was despised. The two litres of wine drunk without fail by Goethe every day led to criticism of his boring moderation.

Historians vary on the date of the Club's foundation, putting it variously at 1742, 1745, 1748 and 1752; not to mention a denial that there ever was such a foundation. The Medmenham cellar fragments only partially assist enquiry into the matter of membership. One can identify 'Francis of Wycombe' as Dashwood; 'Francis of Cookham' is clearly the Francis Duffield who leased Medmenham Abbey to Dashwood in 1751; 'Thomas de Greys' was Sir Thomas Stapleton, a cousin of Dashwood and a neighbouring country squire of Greys Court, near Henley. There is 'Thomas of London' whom Ashe calls an eccentric doctor, Dr Thomas Thompson, Dodington's physician in residence; but Towers thinks it more likely that this was Thomas Potter MP. There are also five men called 'John'.

These Johns are listed as being of Henley, of Melcombe, of Checkers, of Magdalen and of London. John of Henley was a Mr Clarke, a dull but worthy lawyer who acted for Dashwood's proprietorial interests in Buckinghamshire. John of Melcombe was John Tucker, MP for Weymouth and its mayor in 1754. He was also a Navy office cashier during the years when Dodington was Treasurer of the Navy. 'His letters to Dashwood,' Ashe states, 'are among the very few direct proofs from within that the Order did exist as described...' John of Checkers has to be Sir John Dashwood-King, half-brother of the founder; a letter confirms his membership (the 'King' was added to his name in gratitude for a large bequest from an uncle). No historian has yet positively identified the Johns of Magdalen and London, but given the fact that the cellar-books are post 1760, it seems reasonable to suppose that these are John Montagu, Earl of Sandwich, and John Wilkes MP.

There is little to be said about some members. Dr Thomas Thompson, for instance, attended the University of Padua in his youth and in later years received a pension from the secret service. Nobody knows why. Although contemporaries have described him as being extremely slovenly, he aroused Dashwood's respect sufficiently for the latter to commission a memorial tablet to him when he died. Little can also be said about Sir William Stanhope other than that he lived at Eyethorpe and was a younger brother of the celebrated Earl of Chesterfield. Three of the four Vansittart brothers of Shottesbrooke, Berkshire, were associated with the Dashwood circle: Arthur owned the family estate; Robert became Professor of Law at Oxford; and Henry, credited by legend for the introduction of a baboon to Medmenham Abbey, became Governor of Bengal in the service of the East India Company.

Although it is impossible to discern precisely who did and who did not enter the chapter-room, there is a general consensus among historians regarding association with Dashwood. Eric Towers entitled his chapter *Genial Gentlemen All.* We find the poet and satirist, Paul Whitehead; the Earl of Bute, tutor to the future King George III and later to become Prime Minister; George Augustus Selwyn MP, 'the first of the fashionable wits'; Frederick, Prince of Wales; John Wilkes, MP and future Lord Mayor of London; Charles Churchill and Robert Lloyd, two poets celebrated in their time; the Earl of Orford, Horace Walpole's elder brother, whom Raymond Postgate would call 'so silly a man that some considered him feeble-minded'; the Duke of Kingston; the Marquis of Granby; Lord March – that rake known as 'Old Q' – who became the Duke of Queensberry; Joseph Banks, President of the Royal Society; William Hogarth, arguably the greatest English visual artist of the era; Giuseppe Borgnis, a master of interior design; John Hall Stevenson of 'Crazy Castle'; the Chevalier D'Eon, transvestite fencer and secret agent for France; Benjamin Franklin of America and Benjamin Bates, Dashwood's doctor, who would in time deny every accusation. There is also the question of women members.

Most of these names are matters for dispute. For instance, H.T.F. Rhodes associates Charles Churchill with the Monks whilst Raymond Postgate declares that even if Churchill visited once or twice, it was for nothing more than a glass of sherry. However, it is obvious that there was a grouping around Dashwood, that there was a club established for purposes separate from the Divan and the Dilettante, that it was established at some point after 1745 and before 1751 and that within it there existed an outer circle and an inner circle. Some alleged members of this grouping do not strike one as being worthy of close study. For example, 'Old Q', Lord March, can be envisioned attending outer-circle parties with tremendous relish but would have had no interest in religious matters. His main interests in life were women and horses, followed by betting and boozing. As the *Imperial Epistle* from one Kien Long states (1795):

> And there insatiate yet with folly's sport
> That polished sin-worn fragment of the court,
> The shade of Queensb'ry, should with Clermont meet, Ogling
> and hobbling down St James's Street.

'Old Q' seems to have become somewhat jaded in his old age. 'What is there to make so much of in the Thames?' he sighed wearily as he gazed out of his bow-windowed villa at Richmond. 'I am quite tired of it – there it goes, flow, flow, flow, always the same . . .' The Friars and Monks did indeed 'flow, flow, flow', but it was hardly 'always the same'. An early associate of Dashwood was Frederick, Prince of Wales, whom some saw as the future 'patriot king'.

It is no easy task to be Prince of Wales. One is born to be king and possibly groomed to be so but then there is not much to do apart from wait until one's parent dies in order to fulfil one's function. Frederick Louis of Hanover was born son of the future George II of England in 1707. When his father was crowned king twenty years later, the Prince was brought to England. Here he continued to upset his father, who thought him to be an arrogant coxcomb; and he upset his mother too. 'My dear first-born is the greatest ass and the greatest liar and the greatest *canaille* and the greatest beast in the whole world,' his mother Queen Caroline declared, 'and I heartily wish he was out of it.'

Tobias Smollett, author of those delightful classics, *Roderick Random* and *Humphrey Clinker*, did not agree. Smollett wrote:

He was dressed in a coat of white cloth faced with blue satin, embroidered with silver of the same piece as his waistcoat. His hat was laced with silver and garnished with a white feather. But his person beggared all description. He was tall and graceful, his limbs finely proportioned, his countenance open and majestic, his eyes full of sweetness and vivacity, his teeth regular and his pouting lips of the complexion of the damask rose. In short, he was born for love and inspired it wherever he appeared. Nor was he a niggard of his wit, but liberally returned it, at least what passed for such. For he had a flow of gallantry for which many ladies of this land can vouch from their own experience.

Smollett obviously knew the facts there. As Dryden had it of King Charles II in *Absalom & Achitophel*, Frederick 'scattered his maker's image throughout the land'. Throughout his life, Frederick made love to actresses and opera singers. In 1736, he obeyed his father's wishes to marry and produce an heir, the wife being Princess Augusta of Saxe-Gotha, then aged seventeen. She bore him five sons, including the future King George III, and two daughters. This fecundity did not prevent Frederick from fornicating further. His lovers included Ann Vane, daughter of Lord Barnard, who was free with her favours to talented men of rank; though Frederick also had her chambermaid for good measure and had a son by her. There was also his affair with Grace, Countess of Middlesex. Quite simply, he liked sex and women liked him. That was probably because he genuinely liked women.

He was good-natured, he played the cello and sang French songs, he was a talented mimic and he loved amateur theatricals.

One might think him to be a good candidate for the role of patriot king, especially in view of Smollett's opinion, but Geoffrey Ashe does not agree:

> Known as Fred, or (to his family) Fritz, he was a short, vacant-looking, swarthy young man with a big, flattish nose and a weak chin. His English was shaky, so was his education. He could be both timid and vain. He was also a shameless liar... In spite of debts, English as well as Hanoverian, he gambled. There is a story that he joined a Hell-Fire Club, presumably the one at the George and Vulture. Still, at his best he was an affable, generous person... When he exerted himself to be popular, he was.

His quarrels with his father, the King, intensified. George II ordered him out of St James's Palace and the allowance he gave him, £50,000 a year, was just half of what George had received when *he* had been Prince of Wales. Frederick moved to Leicester House, Leicester Square. There he held his court and Dashwood was a regular visitor. One cannot feel too sorry for Fritz on this score, for he also had as his country seat the beauties of Cliveden House on the Thames near Marlow.

The court of Frederick was set up in direct opposition to that of his father and mother. 'Whoever was received at the King's court was excluded from the Prince's; and vice-versa,' Ashe writes. Meanwhile the Prince endeavoured to cultivate both the mob and the elites. He won over the former by giving beef and beer to the poor and personally assisting in fire-fighting in the Temple. 'Crown him!' the London mob roared. He also became the first English royal Freemason as recorded by the United Grand Lodge. His relations with his mother the Queen grew even worse. 'I hope in God I shall never see the monster's face again,' she declared after the birth of his first child. Her wish was granted, for she died without any reconciliation in 1737.

This increased the scope of Frederick's influence. He hated the Prime Minister, Sir Robert Walpole, who had relied so much on the influence of the Queen. He accelerated his endeavours to be regarded as the principal focus of the opposition. He purchased Carlton House in Pall Mall from Lord Burlington for £6,000 lent to him by his increasingly important associate, Dodington. He took an greater interest in political affairs. His ideological position was that the Glorious Revolution had been betrayed and that the opposition should support a monarch eager and willing to restore its formerly promised glory. He attracted supporters by pointing out that the King was an old man and stating that when he died, Frederick would dismiss the entire government and appoint another.

This claim was supported by practical action. The Duchy of Cornwall was in the Prince's pocket and money secured the return of ten opposition members. A further £12,000 ensured the election of two more loyalists to the Prince for Westminster, a slap in the face of his father. His aide, Dodington, had control of another seven seats in Parliament. There were roughly a hundred and fifty Independents – Members committed to no allegiance – and experts calculated that the 1741 election would not give Walpole a majority of more than fourteen seats. Frederick then backed the rising orator, William Pitt. When the War of Jenkins' Ear erupted, Pitt savaged Walpole's policy of peace, invoked patriotism, appealed to the merchants who wanted to take trade away from Spain and forced Walpole's resignation in February 1742.

It seemed to do no good. Walpole might be gone but the system continued. George II remained king, disowning and abusing his son. Frederick alternated between fits of enthusiasm and despondent boredom. Would his father never die? There were fits of petulance and eccentricity. During the Jacobite rebellion of 1745, when Bonnie Prince Charlie's soldiers were pounding the Hanoverian defence of Carlisle, Fritz gave a party which featured an iced cake to represent its fortifications and hired some girls to smash it to bits by hurling little cannonballs. On another occasion at Cliveden, he forced his guests to go gardening in wild, wet February weather then rewarded them with cold food and his own rendition of *Macbeth*.

However, 1747 seems to have marked the inception of a more positive attitude. He came into closer contact with Dashwood. 'At the time of the 1747 election he had invited him, with his friend Lord Talbot, to Carlton House, to explain his proposals for the way the government ought to conduct itself and would when he was king. He intended to "abolish for the future all distinctions of party"', as Eric Towers states. 'Dashwood and Talbot were asked by the Prince to give "the most positive assurances to the gentlemen in the opposition of his upright intention"'. Dashwood's reply was courteous but noncommittal; yet this matter would bear strange fruit.

So would the accidental meeting with John Stuart, third Earl of Bute. At a race meeting in Egham in 1747, rain forced the Prince to shelter in a tent. Lord Bute, who had little money and was simply hanging around, was invited to join a game of whist, and the encounter resulted in an invitation to Cliveden. Bute – pronounced 'boot' – soon became a frequent guest there and impressed the Prince with his gifts for amateur dramatics. In 1750 he was appointed Lord of the Bedchamber. In due course he would become the lover of Frederick's widowed wife, the future Queen Mother, and thence Prime Minister.

Meanwhile, Frederick had another choice in mind: Dodington, an experienced parliamentarian, minister and fixer. Dodington had known Dashwood well for many years: they were both members of the Dilettante. In 1749 Frederick gave Dodington a shadow ministerial job as 'Treasurer of the Chambers' at £2,000 a year. It was understood that when Frederick succeeded to the throne, Dodington would be Prime Minister. Dashwood threw his support behind the plan. Eric Towers observes:

Dodington was busily explaining to Frederick that opposition for its own sake was pointless. What was necessary was to establish a programme to which every right-thinking person in and out of Parliament would happily subscribe, based on principles which only the notoriously corrupt would not cheerfully support. In this way the opposition would be able to attain a moral superiority over the government...

Dashwood agreed. He wanted a patriot king who would appoint his ministers on merit rather than follow the custom of taking on tired old hacks whose sole qualifications consisted of blind party loyalty. There was also a second factor in Dashwood's support for Frederick, as Ashe duly observes: 'It may be significant that around 1749–50 the Prince was dabbling in Magic. Not of a very profound kind: he frequented palmists and kindred fortune-tellers. But still, magic.'

The diaries of Dodington give us further information. There is an entry for almost every day from spring 1749 to autumn 1754. However, there are little gaps following meetings with Dashwood. John Carswell and Lewis Arnold Dralle, who edited *The Political Journal* of George Bubb Dodington (1965), opine that these gaps occur because Dodington had reason not to record the details of these meetings. Events bear out their opinion.

There is a gap on 20 May 1750 from which one can draw no conclusions. However, on 13 September 1750, Dodington records that he visited Dashwood at West Wycombe for political discussions on 10 September, stayed the night, then on 12 September they both visited Cliveden to see the Prince. The entry for 13 September is blank. The entry for 14 September reads: 'Sir Francis and I returned to Wycombe by ten in the morning.'

From the point of view of Dashwood and Dodington, Frederick was perfectly positioned for their plans: nor did he have any particular antipathy to Sandwich. Politically, he genuinely wanted to embody Dashwood's ideals, which would suit Dodington as a future Prime Minister. In religious matters, he appears to have been more than highly sympathetic to Dashwood's ideals, probably even participating in ceremonies familiar to them as a Freemason. Moreover, he was popular with the people.

Unfortunately, 'the best laid plans of mice and men gang aft a'gley', as Robert Burns would say: for Frederick caught a cold which turned into pleurisy and he died in March 1751.

There are two possible epitaphs upon his life. One could say that he was an honourable and decent fellow, ill-treated by his parents, who would have played his part in realising a vision by becoming an excellent king. His wife, Princess Augusta, genuinely grieved for him, though his father merely grunted '*Fritz ist tot*' and looked relieved. Fritz was a disconcerting mixture of strength and weakness.

Arguably he could have had a notably improving effect upon the England of his time. The more cynical, however, concurred with the well-known, anonymous verse:

> Here lies Fred
> Who was alive and is dead;
> Had it been his father,
> I would much rather;
> Had it been his brother,
> Still better than another;
> Had it been his sister,
> No one would have missed her;
> Had it been the whole generation,
> Still better for the nation;
> But since 'tis only Fred,
> Who was alive and is dead, –
> There's no more to be said.

'Oh! If only I had you in a dark wood!' Dodington exclaimed breathlessly to a noted courtesan.

'Why? What would you do there that you can't do here?' she replied tartly. 'Rob me?'

This idea of Dodington as a fat wheezing puffer whose performance could never match his desire, has passed through many books. E. Beresford Chancellor, especially, used him as a butt to kick, a mere knockabout clown. Yet this man would have become Prime Minister if only Frederick, Prince of Wales, had outlived his father.

Many writers have been unkind to him. Charles Churchill, his contemporary, wrote:

Bubb is his name and bubbies doth he chase,
This swollen bullfrog with lascivious face.

In the succeeding century, the poet Robert Browning lashed him as the epitome of eighteenth-century incompetence and corruption. H.T.F. Rhodes wasn't much kinder in the mid-twentieth century, calling him 'a writer of indecent verse, of a salacious diary and...an amateur of obscene Latin inscriptions...His body and double-chinned face were as gross as his conversation.' This body and these features have been immortalised in Hogarth's classic visual portrayal of eighteenth-century political life, *Chairing the Member*.

Our contemporary historians have discerned rather more to this man than some of their predecessors. In the view of Geoffrey Ashe: 'In spite of all ridicule then and since, he has been described by a modern historian as "the key to the Whig cipher of the mid-century, its Rosetta stone." To take a close look at him, at the setting he moved in and the company he kept, is not to wander down a by-path but to follow a highway leading into the heart of public affairs.'

'One whose friendship he cultivated assiduously,' Eric Towers states in his study of Dashwood, 'was George Bubb Dodington, a short, fat, affable man of fifty, who had been a Member of Parliament since he was twenty-four.'

In truth, what sort of man was he? He was born in 1691, reportedly the son of a Weymouth pharmacist, and he was baptised as plain George Bubb. He would die as Dodington in 1762, at the height of the Club crisis, yet he would die as a rich man. This was mainly on account of his marriage to the sister of George Dodington, a country gentleman of Somerset and a governor of the Bank of England. Bubb's wealthy elder brother-in-law purchased Eastbury Towers, Dorset, in 1709, where he tried to build a palace to rival Blenheim. Since he had no issue, he made Bubb his heir conditional upon taking the Dodington name, which Bubb did gladly. He proceeded to inherit an immense, if half-built, palace – whose landed estate gave him control of seven parliamentary seats – and substantial business investments.

The pharmacist's son proceeded to enjoy a very comfortable life. He went up to Oxford and then he enjoyed a long and leisurely Grand Tour. On his return, he took over the parliamentary seat of his brother-in-law in the first parliament of George I and was then sent to negotiate a trade treaty with Spain, where he proved himself to be a successful diplomat.

Initially he was an ally of Prime Minister Walpole and the ruling Whig establishment. Sitting as MP for Bridgwater, he could now fill a dozen seats with his nominees. Small wonder that Walpole had made him a Lord of the Treasury in 1724, his task being to use bribery and corruption to keep the House of Commons quiet. Even so, Dodington continued to speak up in favour of Liberty. He appears to have thought at this time that it could be achieved best by the political principles then in operation. Small wonder, since these had brought him so much benefit. Even so, he entertained Voltaire on occasion of the latter's 1727 visit to Eastbury, hosted him for the summer and spoke at length about his political views. It was from Dodington that Voltaire gained not only his knowledge but also his admiration of the English political system, and Voltaire would use it to provoke what ultimately became a revolution in France.

Ironically, he was the Lord of the Treasury who signed the papers which disposed of the last assets of the Duke of Wharton, the original 'Hell-Fire Duke'. He was a mass of contradictions: or else he was a more complex character than has been apparent. According to some, he was merely a laughing-stock. 'Bubb, sometime known as Silly-Bubb, lacked Dashwood's finer flair for the classic,' state Pat Silver and Jesse Lasky Jnr, in their intriguing essay 'Hell-Fire Dashwood':

His home was a monstrosity of purple and orange silks topped off by too much gilt wood. His fortune was as bottomless as his taste, yet he was of a quixotically frugal nature, refusing to hang paintings because he considered them an extravagance. He would cut up his embroidered silk waistcoats when they grew too small for his expanding belly and have them sewn into a carpet...On one occasion at least he got a laugh out of Charlotte, wife of George III. Bowing deeply before her he was brought up hastily by a loud riiipp! in his satin breeches. No doubt the offending garment found its way into his State Bedroom carpet.

Then there is the matter of his wig. Throughout his life, he retained the shoulder-length style of his youth and was thought in consequence to be deplorably old-fashioned. Yet there is assuredly rather more to him than mere comedy, even though he was disconcertingly fat and thus a favourite target for caricaturists. He was certainly a good businessman. For example, he invested just a few hundred pounds in Vauxhall Pleasure Gardens and sold his half-share for £3,800 between 1743 and 1744 when he discerned that Ranelagh Pleasure Gardens would become more popular. When he lent Frederick, Prince of Wales, the money to purchase Carlton House, Dodington secured his investment by taking out an insurance policy on the Prince's life. As has been seen and will be further demonstrated, he was a clever politician.

He was also a discerning patron of the arts. Anyone who patronises genuinely talented artists deserves a lasting vote of thanks from the nation. Dodington assisted the impoverished poet, Edward Young, at one time patronised bv the Duke of Wharton. One anonymous jealously gibed at Young:

> While with your Dodington retir'd you sit
> Charmed with his flowing burgundy and wit...

'The wit was not often very witty,' Geoffrey Ashe comments, 'but in Bubb's house his feeblest pun would get a laugh, and he was genuinely a fluent talker, a good reader-aloud, a genial personality. In London he frequented a Pall Mall club called "The World" and took Young to it.' Did the Prince of Wales pop across the road from Carlton House, one wonders, or was the club there and did Dashwood attend? One example of Dodington's wit was described by Lady Mary Wortley Montagu: apparently Walpole, still Prime Minister, invited Dodington to attend a frivolous 'secret committee' to discuss a proposal to amend the Ten Commandments simply by deleting the word 'not'. Dodington disagreed, remarking that obligatory adultery would ruin its popularity.

Dodington proceeded to assist James Thomson, poet and author of *The Seasons*, the extraordinary *The Castle of Indolence*, to which we shall be returning, and that rumbustious and stirring national hymn, 'Rule Britannia'. As Ashe rightly states: 'through all parvenu absurdities he retained his energy, his acuteness, his zest for literature, and a degree of public spirit. When the neighbouring town of Blandford Forum was burnt down, he arranged a Treasury grant to aid in rebuilding.' Dodington also assisted one of England's greatest authors, Henry Fielding, who dedicated *Jonathan Wild* to him and went on to write *Tom Jones*.

The political doings of Dodington before 1749 are difficult to follow. Initially he seems simply to be a fixer on the make, acquiescing in the present system and out to make the best possible deal for himself. Failing to find further advancement under Walpole, he was drawn into the ambit of Frederick, Prince of Wales. An annoyed Walpole responded by dismissing him from his lordship of the Treasury in 1739. After Walpole's fall, the principal figure was the Duke of Newcastle, who thought it best to conciliate Dodington and win him over to the Whigs again by making him Treasurer of the Navy. Newcastle was an astute domestic politician, though one cannot forget the bungling of his foreign statecraft. On being told that Annapolis was being attacked, the Duke rushed around shouting: 'Defend Annapolis! Annapolis is at all costs to be defended! Ensure the defence of Annapolis!' He was then overheard to whisper to an aide: 'Pray, where *is* Annapolis?'

In common with Sandwich, First Lord of the Admiralty, Dodington, Treasurer of the Navy, was a member of Dashwood's Dilettante. Some sort of change of heart on Dodington's part seems to have come about during the 1740s. Was this simply because he could see no personal advancement for himself within the establishment and so chose to switch his allegiance to the opposition? The likelihood is that his motives were mixed. After all, it seems improbable that he would patronise authors such as Edward Young, James Thomson and Henry Fielding, all of whom were castigating injustice and the establishment, without being influenced by their excellence. No businessman pays to have his own ideals assaulted. It has been alleged that he joined the Dashwood circle in 1746. In any event, Dodington resigned the lucrative office of Treasurer of the Navy in March 1749. A couple of months later his diary records:

On Tuesday 18th I arrived at Kew about eleven o'clock. The Prince received me most kindly and told me he desired me to come into his service upon any terms and by any title I pleased; that he meant to put the principal direction of his affairs into my hands...He then continued to say that he would provide for my friends, whom he knew I valued more than myself. That he promised...Sir Francis Dashwood the Treasury of the Navy...

Dodington thereby became the unofficial leader of an unofficial opposition but threw himself into the task with enthusiasm. Henry Fielding was promptly commissioned to edit the opposition paper, then called *The Champion*. Subsequently this passed into the editorship of an American friend of Benjamin Franklin, James Ralph, who was also commissioned by Dodington to write a history of England from 1660 to 1715, its purpose being to demonstrate how the Glorious Revolution had been grossly betrayed.

Unfortunately for Dodington, this move turned out to be an inglorious failure when the Prince of Wales died unexpectedly in 1751. He made overtures of peace and sought office once again with the prevailing government, but to no avail. There was a further disaster in the 1754 election, which Dodington fought fiercely at Bridgwater. His diary records: 'Sunday, Monday, Tuesday, spent in the infamous and disagreeable compliance with the low habits of venal wretches... Wednesday, came on the election, which I lost by the injustice of the Returning Officer. Thursday, left Bridgwater for ever.'

Bubb had the resilience to bounce back. He made many calls on Princess Augusta, the future Queen Mother. Eighteen months after the disastrous Bridgwater defeat, Dodington returned to power, once again as Treasurer for the Navy.

'To be Treasurer of the Navy was an interesting and rewarding appointment!' Towers states correctly, 'the task was to raise money in the City for the upkeep of the Navy, a banking job in effect, and in the normal way of politics at the time a proportion of the money flowing through the Treasurer's office found its way into the Treasurer's private account.' Unfortunately, when Pitt took over the reins of government, Dodington was once more dismissed.

One might laugh at Dodington but the man was irrepressible. New opportunities opened up to him in 1756, when King George II set up an establishment for his grandson and heir, Prince George. As Ashe states:

> Once again Bolingbroke's Patriot King seemed a possibility. If Prince George could be made to realise his duty, and the power which the Crown still had, he might do what the Duke of Wharton had been the first to demand. He might restore what the opposition insisted was the true Constitution. He might break the grip of the Whig oligarchy, end corruption and placemanship, deliver Parliament from the grandees and manipulators, and govern his people with equal hand through ministers of different parties and no party. In other words he might restore public Liberty as the Medmenhamites conceived it.

Trust Dodington to have discerned a new opportunity! He knew that Lord Bute was not only tutor to the Prince but lover of the Princess Augusta, future Queen Mother. Bute was a member of the Dashwood-Dodington circle. Dodington persuaded Lord Holderness to resign as Secretary of State for the Northern Department, making way for Lord Bute, within a year of the Prince coming to the throne as King George III. Dodington continued to intrigue. Shortly afterwards, in 1761, the Earl of Bute replaced William Pitt as Prime Minister and Dodington became Lord Melcombe.

'I came to wish you joy,' said Horace Walpole, for once gentlemanly enough to congratulate a man he detested.

'I imagined so,' Dodington replied, obviously overjoyed at his long-awaited elevation, 'and came to receive it.' As part of his celebrations, he finally embraced the modish custom of the time and took to wearing a short wig.

He continued to rejoice in his long, old friendship with Dashwood, no doubt recalling the letter he'd written years before on the occasion of Dashwood's marriage, which argued the advantages of domestic affection and pointed out the tedium of casual affairs. He also enjoyed La Trappe, the villa near the present Hammersmith Bridge, which he had had restored at vast expense. The designer was a fashionable Italian who gave it a stucco front, a balustrade, a pillared Temple of Venus, a bathing hut, a bugle-shaped pattern of white stones on his sloping lawn to form his family crest; and in the interior, garish frescoes filled with pink-bottomed cherubs, tapestries, antiques, gilt, a marble chimney-piece from which fake stalactites drooped, and a sculpture gallery eighty-five feet long with the roof supported by seventeen-foot pillars of Italian marble, the same marble also adorning the floor.

'Some visitors,' Dodington wheezed as he proudly displayed it to the Duke of York, 'think that this gallery ought to be on the ground floor.'

'There is no need to worry, Mr Dodington,' the Duke answered, 'it soon will be.'

Yet the balance of evidence is that La Trappe was not merely an ostentatious eruption of *nouveau riche* vulgarity. Dodington appears to have been emulating Dashwood. The name itself – La Trappe – alludes to Trappist monasteries and therefore reminds one of the Monks of Medmenham. Dodington referred to the place as 'my convent'. His 'monks' were three resident companions including his physician, Dr Thomas Thompson, who was also a Medmenham Monk.

It is all too easy to underestimate this genial, civilised upstart snob and eccentric and to deplore the fact that he had much more money than taste. Those who laughed too hard had the grins wiped off their faces when he fixed them in Parliament. He was a key player in bringing down Pitt and bringing in Bute and a prime mover in conciliating the 150 independents so as to maintain Bute in power. It is hardly surprising that Bute invited him to become First Lord of the Admiralty.

'Joy Joy Joy to my dearest Lord,' Dodington wrote delightedly, 'this is the greatest happiness I could wish for in this life.'

He would never drink from this particular cup of joy. In the summer of 1762, worn out by years of dames and drink, the seventy-one-year-old Dodington fell down a flight of stairs and died.

His will named Dashwood as executor and created a legacy of £500 to erect a monument to their friendship. Dashwood responded by constructing a six-sided mausoleum at West Wycombe and Dodington was the first to be laid to rest there.

Dodington's venality and political machinations may be forgotten by all except historians of the period. His artistic patronage of Young, Thomson and Fielding and his warm friendship with Dashwood should be remembered.

> May I (can worse disgrace on Manhood fall?)
> Be born a Whitehead and baptised a Paul?

Charles Churchill, Whitehead's acquaintance and contemporary, wrote that. Some called him 'The Atheist Chaplain'. Robert Lloyd, fellow Medmenhamite and poet who took Churchill's side in the later quarrel with the Club, termed him 'Learned in lechery, a sedulous and patient seducer and a veritable troubadour of blasphemy'. This makes him sound rather interesting.

Paul Whitehead was born in 1710, the son of a tailor, and died in 1774. He wasn't a particularly good poet but he had undeniable talent as a versifier and satirist. He began his career as a writer and a rebel, he hurled invective against the ruling establishment, and he aroused the disdain of Dr Johnson. A spell in debtors' prison only increased his anger. Sir John Hawkins described his conversation as being 'desultory, vociferous and profane'. He attacked the Freemasons and travestied their annual march by organising a parade of tramps and beggars in mock-Masonic regalia. This aroused the laughter of Dashwood and the intrigued attention of Frederick, Prince of Wales, a Freemason himself. In common with most gifted satirists, Whitehead found himself in receipt of tempting establishment offers if only he could tone it down just a little bit. Prince Frederick employed him to write propaganda against his enemies and Whitehead performed the task with relish. Dashwood knew talent when he saw it and brought Whitehead into his circle. The latter required a living and had administrative gifts. Dashwood made Whitehead the steward of the Friars.

Whitehead's duties were not too onerous. He planned much of the ritual, supervised the consumption of wine and food and collected the subscriptions. In other words, he was the master of all details of logistics which bored Dashwood. As Charles Churchill wrote:

> Whilst Womanhood in the habit of a nun
> At Med'nam lies, by backward monks undone;
> A nation's reckoning, like an alehouse score
> Which Paul the Aged chalks behind the door.

His critics declared that he had sold out his former radical principles. The portrait painted by J. Downman in 1770, and now in the National Portrait Gallery, does indeed show a face that

H.T.F. Rhodes describes as being 'both complacent and crafty'. Raymond Postgate disparages his letter to John Wilkes, in which Whitehead announces his decision to abandon his formerly democratic principles, and deplores him as a mere mercenary. Moreover, he married a rich woman who was half-witted, although he always treated her kindly. One contemporary recorded after a visit that this wife suddenly pointed at the valley below the Twickenham estate her money had brought him and said: 'Look, dear: there are cows.'

'Yes, my dear,' Whitehead replied impassively, 'there are indeed cows. But they are very nice cows.'

Once Bute was Prime Minister in 1761, Dashwood rewarded his steward with the sinecure of 'Deputy Treasurer of the Chamber', which carried a salary of £800 a year. Small wonder that Whitehead wrote:

> Safe in the harbour of my Twickenham bower
> From all the wrecks of State and Storms of Power,
> No wreaths I court' no subsidies I claim;
> Too rich for want, too indolent for fame.

Yet when Bute's ministry came under attack, Whitehead was a target.

> Once on a time, as Fame reported,
> When Friar Paul St Francis courted,
> Thus Francis answer'd, You're no Novice,
> You well deserve the Jewel Office.
> A Place of Trust your Faith will suit,
> You shall demand it as Laird Boot,
> Your MANNERS, Morals, Virtues, Grace,
> Call loudly for a goodly Place.
> Success attend you, I'll be blunt,
> My dearest Brother, here is —

Well, it's rather obvious what the author thinks of Bute. The MANNERS referred to the satirical work of twenty years before which had launched Whitehead's reputation. 'Friar Paul' refers to Whitehead himself, 'the Jewel Office' and 'A Place of Trust' refer to well-paid government sinecure. The verse was published in *The Public Advertiser*, edited by Henry Woodfall, whom John Wilkes, foe of Bute's government, knew well. Towers suggests, probably rightly, that the words were written by Wilkes's friend and fellow fighter, Charles Churchill. The text was accompanied by a print which depicted Dashwood in a monk's habit, seated at his devotions before an altar with a glass of wine in his hand and *Hymns by Ovid* by his side, gazing reverently upon a replica of the Venus de Medici. Beside Sir Francis, there stands Paul Whitehead.

The assaults of Wilkes and Churchill had a poor effect on Whitehead's health. It is said that he spent the last three days of his life assiduously burning the Club papers. In December 1774, Whitehead died at his London lodgings in Henrietta Street. His will stated:

> I do hereby charge and direct my Executrix . . . to raise my Body to be opened, that the faculty may if possible discover after I am dead what they seemed to be totally ignorant of while I was living, the Cause of my death; and I do further order that my heart be taken out and disposed of as follows: I give to the Right Honourable Francis, Lord le Despenser, my heart aforesaid, together with Fifty pounds, to be laid out in the purchase of a Marble Urn, in which I desire it may be deposited and placed, if his Lordship pleases, in some corner of his Mausoleum, as a Memorial to its Owner's warm attachment to the Noble Founder.

What is one to make of this man? Was he simply a radical satirist who turned his coat the instant he was offered money for a new pair of britches? This seems unlikely, though one must allow that in common with most men without means, he was on the make. Even so, he never went over to the Whig side so despised in his early satires. He went over to the Independents as represented by Dashwood. Dashwood gave him a comfortable living, introduced him to certain matters of religion with which Whitehead had been hitherto unfamiliar but which he subsequently embraced, and urged that his negative cynicism be transmuted into an optimistic pamphleteering for the ideal of a Patriot King. Whitehead did well out of that deal. Perhaps also he saw the vision described by his enemy Charles Churchill:

> Dashwood shall pour from a communion cup,
> Libations to the goddess without eyes...

Thomas Potter, son of the Archbishop of Canterbury, exhorted his friend John Wilkes to visit him in Bath 'if you prefer young women and whores to old women and wives, if you prefer toying away hours with little Sattin Back to the evening conference of your Mother-in-Law... but above all if the Heavenly inspired passion called Lust have not deserted you'.

'I poison all my friends' morals,' Potter boasted. He has been called 'Wilkes's Evil Genius'.

> He drank with drunkards, lived with sinners
> Herded with infidels for dinners.

Raymond Postgate fulminates over the relationship in his biography of John Wilkes. 'Potter ruined Wilkes financially as well as morally for he introduced him to the Jews...' he writes. Was it really just the Jews? Undeniably, seventeen years later, the supporters of the Bill of Rights were attempting to pay off Wilkes's resultant debts. Postgate fumes further on the matter of the Medmenham Monks:

All the monks were atheists, deists, or merely without interest in religion... They altered the ceremonials of the Roman Church to the extent of substituting the Bona Dea, the pagan goddess of fertility, for the Almighty, and this simple change gave them the same elementary pleasure as writing four-letter words on a lavatory wall does a schoolboy.

Dear me, this is quite shocking. Postgate then adds that it was all 'Nothing but an adolescent prank.'

Thomas Potter (1719–59) was born with every possible advantage. He had good looks, he had a fortune at his disposal and he had wit. In common with Whitehead, he was not a particularly distinguished poet but he could write highly amusing satirical verse. With Wilkes he composed a salacious parody of Pope's *Essay on Man*: they called it *Essay on Woman* and it would eventually cause a scandal which would divide the Friars. It was addressed to the beautiful Fanny Murray, mistress of Beau Nash, Lord Sandwich and many other bucks and probably a woman member at Medmenham.

He was the son of a former Archbishop of Canterbury from whom he inherited a substantial estate at Aylesbury. In spite of this he spent his fortune so fast that he had to marry twice for money. He didn't give a damn about anyone or anything and his conduct was thought to be scandalous, even by the lax standards of his time. He was a compulsive womaniser, and he could be mischievous too. When the Bishop of Warburton sternly defended the morality of the Christian religion in a series of pamphlets, Potter responded by seducing the man's wife. His other pleasures were somewhat more morbid. He enjoyed watching public executions and liked to fornicate in graveyards.

His wealth, handsome face and easy charm gave him a ready place in Parliament, where he sat as an Independent Member for Aylesbury and later for Okehampton. He became secretary to Prince Frederick. The offices of state he enjoyed included those of Paymaster-General and Vice-Treasurer for Ireland. Hogarth immortalised him in a splendid satirical picture inspired by the 1754 General Election. Here Potter sits in his modish white wig and blue-grey velvet suit, reluctantly accepting the kisses of the publican's fat wife as he feasts his local, drunken supporters at a tavern. A brick is flying in through the window; but Potter won the election.

By this time he was good friends with Dashwood, who impressed him greatly. 'I know the nothingness into which the genius of a Potter is apt to shrink under a superior influence,' Potter observed wryly with uncharacteristic modesty. Perhaps Dashwood guided his instinctive anarchy into more constructive pursuits. It was Potter who became the conduit between Dashwood and John Wilkes, his friend, boon companion and fellow-fornicator. Potter introduced Wilkes to the powerful Lord Grenville, then made a deal with Pitt whereby Wilkes took over as Member for Aylesbury and Potter moved to Okehampton. The Aylesbury election of 1757 cost Wilkes the substantial sum of £7,000 – for which his creditors would be baying in years to come – but it did not bring the man into the mainstream.

Potter continued to wench and booze throughout the 1750s. In consequence his moods alternated between an amused cynicism and a dark despair. Eventually he fell ill from what he termed 'a petty triumvirate' of gout, scurvy and palsy. By 1758, he was on a milk diet. According to legend, this did not prevent him from spending all night on a gravestone whereby he caught a fatal chill. He died in 1759.

Potter was both a classic rake and a genuine wit. It is hard to discern any harm he did to anyone in his private life. There remains the irony that it was Potter who brought Wilkes into the Friars, a grouping which had graced the former's aspirations, and it was Wilkes who became the instrument of the Friars' fall from power.

George Selwyn MP (1719–91) has been called 'the first of the fashionable wits'. 'He was refined and sensitive,' states Rhodes, 'and lacking in the "hell-fire" spirit as it was commonly understood.' Indeed, some historians have doubted whether he was a member at all, but one is inclined to concur with Ashe that his membership is 'fairly well attested'.

At Eton he was a contemporary of the poet Gray, author of the exquisite *Elegy in a Country Churchyard,* and of Horace Walpole. He went up to Hertford College, Oxford in 1739 but was expelled in 1746 for toasting 'queer deities' from a chalice which included blood from his own arm in a parody of Christian communion held at a tavern on the High Street, near St Martin's Church. Just one year later, he became the Member of Parliament for the family borough of Ludgershall. From 1754 to 1780 he was the Member for Gloucester.

Opinions vary about this man. It cannot be denied that in common with Thomas Potter, he had a morbid fascination with death and its many modes. How he loved to attend public executions! One of the ghastliest of the century was that of Robert Damiens, who had tried to assassinate King Louis XV; it took place in the Place de Crève, Paris, 1757, in front of a large crowd of men and women. After preliminary torture in private, Damiens was led out before the public and a horse was harnessed to each limb. He was literally pulled limb from limb. It took hours for the man to die and one gracious lady declared her sorrow for the sad toil of the horses. George Selwyn arrived to watch this disgusting spectacle, disguised as a washerwoman, and couldn't find a seat. The executioner's sharp eyes penetrated the disguise. 'Let this gentleman through!' he cried, 'he is a famous English amateur!'

As Professor Mario Praz demonstrates in *The Romantic Agony*, Selwyn attained cult status among certain French authors. 'The Honourable George Selwyn' is the epitome of the gentleman-sadist in Edmond de Goncourt's decadent novel *La Faustine*.

Selwyn made no secret of his interests. After the execution by beheading of Lord Lovat, Selwyn was heard to murmur: 'My dear Lord Lovat, your Lordship may now rise.' 'I suppose you'll be coming to see me hanged,' one Lord remarked to Selwyn on the opening night of a play he'd written. 'Oh no, my Lord,' Selwyn answered, 'I never go to rehearsals.' The man was a noted necrophiliac. 'Show Mr Selwyn up,' Lord Holland said as he lay on his deathbed, 'If I am alive, I shall be pleased to see him; and if I am dead, he will be pleased to see me.'

So far he sounds like a real charmer; the curious thing is that many insist he actually was. Horace Walpole, his lifelong friend, declared: 'Few knew him so well, and consequently few knew so well the goodness of his heart and nature.' E. Beresford Chancellor, like Lord Macaulay on Leigh Hunt, exhorts the reader to 'have a kindness' for Selwyn, insisting that his heart was true, his affections were kindly, his wit was exquisite and his manners were irreproachable.

No one disputes that he was a dandified, somewhat somnolent man with a lazy, drawling manner of speech. After listening at length to the account of a Mr Bruce of his travels in Abyssinia, climaxed by Bruce's remark: 'I only saw one lyre there', Selwyn responded with 'Yes, and there's one less since you left the country.' He was told that Fox, rake and politician, was attracted by Mrs Robinson, a notorious courtesan. 'Well,' he drawled, 'whom should the "man of the people" live but with a woman of the people?' An acquaintance informed him that a mistress had passed from the grandfather to the father and thence to the son, exclaiming: 'There's nothing new under the sun!' 'Nor under the grandson,' said Selwyn.

He upset Sandwich, whose grandfather was accused of sodomy and then drowned at sea, by saying how sorry he was to learn that the man had 'gone to the bottom'. Meanwhile he spent much of his time at White's and at Brook's and was something of a degenerate gambler. Few matters troubled his tranquil life apart from one occasion in the 1761 election when he complained that two of his voters had been murdered. The agent for his rival was a man called Snell, who apparently lured the intended victims into a post-chaise 'where, being suffocated with the brandy that was given them, and a very fat man that had the custody of them, they were taken out stone dead'. One wonders if Selwyn rushed to see the corpses.

If Selwyn did any harm, it was only to the dead, who, after all, are beyond it. Nor should we forget that his sister left us a legacy in her descendant, Sarah, 'Fergie', Duchess of York. It is impossible to tell whether Selwyn was a member of the inner or the outer circle but certainly he brought a macabre neo-Gothic aspect to influence Dashwood's doings.

Few eighteenth-century clubs admitted women but the Friars did. Who were these women? Walpole refers to the frequent importation of 'nymphs' to Medmenham Abbey. It is probable that they came from the London bordello of Charlotte Hayes and were brought in purely to satisfy the carnal lusts of the Friars. However, whores were not the Friars' only female associates. One was that remarkable and attractive woman, a noted 'bluestocking', a friend of both Wharton and Dashwood, Lady Mary Wortley Montagu.

'There is no part of the world where our sex is treated with so much contempt as in England,' she wrote indignantly in 1753. 'I do not complain of men having engrossed the government... but I think it the highest injustice... that the same studies that raise the character of a man should hurt that of a woman.' By this time she had honestly earned a reputation as the wittiest and most intelligent woman in the country, having also been a noted beauty in her younger years.

Lady Mary knew Wharton and his Schemers' Club back in the 1720s. Her pretty face and delectable figure had made her the toast of the Kit-Kat Club. As the wife of a diplomat, she went to Italy and Turkey, writing books on the arts of travel in consequence. After thirty years of marriage, she separated from her husband and met Dashwood in Florence around 1740, when she was enjoying the company of Horace Walpole. Then she went to live in Twickenham with Dodington as a neighbour in nearby Hammersmith, just down the river. In earlier years, the poet Alexander Pope had made unwanted sexual advances to her in 'Twickenham's bow'r' and on being turned down politely, had savaged her in verse. Lady Mary remained highly displeased with Pope's churlish conduct but laughed it away; meanwhile she cast a wry eye upon the politics of the time. She described a visit to the House of Commons as being like going to the theatre:

There's a little door to get in and a great crowd without, shoving and thrusting who shall be the foremost. People who knock others with their elbows, disregard a little kick of the shins and still thrust heartily forward, are sure of a good place.

A diary kept by a local tailor records 'EIGHT LADIES WHITE HABITS, made to original design' for delivery to Medmenham Abbey. For whom were these intended? It is not certain but the probability is that the wearers included 'the Sultana Walcotonia', whom Dashwood had brought as a guest to the Divan Club and who was in fact his half-sister, Mary Walcott. Was Lady Mary Wortley Montagu a member too? There is a portrait of her at West Wycombe, in Turkish dress, one of several commissioned by Dashwood in 1745 when he founded the short-lived Divan Club for old Turkish hands, of which she was one; yet puzzlingly enough, there is no evidence to suggest that she was a member of the Divan Club. It initially seems unlikely that she was a member of the Monks of Medmenham, for she was born in 1689 and died in 1762. She lived abroad during the 1750s. By 1760 she was seventy-one years of age. Even so, she was a friend of both Dashwood and Dodington and a daughter of hers married Lord Bute. In that era, there was nothing unusual about an elderly lady of wit and of means associating with wealthy rakes; it had been archly portrayed by William Congreve's Lady Wishfort in *The Way of the World* in the preceding century. Ashe is probably right in terming her an honorary member.

It is also not known if Frances, Countess Vane, was a member though this has been suggested and is plausible. Born Frances Anne Hawes, she was introduced to society at the age of thirteen and fell in love with Lord William Hamilton two years later. When both families opposed the match, they eloped. Unfortunately her husband died after a year of marriage. Frances then married Viscount Vane, who seems to have been most disappointing sexually for she kept running away from him. Lord Egremont wrote in his *Diary*, 1737:

I read this day in the newspapers my Lord Vane's advertisement offering £100 reward to him that should discover his lady, who for some time had eloped from him. One would think he had lost some favourite spaniel bitch, for he describes her person very particularly, even to the clothes she wears.

In 1739 Lady Mary Wortley Montagu wrote to Lady Pomfret:

Lady Vane is returned hither in company with Lord Berkeley. I am told that she does not pique herself on fidelity to any one man (which is but a narrow way of thinking) but she boasts that she has always been true to her nation and, notwithstanding foreign attacks, has always reserved her charms for the use of her own countrymen.

'When my affairs were brought to that issue', Lady Vane wrote in self-justification, 'I made no hesitation in my choice, putting myself under the protection of a man of honour, whom I esteemed, rather than suffer every sort of mortification from a person who was the object of my abhorrence and contempt.' Ignoring Lord Berkeley, she adds: 'From a mistaken pride, I chose to live in Lord Bolingbroke's house, rather than be maintained at his expense in any other place.'

Lady Vane had clearly been influenced by *Fanny Hill: Memoirs of a Woman of Pleasure*, for in 1751 she persuaded Tobias Smollett to insert her witty, autobiographical parody, *Memoirs of a Lady of Quality*, into his novel, *Peregrine Pickle*. Returning to Twickenham, with Dodington as a neighbour, she praised her lover, one Sewallis Shirley – a Dilettante member and a friend of Dashwood – as a truly sympathetic companion. This did not prevent her from simultaneously bestowing her favours upon Lord Charles Hey and the Earl of Cholmondeley, in spite of her advancing years. Although her membership is founded upon rumour, she would have been an ideal candidate.

The same can be said of Lady Betty Germain, another female rake of her time. Curiously enough, she was in possession of the Aztec scrying stone of the Elizabethan magician, Dr John Dee,

which then passed into the hands of Horace Walpole and which
now reposes in the British Museum. There was also the celebrated courtesan, Fanny Murray, to whom Wilkes and Potter
dedicated their *Essay on Woman*. Sandwich took her as his
mistress and brought her to Medmenham Abbey.

Other than these, the names of the Nuns are unknown apart
from one puzzle. Dashwood was kind to the mysterious woman
whose name has survived in legend as 'Saint Agnes'. Who was
she?

There are three possibilities. One is that she did not exist. A
second is that she was a tart whom Dashwood liked and whom
he rescued from a life of depravity, making her the housemaid of
the Monks. A third is that she may have been an illegitimate
daughter doing the same duty. However, one cannot concur with
the Lasky-Silver hypothesis that she 'possibly lived in the secret
chamber' of the West Wycombe caves. The caves are so cold, even
in high summer, that nobody could live there.

'Sister Agnes' was introduced at the Abbey by Paul Whitehead.
Her background lay in the shady side of bookselling. She eventually married a Monsieur Perrault and went to live with him in
France. She may have been the midwife to illegitimately born
babies.

Obviously there were other women too but there is no way of
telling who they might have been. Legend has it that they wore
masks to meetings. The Friars, being gentlemen, would have
taken care not to give away the names of debutantes and married
ladies. It is clear, however, that the suggested Nuns were women
of spirit. Regrettably, it is not known if this entitled them to enter
the secret chapter-room of the inner circle. Possibly they were
there not simply to arouse the penis, as the hired whores could
do only too well, but to delight the male mind with their wit and
conversation.

How many men can listen to an attractive and/or interesting
woman for long before becoming either utterly exasperated or
wholly entranced and consequently influenced? The eighteenth
century recognised the all-pervading influence of women. This

is why the London mob derisively termed the so-called 'Hell-Fire Ministry' of 1761–3 the regime of 'the Boot and the Petticoat'.

6

William Hogarth

William Hogarth (1697–1764), thought by not a few to be his century's greatest artist, produced a number of portraits of various Friars. This has led some to argue that he was one of their own, though others state that he wasn't even a member of the outer circle. This cannot be established one way or the other, but it is certain that he was well acquainted with a number of the leading Friars, and that his art has given us clues which may lead to further understanding of their activities.

He came from a shabby-genteel middle-class family of London. His father was a schoolmaster and a minor classical scholar. According to Hogarth, his father did little more for him than 'put me in a way of shifting for myself'. As a teenager he became apprenticed to a silversmith, where he learned the craft of engraving, though he also undertook his own experiments in artistry. He had his own shop by the age of twenty-three, where he earned a modest living by engraving book illustrations, business cards and tickets upon copper. Gradually he proceeded to acquire a growing reputation for his moral and satirical engravings and paintings, of which the best known is probably the eight scenes of *The Rake's Progress*, begun in 1732. Meanwhile he fought successfully for a law to protect the copyright of artists and the so-called Hogarth Act was passed in 1755. This marked the beginning of his financial independence, allowing him to experiment further. He became the first English artist to attract a European reputation.

Although Hogarth's aesthetic theories would have little effect in his own time, they would have substantial influence upon Romantic literature. He wanted art to be individual and English, rather than slavishly derivative of French or Italian renderings of classical themes. He drew directly on to paper or canvas without recourse to preliminary sketches. Contemporary life was his primary source of subject-matter. He wished to celebrate the virtues of the society around him and to excoriate its vices. Technically, he drew on a formidable acquaintanceship with the traditions of European art, insisting upon a balanced harmony of composition, but ensuring that every detail symbolised a message.

One would expect the paths of Hogarth and Dashwood to cross. They had so much in common: a love of the arts, sociability, outspokenness and a liking for London low life as well as urban sophistication. Both men were eminently clubbable. Probably they first met at the Society of Beefsteaks, of which Hogarth was a founder-member. They were also both governors of the Foundling Hospital for orphans, set up by Hogarth's friend, Captain Thomas Coram, to rescue babies abandoned to starve in alleyways. We have already inspected Hogarth's portrait of *Sir Francis Dashwood at his Devotions*, commissioned by Lord Boyne and based upon an original by Knapton. Closer inspection is rewarding.

The Gothic landscape in the background, the friar's habit of Sir Francis, the figurine of the goddess and the face of Sandwich in the halo directly behind Dashwood's head have already been noticed; also the fact that his left hand is laid upon his heart. One cannot see the thumb but presumably it is touching the heart itself. The thumb of the left hand touches the left ankle of the reclining naked figurine of the goddess and the forefinger is extended to form a sign resembling horns. This sign is still used in some esoteric groups today to symbolise male sexual energy. Between and behind the devotee and the figurine, there is a skull denoting the mysteries of death which accompany those of sex. It is not clear which particular book lies between the two upon the altar but its presence indicates Dashwood's veneration for the

notion of a sacred, divinely inspired text. The rosary hanging
upside down from a stake to Dashwood's right displays his
contempt for Christianity. Beneath it, there is a dish. This could
well symbolise the Holy Grail; alternatively, it is also a symbol for
Earth. The fruits of the Earth are shown spilling out of it, along
with oysters. These reinforce the theme of Dionysus and Venus for
the fruit consists of grapes, sacred to Dionysus as god of the vine;
and oysters are sacred to Venus, for this goddess was born out of
an oyster shell. There are two glasses for the two lovers. One is
full. The other has been overturned but has spilled flowers upon
the floor.

Thomas Potter and George Bubb Dodington both appear in
Hogarth's political satires. *The Candidate* (1754) shows Potter
wearily arousing support, submitting to the unwanted kiss of the
innkeeper's fat and unattractive wife on his lap and buying endless
drinks for his drunken constituents at the tavern table. Clearly,
Potter had his enemies in this hotly contested election, as is shown
by a brick flying in through the window to flatten one of his
supporters. *Chairing the Member* (1754) shows Dodington carried
in chaotic triumph by his riotous supporters amidst scenes of
drunken disorder, ironic in view of the fact that Dodington lost
that particular election.

In 1757, Hogarth was appointed Royal Serjeant Painter. Bute's
ministry confirmed this appointment in 1762. Hogarth drew a
pro-Bute cartoon in appreciation and was promptly savaged by
Wilkes, but hit back with caricatures of both Wilkes and Charles
Churchill. Wilkes is depicted with a grossly exaggerated squint,
leering at the spectator with an evil grin like an ugly demon as he
holds aloft a banner for Liberty. Hogarth appears to be implying
that Wilkes is using a popular cause merely to advance his own.

Churchill is portrayed as a big bear wearing a large, floppy and
carelessly tied scarf. His right paw cradles a massive tankard of
ale, his left arm a tree which could also stand as his staff, and
upon which leaves are pinned with words inscribed on them.
From top to bottom, the first reads 'Lye 1', the second is unclear,
and there follow 'Lye 5', 'Lye 8', 'Fallacy', 'Lye 10', 'Lye 12',

'LYE 15' and 'Lye 23' – a clear indication of both Churchill's passion for truth and his method of polemics. At the base of this tree or staff, there is an artist's palette. A big and fierce mastiff or boxer dog sits by Churchill's right, its paws upon its master's *An Epistle to Hogarth*. It is difficult to identify the precise nature of the object reposing on top of three books directly in front of the bear but it is a cylinder made of metal with a slot in the top, a handle on one side and a key on the other, this leads one to think it a collection tin, thus satirising Churchill's interminable financial troubles. The topmost book is a collected edition of *The North Briton*, bound in boards. Beneath that, similarly bound, is the play *A New Way to Pay Old Debts*. It is almost impossible to make out the title of the third book, though it has better binding. A candle snuffer has been carelessly discarded on the floor before them, a reference to the subject's keeping of irregular hours. Ironically enough, both the painter and the subject died in the same year, 1764.

The essence of a good satirist is that he really does care about improving the society around him. Hogarth set out to depict his society truthfully. *Marriage à la Mode*, for instance, is a witty and biting assault on the marital customs of the upper classes. *Four Stages of Cruelty* (1751) is an impassioned indictment of inhumanity, including that of man to animals. *Beer Street* extols the idea of a hard-working, moderately prosperous community rejoicing in a good time while *Gin Lane* deplores degeneracy. Benjamin Franklin would have approved of *Industry and Idleness*, which extols the rise, by dint of hard work and application, of the industrious apprentice.

As a courageous pioneer, Hogarth was often at odds with the art establishment of his time, clashing early on in his career with the Earl of Burlington, who wanted a neo-classical revival. He deliberately employed engraving techniques which made his prints cheaper than hitherto, thus making them more readily available to the general public, but was criticised for his commercialism. No one could deny the excellence of his draughtsmanship or the thoroughness of the teaching at the drawing school he had established in 1734 but his endeavours to be accepted as a painter of history were a failure. In the succeeding century John Constable remarked: 'Hogarth has no school, nor has he ever been imitated with tolerable success.'

It does seem most unlikely that Hogarth was a member of the inner circle of the Friars. His middle-class background, in which he took genuine pride, would have been off-putting to Sandwich, and Hogarth would have found the conspicuous consumption of the Friars to be distasteful. He may or may not have been a member of the outer circle, but since he was a convivial imbiber, no prude, stimulating in conversation and a respected painter and engraver, much in demand and esteemed by lovers of art such as the Friars, his association is more than likely. Let us not forget that he portrayed at least eight of the other associates.

Hogarth's masterpiece is probably his *Self Portrait* (1745). Here he sits with a sardonic and slightly grumpy expression, with eyes of flinty integrity and a jaw set firmly in challenging belligerence, with his dog Trump sitting by his side and looking remarkably similar. The three books before him are by Shakespeare, Milton and Swift, with whom he obviously compares himself. Next to them there is a palette inscribed with a sinuous line which he called 'the line of beauty' and which he held to exemplify the wonder, profusion, complexity, subtlety and variety to be discerned in nature.

Dashwood founded the Friars. But it took Hogarth to create the visual images which encapsulate the essence of the group and by which Dashwood should be remembered.

7

Medmenham Abbey

Legend has it that a boat was provided for those who wished to come by river from London when the Abbey was activated in 1752–3. If so, one arrived and docked at the Abbey orchard, which was dominated by a statue of Priapus brandishing a flame-tipped phallus and beyond it a statue of Venus stooping to pull out a thorn from her foot, with her beautifully sculptured buttocks blocking the entry to a small cavern. Instantly one recognises a celebration of male and female energies. This place requires closer inspection.

Dashwood wanted to resurrect the vision of Rabelais amidst the paradoxes of his own times. He was also inspired by two English poets who had been patronised by Dodington: Edward Young and James Thomson. Dr Edward Young, former tutor to 'Hell-Fire' Philip, Duke of Wharton, is known mainly for his poem *Night Thoughts*, which defends the idea of immortality. Its portrayal of gloomy landscapes enunciates a sensibility which would be called 'Gothic'. James Thomson wrote *The Seasons* and 'Rule Britannia' but was of more interest to Dashwood on account of his *The Castle of Indolence*, which evokes a vision similar to that of Rabelais, conjuring a place where 'freedom reigned, without the least alloy', and continuing:

> For why? there was but one great rule for all:
> To wit, that each should work his own desire,

And eat, drink, study, sleep, as it may fall,
Or melt the time in love, or wake the lyre,
And carol what, unbid, the Muses might inspire.

Yet Thomson, unlike the extravagantly industrious Rabelais, clearly suffers from shame and guilt over this idyll where members have been told: 'Ye sons of Indolence, do what ye will.' Sir Industry comes to wreck it. 'Is happiness a crime?' the members ask him. Sir Industry responds by waving his 'anti-magic' wand, sending them all out to work and blasting the Castle. Thomson was the son of a Scottish Minister of the Kirk and throughout his life felt ashamed of his own indolence.

Medmenham Abbey, on the Thames near Marlow, was roughly six miles south of West Wycombe, where Dashwood was organising an exceptional programme of reconstruction. It had been built around AD 1200 to house about a dozen Cistercian monks. After King Henry VIII dissolved the monasteries, it eventually passed to the Duffield family. The Duffields endeavoured to make of it a mock-Tudor manor house, adding timbered walls, tall chimneys, another storey with accompanying sloping roof and basement accommodation for the servants. Francis Duffield, a young lieutenant in the Horse Guards, lived mainly from his farm rents but spent too much on horses and pretty women. In 1751 he was pleased to lease the Abbey to Dashwood, to join the Friars and to take up residence in another place he owned.

Dashwood brought in the builders, the interior designers and the gardeners. One of his first actions was to have the statue of a Virgin and Child removed. He must have pondered long and hard over the design. One possibility was the fashionable Italian neo-classicism which was influencing so many of his contemporaries. After all, he had viewed the brothel art and other works during the first excavations at the House of Mysteries at Pompeii and a replication of these could be a tempting prospect. Giuseppe Borgnis was brought over from Italy in 1751 to work upon the interiors at West Wycombe House and also to paint frescoes at the

Abbey. Maurice-Louis Jolivet, Dashwood's West Wycombe landscape gardener, received further employment at Medmenham.

There was another temptation, the new fashion known as 'Gothic'. This harked back not to ancient Roman classicism but to contemporary notions of the Middle Ages. Betty Langley, a Twickenham landscape gardener and builders' merchant, had her highly influential manual *Gothic Architecture Improved by Rules and Proportion* published in 1742. Sir William Stanhope, a friend of Dashwood, had Gothic ruins erected in his park at Eyethorpe. Lord Temple, another acquaintance, wanted 'a Gothic Temple of Friendship' built in his park at Stowe, which included a cottage called 'St Augustine's Cave', covered with obscene Latin inscriptions. In 1748 Horace Walpole began building his Gothic mansion at Strawberry Hill, which included battlements, cloisters and an armoury. William Beckford scornfully dismissed Strawberry Hill as 'a Gothic mousetrap', yet erected his own Gothic folly at Fonthill Abbey, Wiltshire, thirty years later, in addition to contributing to the Gothic-literary tradition with his novel *Vathek*. At Medmenham, Dashwood made sure that there was a ruined tower, a cloister and 'hermits' cells'.

The visitor to Medmenham would be bombarded by a variety of aesthetic sensations. The first shock was the statue of Priapus. Beneath it was the inscription PENI TENTO NON PENITENTI – a penis tense, not penitence – and the phallus of the statue was tipped with flame. This deity has been described in terms varying from devotion to denunciation. According to myth, Priapus was fathered by Pan upon Venus-Aphrodite and born with a permanent erection. He became part of the wild entourage of Dionysus-Bacchus and god of beekeepers, farmers and fishermen. Tales have it that he rode upon an ass, a sacred beast in many ancient writings. The Bible reminds us of the talking ass of Balaam, a creature who gave him the truth during a moment of crisis; of the birth of Jesus between an ox and an ass and indeed of the alleged fact that Jesus rode into Jerusalem on the back of an ass. In ancient Egypt the ass had often been venerated as the symbol of Set, god of the mysteries of sex and death. It was still held sacred in the latter days of ancient Rome when Apuleius wrote *The Golden Ass*, an exquisite novel about a man who is turned into a donkey for being gross but who is restored by the religious and magical rites of the goddess Isis.

We are looking, then, at an expression of primordial male energy. This is reinforced by the pedestal. According to Wilkes this displayed 'a whimsical representation of Trophonius' cave from which all creatures were said to come out melancholy. Among this strange and dismal group you might however remark a cock crowing and a Carmelite laughing, and the words: *Gallum Gallinaceum et Sacerdotem Gratis.*' This last is a Latin jest telling one that everyone is sad after sexual intercourse apart from a cock and a priest, who get it for nothing. It is not too difficult to interpret the symbolism here. Trophonius was the builder of Apollo's temple at Delphi and myth has it that after his death, his ghost haunted the temple and inspired the priestesses of the sun god to give enquirers truthful oracles.

This solar-phallic theme is further reinforced by a statue of a cock, copied from one in the Vatican, showing a man's body and neck with a cock's head crowned by a phallus. The cock's head is a totem of the sun god. Pre-Christian inscriptions referred to the cock as 'The Saviour of the World'. 'The figure represents the generative powers of Eros, Osiris, Mithras and Bacchus, whose centre is the sun incarnate in man,' Richard Payne Knight rightly stated in his illuminating study, *A Discourse on the Worship of Priapus*. Knight would in time become a member of the Dilettante Society that Dashwood had founded. Nor should one forget that in voodoo ceremonies, the cock is solemnly sacrificed to the goddess. Dashwood was reaching back not to an anti-Christian tradition, but to one that was pre-Christian. One can see this reiterated in the joke that the priest joins the cock in getting sex without sadness and for nothing. In pagan times the priest was regarded as embodying fertile virility. Even today in India, 'holy men' are followed by hordes of women hoping for healthy impregnation. Only Christianity, and specifically Roman

Catholicism, insists that the priest should be a neutered, sexless being.

It is the goddess that awaits us on our next turn and female sexuality is represented by her enchantingly proportioned buttocks, whilst a Latin inscription informs the visitor that entry by the wrong route is deplored here. There is the goddess known and hymned under so many names: Aphrodite, Venus, Isis and *Bona Dea*. Obviously this is not a matter solely of phallic worship. Her bottom blocks the entrance to a cave and one may recall that Trophonius, Apollo's Delphi architect, retired to one. In time Dashwood would create at vast expense an astonishing network of caves at West Wycombe, but his vision began at Medmenham where he worshipped *Bona Dea*.

According to Greco-Roman myth, Venus-Aphrodite was created when Zeus castrated his father, Chronos-Saturn; The blood spilled into the sea, was transformed into white foam upon the waves and, as painted unforgettably by Botticelli, the goddess emerged from an oyster shell and walked ashore naked upon the sands of Cyprus. The gods could not find words to describe her astounding beauty and the powers of lust she aroused in them. The goddesses were jealous, though they could not deny her charm, for she embodied the magic of womanhood. She was sweet and forgiving to any genuine worshipper but whenever she felt slighted, she was implacable in revenge. When the girls of Amathus denied her divinity, she turned all of them into prostitutes.

Dashwood adored this goddess, as the portraits by Carpentiers, Hogarth and Knapton display. The nature of his worship has been both assailed and misunderstood. John Wilkes, after falling out with the Friars, exclaimed: 'How can any man take such pains to show public contempt of all decency, order and virtue?' It was 'all Greek' to Wilkes. He mocked the building which followed after the statue of Venus and which was called both 'The Temple of Cloacina' and 'This Chapel of Ease'. All he could see was the members' lavatory.

Horace Walpole serves as a useful but similarly blinkered guide.

'The Abbey is now become remarkable by being hired by a set of gentlemen who have erected themselves into a sort of fraternity of monks and pass two days in each month there,' he wrote. 'Each has his own cell into which they may carry women. They have a maid to dress their dinner and no other servants. Over the door is written this sentence from Rabelais: "FAY CE QUE VOUDRAS"' [Do what thou wilt.] 'The decorations may be supposed to have contained the quintessence of their mysteries,' he continued in his *Journal of Visits to County Seats*, 'since it was impenetrable to any but the initiated.'

The interior gave the guests every possible comfort. There was a drawing room which Wilkes declared to be furnished largely with damask sofas of green silk amidst ornate Roman decorations 'conducive to conviviality'. Outside on the landing, male and female polarities were affirmed once more in the shape of two statues standing guard: Harpocrates and Angerona. Harpocrates was the child god of silence in Ancient Egypt; Angerona was the goddess of silence in Ancient Rome. Laurence Dermott comments in his *The Constitution of Freemasonry* (1801) that 'the Egyptians worshipped Harpocrates, the god of silence, for which reason he is always pictured holding his finger to his mouth. The Romans had a goddess of silence named Angerona, which was pictured like Harpocrates, holding her finger on her mouth, in token of secrecy.'

Glazed and framed prints of the kings and queens of England were hung upon the walls of the Abbey. Paper had been pasted over the face of Henry VIII for closing down the monasteries. One continued to the dining room. Parson Woodforde, a contemporary, noted in his *Diary* that for dinner he served four guests 'leg of mutton, boiled and capers, a boiled fowl and a tongue, a batter pudding, a fine turkey roasted, fried rabbits, tarts, custard and jellies. Almonds, raisins, oranges and apples after. Port wine...porter and ale, etc.' He was merely a country vicar with a modest living. The Friars obviously feasted even more lavishly and rejoiced in the fact that this feasting was supported by a virtually inexhaustible wine cellar. Probably they agreed with

Dr Johnson's aphorism: 'Claret is for boys. Port is for men. But he who aspires to be a hero must drink brandy.'

In the spirit of Rabelais, the Friars and their guests drank to venerate Dionysus-Bacchus, the ancient Greek god credited with introducing fermented grape juice to humanity. Wine had a wide variety of effects. It made some dull, sleepy and stupid; it made others crazy, violent and lascivious; and in some it inspired their finest ideas and ideals of creation, enabling civilisation to be brought out of barbarism. Dionysus was one of the many sons of Zeus fathered on mortal woman, and in his case, it was Semele. Indeed, the early career of this slim and delicately handsome youth consisted of lust and drunkeness with music gladly supplied by that ageing veteran of a rocker, Silenus. Dionysus caused chaos wherever he went. King Pentheus, the epitome of order and stern reason, had Dionysus flung into gaol for disturbing the peace and awakening people into an ecstatic enlightenment. Dionysus escaped from prison in a miraculous manner, after which an inquisitive Pentheus was torn to pieces by the women followers of Dionysus upon whom he had been spying and who included his own mother, as *The Bacchae* by Euripides describes so unforgettably.

Alas! Youth does not last for ever. The young, slim and effeminate youth who had brought the gift of wine to the world was in middle age a jovial toper, surrounded by a raucous crowd of centaurs, nymphs, satyrs and bacchantes raving around the ass upon which he swayed so riotously. Small wonder, as Livy records, that the celebrations of the Bacchantes were forbidden by the Roman senate in 168 BC. Small wonder too that the ceiling of Dashwood's dining room at West Wycombe is graced by Giuseppe Borgnis's paintings of Bacchus and his entourage celebrating a loving and laughing carousal.

Dionysus-Bacchus is a solar-phallic deity. As we have seen, another aspect of the sun as incarnated by Apollo was also venerated at Medmenham: the cave of Trophonius is replicated on the pedestal of Priapus. It was the late nineteenth-century German philosopher Nietzsche who best explored the aspects of

Dionysus and Apollo, compared and contrasted as solar-phallic deities. He argued convincingly in *The Birth of Tragedy* that we find an uneasy antithesis in Ancient Greek culture between two modes of apprehension. Both Dionysus and Apollo stand for man's upright place in the sun. However, Apollo stands for classicism and order, Dionysus for romanticism and chaos. In Dashwood one discerns an attempt at reconciling these two apparent opposites so as to create a fruitful synthesis.

Dashwood was a man committed to all the civilised trappings of eighteenth-century civilisation but he also loved the intoxication of the vine. In *Hieroglyphics* by Arthur Machen, strong drink is portrayed as a symbol of divine ecstasy. Machen cites principally *The Iliad* of Homer, *Gargantua and Pantagruel* by Rabelais (naturally); and *The Pickwick Papers* by Charles Dickens, in which excessive quantities of milk punch are consumed with relish. A century earlier, John Wilkes had praised 'the divine milk punch' of Sir Francis Dashwood.

Again in the spirit of Rabelais, there was a fine library which included the classics, ancient and modern, and also erotic literature. There was the *Kama Sutra*, inscribed and presented by Sir Henry Vansittart. This is not a pornographic work. *Sutra* means a scripture, *Kama* refers to a Hindu god of love; therefore the *OED* defines the *Kama Sutra* as 'an ancient Sanskrit treatise on the art of love'. It embodies a notion alien to Christianity, that the sexual act is sacred, both to the divine within us and the divine without us. It is a most holy sacrament.

Masturbation can be a sacred act too, providing that it is pledged to the goddess. One encounters these ideals repeatedly in studying holy Tantric texts; pious Tantrics would rightly regard the Christian notion of sex as sin as being a perversion and blasphemy of divine truth. It seems that Sir William Stanhope had some grasp of this notion, for in 1758 he sent some books to Dashwood, 'hoping they will now and then occasion an extraordinary ejaculation to be sent up to Heaven'.

If one worships deities such as Dionysus-Bacchus (and Priapus) and Venus-Aphrodite, then one will seek means of greater communion with them. To this end, there were books of ceremonial magick reposing in the library giving methods as to how this could be done. Dashwood had purchased the bulk of these in Venice. The word 'occult' means 'hidden', though it can also be defined as 'rejected knowledge'.

Clues for our approach to the Abbey can be found in Wilkes's and Walpole's descriptions of the statues and architecture. Everything was done to some end. Obviously the Friars wanted to drink and fornicate, as one discerns from Horace Walpole's jealous reference to the constant importation of 'nymphs and hogsheads' to the Abbey. Walpole adds that the bedrooms or 'cells' were 'fitted out for the private pleasures of each monk'. Wilkes mentions an *Idolum Tentiginis*, a phallic hobby horse used in ancient fertility cults, which gave masturbatory pleasure to every woman who sat upon it. Here was a place where one could eat, drink, be merry and make love to any willing partner to one's heart's content. So far, so civilised; but there remains the matter of the chapter-room.

The silence and secrecy surrounding this place settles the question as to whether there was anything more to the Monks than the aesthetic sensibilities of Sir Francis. Walpole and Wilkes never entered this sacred space and were reduced to guessing. We are confronted by a closed door, dividing the inner and outer circles. Horace Walpole saw the changing room of those who entered the temple and noted white hats, jackets, and trousers which he called 'more like a waterman's than a monk's'. He does not appear to have drawn the inference that Charon, ferryman across the River Styx for the dead in Greek mythology, was a waterman too.

William Hogarth painted the three Vansittart brothers wearing blue tam o'shanters with the motto *Love and Friendship* inscribed around the brim. The Nuns allegedly wore white robes upon which were inscribed mottoes embroidered in silver. Lord Temple felt grateful merely to be admitted to the outer circle at Medmenham Abbey in 1754. 'It is very gracious of the pious Aeneas, after his love-feast, to keep up friendship with one who has so slender a claim to be admitted to the table of the Saints,' he wrote in epistolary gratitude; 'I shall only now and then drink to the pious moments I have spent in your wicked company.' Temple wasn't a frequent guest because most members called him a bore.

Wilkes stated that the outer circle 'used to sacrifice to mirth, to friendship or to love, never to fortune nor ambition'. He added, in an article for the *Public Advertiser*, 1763: 'No profane eye has dared to penetrate into the English Eleusinian mysteries of the chapter-room, where the monks assembled on all solemn occasions, the more secret rites were performed and libations poured forth in much pomp to the *Bona Dea*.' Horace Walpole visited Medmenham without invitation by bribing the servants and declared of the chapter-room: 'Nobody is suffered to go into it but the members. It is said to be furnished with bawdy pictures.' There was 'a mock celebration of the ridiculous rites of the Monkish orders', John Wilkes wrote in an article for *The Political Register* in 1768. But neither Walpole nor Wilkes really knew what went on inside the chapter-room, among the inner circle.

Obviously some Friars entered this room to do something concealed from the others. This gives the lie to the argument that Dashwood was merely running a social club. Unfortunately, working out just what did take place among the inner circle in the chapter-room is not an elementary matter at all. Whatever went on behind closed doors has on the whole been lightly dismissed by historians as some silly mockery of Christianity. If this was the case, one wonders why all the members couldn't enter into genial jesting over a subject which none took seriously. Montague Summers saw the secrecy as being evidence of satanism but he saw satanism everywhere.

Political controversy produced a print published in 1763 which purports to tell the truth. Dashwood and Whitehead are shown worshipping an image of Venus. There are two books next to them: *The Art of Love* by Ovid and a book of 'evening prayers'. It is nonsense to suggest that the Medmenham meetings were merely a joke, for no joke goes on as a series of meetings for twenty-five years. Occasional meetings continued until 1777, when Dashwood gave up the lease and the Abbey was sold to a Robert Sawyer of Heywood, Berkshire. The Abbey had been stripped bare by then, for in 1766 we find founder member John Tucker writing to Dashwood in terms of pained complaint: 'I was last Sunday at Medmenham and to my amazement found the Chapter Room stripped naked.' This implies that the room was available to members of the inner circle for their private devotions. It also implies that the various ornamentations had been taken to another venue.

What we have here is a compound of paganism, occultism, and worship of the male and female generative organs, a religious deployment of sexual energy appearing to derive from Indian Tantricism and Western Bacchic rites. This theme will be reiterated as we explore the house, church, mausoleum and caves at West Wycombe Park. The clues here will enable us to unlock the closed door of the chapter-room. The key, which consists of a conjunction and communion of the male and the female, is shown in Dashwood's pouring into a communion cup 'Libations to the Goddess without eyes...'

8

The Boot and the Petticoat

The amorous activities and mysterious religious ceremonies continued unabated for the Monks of Medmenham during the 1750s. Meanwhile, what of the politics? Frederick, Prince of Wales, who had epitomised the ideal of the patriot king, was dead; but now another player entered on the scene, John Stuart, third Earl of Bute (1713–92). Although he came from a relatively old Scottish family, Bute's property consisted solely of the island of that name. He had little money but he did have a pedigree, for he was descended from a bastard son of Scotland's King Robert II, and this Eton-educated man parlayed his ancestry into a marriage with Lady Mary Wortley Montagu's daughter. At first Lady Mary fiercely disapproved of the match, but she was reconciled when Bute proved himself to be a kindly and attentive husband who made her daughter happy. Money remained a problem, however, and Bute took a house in Twickenham at just £45 rent a year.

Luck had led to a meeting with Frederick, Prince of Wales, who took a liking to this tall, dark, handsome man of many talents. The two became firm friends. Bute's leisure interests were botany, music, amateur dramatics and mathematics. These pleased the Prince and soon enough Bute was supervising gardening at Kew, music at Carlton House, amateur dramatics at Cliveden; and tutoring Frederick's son, the future George III, in mathematics. The Prince made Bute a Lord of the Bedchamber.

Bute also won the favour of Frederick's wife, Princess Augusta, a strong, handsome woman. When her husband died, she appointed Bute as Groom of the Stole, in effect the salaried head of her official household. King George II detested Bute, simply for being a Stuart and a friend of his late son. He declined to receive the Earl but acceded to the appointment, telling the Duke of Grafton to slip the gold key – the badge of office – into Bute's pocket. By contrast, the future King George III liked and respected his tutor. 'Remember that when you are King, you must be ruthless,' Bute told him. Meanwhile, although his marriage to Mary Montagu was quite happy, Bute was reputed to be enjoying an affair with Lady Howe; and then, it was said, Princess Augusta. He was holding a golden key indeed.

Dodington and Dashwood cultivated Bute. He was intelligent, charming and socially accomplished, if somewhat vain. Some doubted his abilities, including his late patron, Prince Frederick. 'Bute is a fine showy man,' Frederick had said. 'He would make an excellent ambassador in a court where there was no business.' His connection with the Friars is tenuous. Ashe suggests that he could well have been the 'John of London' listed in the cellarbooks. Certainly he was a member of the Dashwood–Dodington circle. He continued to visit Princess Augusta in a curtained sedan chair borrowed from Miss Vansittart, sister of the three brothers who were Medmenham Monks. He waited in the wings as he watched political developments.

The Seven Years War affected the fortunes of all politicians. England had allied with Frederick the Great of Prussia, under the Newcastle-Pitt ministry. As usual, the enemy was France, allied with Austria, Russia and Sweden. Pitt's policy was one of imperialism. 'We must win Canada on the banks of the Elbe,' he declared and Britain funded Frederick whilst engaging in naval battles and colonial land assaults. In the course of this war, there occurred the sordid tragedy of Admiral Byng, who retreated in good order before a vastly superior show of French force and who was unjustly hanged for cowardice. The Monks of Medmenham united behind Dashwood in his honourable House of Commons protest to absolve Byng from all charges brought against him. The

French admiral, the Duc de Richelieu, who had conquered the British colony of Minorca in 1756 and then forced Byng's small squadron into retreat, was nevertheless a chivalrous foe, for he sent testimony to the court which exonerated Byng of all blame. Richelieu was a notorious rake and he had been a friend of Philip, Duke of Wharton, the original Hell-Fire clubman; he did not want his foe to be treated unfairly. Unfortunately, British public opinion was outraged by the loss of Minorca and the government wanted Byng to be its scapegoat.

Dashwood's courageous defence of Byng received a poor reception in the House of Commons. Dodington went in to bat for Byng. Horace Walpole described his speech as being 'bold and pathetic', Dodington subsequently losing his job as Treasurer of the Navy; yet even Walpole felt compelled to write in defence of Byng. Paul Whitehead penned a pamphlet but none of these endeavours succeeded, for Byng was judicially murdered.

The subsequent accession to power of William Pitt the Elder is notable for his speeches, which stirred a nation, and his successful prosecution of the Seven Years War. Clive won in India. Wolfe took Quebec. Howe smashed French naval might at Quiberon Bay. Dodington then felt that all British war aims had been achieved and argued for the making of a civilised peace. Bute agreed with him, all the while making contacts and conferring with those who could deliver votes. Pitt disdained proposals of peace. Dodington intrigued to have Pitt dismissed from office, calling him 'a ranting buskineer' and 'a most impracticable colleague'.

On 25 October 1760, King George II died as grossly as he had lived: upon a lavatory seat. Two days after the burial, Dodington called on Bute, having discerned potential in a man who had never held any political office. Dodington ensured that Bute replaced Lord Holderness as Secretary of State for the Northern Department on 25 March 1761. Then Spain, allied with France, threatened an entry to the war. Pitt demanded a pre-emptive strike against Spain. Bute opposed this measure. Pitt lost power.

It was a case of the spoils of office for the Monks of Medmenham. The King was George III, who adored his tutor

Bute, as did the king' s mother, Princess Augusta. Bute became Prime Minister. He appointed Dashwood as Chancellor of the Exchequer. Dodington was elevated to the peerage as Lord Melcombe. Sandwich was given a Crown sinecure with a promise of return to the Admiralty in the following year. The way seemed clear for a new patriot king, guided by his Prime Minister, to lift the country out of the rut of petty party politics and to wrest it from the greedy grasp of the Whig oligarchy. Bute took office in good faith and yet, as Thackeray would declare: 'he was hated with a rage of which there have been few examples in English history'. Some called this 'the Hell-Fire Ministry'.

Bute was an old-fashioned Tory committed to the ideal of a patriot king, a role he hoped his princely pupil would exemplify. King George III was well intentioned but lacked intelligence. He favoured a benevolent authoritarian paternalism and Bute encouraged him in embracing this notion. The King genuinely wanted to improve the lot of the common people. Meanwhile, Bute ensured that his Medmenham associates were rewarded. Paul Whitehead was given £800 a year as 'deputy treasurer of the chamber'. 'Old Q', the Earl of March, was made a Lord of the Bedchamber, a Knight of the Thistle, and a Scottish representative peer. William Hogarth, who painted and drew so many of these men, was confirmed as 'Serjeant Painter'. Henry Fox, a Medmenhamite according to some, was appointed Leader of the House of Commons. Bute declared to the King that 'most of our best authors are devoted to me'. He gave Dr 'Dictionary' Johnson a pension of £300 a year; he patronised John Home, a former tutor of the King, James Macpherson, who had skilfully faked the Gaelic epic of *Ossian*, and the novelist Tobias Smollett, who set up a journal to propagandise on behalf of Bute. It was called *The Briton*. Unfortunately, the Prime Minister did not trust the people and therefore never appeared in public without a bodyguard of prize-fighters. Still more unfortunately, the King fell asleep when Bute was explaining to him the importance of arts and letters.

The so-called 'Hell-Fire Ministry' instantly ran into difficulties.

Horace Walpole wrote in June 1762:

> The new administration begins tempestuously. My father was not more abused after twenty years than Lord Bute is after twenty days . . . the coins of the King were the worst that had appeared for above a century and the revenues of the Crown were so soon squandered in purchasing dependents, that architecture, that darling art of Lord Bute was contracted from the erection of a new palace, to altering a single door-case in the drawing room of St James's . . .

Bute was unused to the hurly-burly of practical politics. His first difficulty was that he was a Scotsman at a time when there was much prejudice against the Scots.

'Sir, I think you are a Scotsman,' Johnson had growled at Boswell when they first met. 'Sir, I am indeed from Scotland,' Boswell answered, 'but that I cannot help.'

'That, sir,' Johnson retorted scornfully, 'is a matter which a great many of your countrymen cannot help.'

The London mob did not appreciate the Scots either. The mob did not have the vote, which was then confined to owners of property, but in an era when voting was public, the mob's muscle could be employed to swing elections, for they were a lawless lot with little to lose. In London especially, it was vital to secure the backing of the mob. If they rioted, honest citizens might well vote for a change of regime. John Wilkes knew this but Bute did not.

A further thorny matter was that of economics. Dashwood's many qualities did not equip him to manage the finances of a nation. His Budget of March 1763 was a fiasco. 'I am not for an extension of the excise laws but for an enlargement of them,' he declared, leaving his own supporters to ponder this contradiction. He proposed to raise £3,500,000 in revenue via annuities of 4.5 per cent and a tax upon cider. 'All the whole total is anything for peace and quietness' sake,' the Chancellor said. Although the essential principle of the cider tax was reasonable and would be employed in modified form by subsequent governments, it caused outrage in the West Country. An anonymous wit savaged the administration:

> The King was going to Parliament
> A numerous crowd was round him
> Some hurra'd him as he went
> And others cry'd – confound him!
> At length a shout came thundering out
> Which made the air to ring, Sir;
> All in one voice cry'd no excise,
> No BUTE, no Cyder King, Sir.'

Foreign policy provoked a further problem. Pitt had wanted to continue the Seven Years War; Bute wanted a civilised peace, and to this end he signed the Treaty of Paris on 3 November 1762. The triumphs of Clive in India, Wolfe in Canada and Hawke's at Quiberon Bay gave England the French surrender of all claims to Canada, Nova Scotia, Grenada, St Vincent, Dominica, Tobago, Senegal, and all lands and rights in India acquired since 1749, which meant most of Bengal. The Mediterranean island of Minorca, lost to the French and not won back by the unhappy Admiral Byng, was returned to England. Spain agreed to cede Florida to Britain. Bute stated that he hoped his moves as a man of peace would be inscribed upon his tombstone.

'The sooner the better,' said some anonymous critic, and John Wilkes called this treaty 'the peace of God which passeth all understanding'. Why? Some claimed that Bute had abandoned England's ally, Frederick the Great of Prussia, and left him to fight his own battles. London merchants objected to Bute's conciliatory moves in returning the sugar islands of St Lucia and Guadeloupe to France along with cod-fishing rights off Newfoundland, and in giving Havana, Cuba, back to Spain. It was a tight vote in the House of Commons and it was managed with the methods customary at the time. 'A shop was publicly opened at the Pay Office, whither the Members flocked and received the wages of their venality in bank bills, even to so low a sum as two hundred pounds for their vote on the treaty,' Horace Walpole wrote indignantly. 'Twenty-five thousand pounds, as Martin, Secretary of the Treasury, afterwards owned, were issued in one morning, and in a single fortnight a vast majority was purchased to approve the peace.' Secret service records show that the fund was £15,000, roughly £800,000 in today's terms. Sir Robert Walpole, Horace's father, would not have thought twice about this expenditure and so it is hard to understand his son's self-righteous outrage.

Bute won the vote on the treaty. This did not save him from being savaged by his enemies, John Wilkes, Charles Churchill and Robert Lloyd writing in the broadsheets and discrediting his every action. Rumours spread, accusing him of being the lover of Princess Augusta, 'the petticoat', and mother of the king, a matter which has not been proven one way or another. Bute was a civilised and humane man, albeit somewhat vain and snobbish. He had solved his financial problems by marrying the daughter of the coal magnate, Edward Wortley Montagu, which brought him a dowry approaching £1 million. He felt that he was doing his best for the kingdom, and he simply could not take being ridiculed by the press. His minders could defend him from immediate physical violence but no one would enjoy being hissed publicly or having stones thrown at one's carriage. The London mob's abusive placards of 'The Boot and the Petticoat' upset him dreadfully. The sensible though limited achievements of his so-called 'Hell-Fire Ministry' can be defended, for Bute genuinely felt that he had exercised his abilities to the utmost to benefit the finances and foreign policy of the nation. He had reckoned without the man the King called 'that Devil Wilkes'.

9

'That Devil Wilkes'

Few men have caused so much controversy as John Wilkes. Lord Bute's son called him 'a goggle-eyed son of a bitch'. Pitt the Elder declared him to be 'a blasphemer who did not deserve to be ranked among the human species'. According to an anonymous critic: 'There was no corruption that he had learned anywhere but he was able to duplicate it . . . there was not a friend Wilkes would not sacrifice for a scurvy jest'. Yet it was added: 'Wilkes has every vice but one – he is not an hypocrite.' Charles Johnstone, author of *Chrysal*, had a more favourable opinion: 'His wit gave charm to every subject he spoke upon.' Rhodes refers to Wilkes's 'robust agnosticism' and observes that 'it is tribute to Dashwood's remarkable personality that he retained the loyalty of so heretical a member for so long'. Ashe states astutely: 'Conspicuous for wit, political flair, journalistic verve, disreputability and scorn for religion, Wilkes was the test case; the man who could make Libertinism and Liberty go together if anyone could.' He would traumatise his era.

John Wilkes (1727–97) was the son of a London merchant. He had extravagant tastes and soon ran up debts that would plague him throughout his life. These caused him to marry a sleepy and somewhat physically unattractive but pleasant woman who had some money. He remained a rake but he was kind and considerate to her, and the daughter his wife bore him absolutely adored her father. In the course of his carousing, Wilkes met Thomas Potter.

As mentioned, some called Potter 'Wilkes's Evil Genius'. Potter, a Medmenham Monk, introduced Wilkes to Pitt and his brother-in-law, Earl Temple of Stowe in Buckinghamshire. In 1754 Wilkes was made High Sheriff of Buckingham and used his wife's money to buy a house in Aylesbury. In the same year, he was put up as a parliamentary candidate for Berwick and lost. Three years later, he was returned as the Member for Aylesbury. He had Thomas Potter to thank for that, though it greatly increased his debts. 1757 was also the year in which Potter introduced Wilkes to Dashwood, who liked him sufficiently to appoint him his lieutenant-colonel of the Bucks Militia and who invited him to join the Friars in the following year.

Wilkes obviously enjoyed his initial period at Medmenham Abbey. The cellar-book fragments record his name more often than anybody else's. He was drinking wine for his 'private devotions' on 28 August, 4 and 5 September 1760. A letter to Lord Temple mentions coming from 'Medmenham Abbey, where the jovial monks of St Francis had kept me up till four in the morning'. Wilkes praised Dashwood's imagination and called him a man of 'very real mental abilities', although he was never invited to enter the chapter-room.

He was not merely a middle-class aspirant to fame and fortune, not merely a wit, rake, sceptic and debauchee. Women loved him even though, as portrayed by Hogarth, he had an awful squint. 'Give me half an hour to make up my face,' he retorted to the taunts of men, 'and I'll seduce a woman ahead of the handsomest man in Europe.' He would fulfil his boast later in Paris, where he seduced in one night a woman Casanova had besieged for six months without success.

Wilkes had allies in the shape of two poets, Charles Churchill and Robert Lloyd. It is difficult to find Robert Lloyd interesting or to make him interesting. Even his friend Wilkes declared he was 'scampering around the foot of Parnassus on his little Welsh pony'. Lloyd had known Charles Churchill at Westminster School, where the former had been a bright scholar, but, as Ashe puts it, he 'drifted dismally into teaching and composition of petty, self-pitying verse'. It was Churchill who introduced Lloyd to the Friars, having himself been introduced by John Wilkes. Lloyd must have been delighted, for at the Abbey there was a hedonistic refuge from both poverty and chastity. Posterity has not been impressed. Postgate calls him 'an amiable and simple Welshman...he wrote lengthy, flowing ephemeral satires in undistinguished verse'. 'A poor and miserable Welsh schoolmaster,' Eric Towers observes of this Medmenham Monk, 'who was known to Churchill and who suffered the indignity of dying in debtors' prison through not attending to his job.'This occurred in 1764. There is little to add other than the fact that he was a decent chap who was kind and loyal to his friends.

Charles Churchill was a different kettle of fish altogether. Anyone who thinks that poets are wimps should have met him. 'Huge and clumsy...' Postgate writes, 'his legs and arms astonishingly thick'. Hogarth portrayed him unforgettably when he caricatured Churchill as a bear with a beer tankard in his paw and a mastiff at his feet. 'His fame in life was enormous,' Postgate observes, 'his eclipse after his death was rapid.' His *Collected Works* were published posthumously in 1804 and the editor's preface gives one an intriguing insight into the tastes of the time, for it calls Churchill 'often as contemptible a poet as Donne, yet he frequently rose as high as Dryden'.

Rhodes gives the man credit where it is due: 'Despite the atmosphere of scandal and violence which surrounded his private life, he was generous to his friends and charitable to the poor.' Churchill had been born the son of a London parson and was educated at Westminster School. Before the age of eighteen, he made a girl pregnant. His father forced him to marry her and more or less bludgeoned the son into the job of curate at Rainham, Essex. He had no vocation for the job whatsoever. He moved to the curacy of South Cadbury, Somerset and was equally miserable there. The death of his father in 1756 enabled Churchill to move to London, where he taught at a girls' school.

London suited Churchill's tastes. He swaggered around in a gold-laced hat, a blue coat, white silk stockings and silver-buckled shoes as he constantly visited the theatres, the taverns and the broth-els. His poetry won him an increasingly formidable reputation.

'His genius was biased by personal animosity,' Chalmers writes in his *Life of Churchill*, 'and where he surpasses all other writers, it is not in the keenness, not of legitimate satire, but of defamation. His object is not to reform, but to revenge, and that the greatness of his revenge may be justified, he exaggerates the offence of his subjects beyond all bounds of truth and decency.'

As Churchill himself would write:

> From Hell itself his characters he drew,
> And christened them by every name he knew.

John Wilkes was feeling mean and vicious. He was heavily in debt and despite his membership of both Parliament and the Friars, he had not been offered a job in Bute's government. His friend and ally, Thomas Potter, was dead. Now his new friend, Charles Churchill the poet, urged him to fight for the principles which the latter perceived to be right.

Wilkes proceeded to savage the Bute ministry, initially for few purposes other than the self-righteous indignation of a man who feels rejected. In time, though, this feeling would grow to be more profound. To the task he brought undoubted courage and acute wit. Wilkes could sense a weakness in an enemy and took joy in stripping away the veneer so as to expose it to the world's ridicule. Bute had commissioned Smollett to edit *The Briton*, essentially propaganda for Bute's ministry; very well, then, Wilkes and Churchill brought out *The North Briton* as their weapon of satire. It is probable at that point that Wilkes could have been bought by a reasonable proposition from Bute, for then he had very few principles other than those of enlightened self-interest. By contrast, Charles Churchill had his faults but lack of principle was not among them.

In March 1763 Ben Jonson's *The Fall of Mortimer* was published with a scathingly satirical introduction by Wilkes. This compared

Bute, lover of the Queen Mother, to Mortimer, that wheeling and dealing lover of the wife of Edward II who was mother to Edward III. Eric Towers declares of Wilkes: 'Like Pitt before him, he planned to make such a nuisance of himself that the administration would buy him off with a well-paid position.'

The government responded by firing warning shots over the bow of Wilkes's ship. Wilkes answered by increasing the acidity of his attacks. The government replied by issuing general warrants for the arrest of the publishers and editors and those connected to *The North Briton*. Wilkes defied it, announcing in print that 'Those few, those very few, who are not afraid to take a lover of liberty by the hand, congratulate me on being alive and at liberty.'

As we have seen, Bute resigned on 8 April 1763. Dashwood, mocked mercilessly by Wilkes over the cider tax and his fumbling though well-intentioned expostulations over finance in the House of Commons, was kicked upstairs to the House of Lords as Baron Le Despenser, the premier baron of England. Under the new ministry of Grenville, Lord Sandwich returned to his beloved post as First Lord of the Admiralty. There was still a possibility of domestic peace; but Sandwich couldn't bear Wilkes. Once again, no offer of office was made to Wilkes under the new ministry.

Number 45 of *The North Briton* was issued on 23 April 1763. Wilkes went wild. He damned the government as a bunch of degenerate and corrupt time-serving hacks who had no concern for the nation. Then he condemned Bute's Treaty of Paris as a sell-out of the Seven Years War and presented himself as a patriot. Certainly Wilkes aroused the London mob. The address of congratulation had to be presented to the King by a delegation representing the City of London, and they were booed and hissed by the mob all the way to St James's. However, Wilkes refrained from a personal attack upon Dashwood.

'It is perhaps singular with respect to this periodical that it was conducted upon principles different to any other,' Wilkes wrote many years later:

No private tie had been broke, no connexions dissolved, nor

any attack when there was friendly intercourse. Sir Francis Dashwood will be on record as a remarkable proof of this observation. He was certainly as Chancellor of the Exchequer the best mark an Opposition could wish. He was spared by *The North Briton* and it was believed he owed that indemnity to private connexions with Mr Wilkes. He was one of the Monks of Medmenham and used to attend the Chapters very regularly. He afterwards neglected those meetings and gave us the reason that he did not choose to meet Mr Wilkes, who was an enemy of Lord Bute. Mr Wilkes desired their common friends at the Abbey to represent to Sir Francis the nature of such an institution, in which party he had not the least concern.

Definitely Dashwood took no part in the proceedings which followed the publication of number 45. Wilkes was arrested under a general warrant and imprisoned in the Tower of London. There, perhaps, he reflected upon his method of journalism, one which he would later explain to the economist, Adam Smith: 'Give me a grain of truth and I will mix it up with a great mass of falsehood so that no chemist will ever be able to separate them.'

Wilkes languished in the Tower for a time but, as always, he hit back. Without even meaning to establish the principle and only to get himself out of gaol, he struck a blow for English liberties in challenging the legality of a general warrant. Essentially this entitled the authorities to arrest and imprison anyone suspected of subversive activities without even naming him or her. Wilkes's case established the illegality of a general warrant and is now enshrined as a major principle of British constitutional law. The authorities had to release Wilkes in May 1763, the mob saluted him with fireworks and a procession and for the first time, the cry of 'WILKES AND LIBERTY!' rang through the streets of London.

It was a temporary triumph, for the damage had been done. The King was outraged over the fact that Wilkes had called him a liar in print. The officers of the law had raided the offices of *The North Briton* and come away with incriminating evidence. For

Wilkes it was like a poker game in which the stakes were being upped. Dashwood tried to make peace. In the globe atop the curious church of St Lawrence, he invited Wilkes and Churchill to discuss serious matters.

'As to secrecy, it is the most convenient Place imaginable,' Wilkes would write, 'and it is whispered that a Negotiation was here *entamée* by the noble Lord himself with Messrs Wilkes and Churchill. The event will show the amazing Powers of his Lordship's oratory; but if from Perverseness neither of these gentlemen yielded to his wise reasons, nor to his dazzling Offers, they were both delighted with his divine milk punch.'

Wilkes had not yet realised at least one basic truth which Dashwood was endeavouring to explain to him: to wit, that the establishment could do much more harm to him than he could do to the establishment. Wilkes thought that he was tough enough and clever enough to take anything that the establishment tried to throw at him. Soon enough he would experience the painful fact that when it came to being mean and vicious, the establishment made him look like Mr Nice Guy.

10

Mean and Vicious

The autumn of 1763 saw the establishment moving to crush John Wilkes. The House of Commons resolved to read out the King's message: 'His Majesty having received information that John Wilkes Esquire, a Member of this House, was the author of a most seditious and dangerous libel...' By a vote of 273 to 111, the Commons decided that *The North Briton* number 45 was 'a false, scandalous and seditious libel, containing expressions of the most unexampled insolence and contumely towards His Majesty, the grossest aspersions upon both Houses of Parliament and the most audacious defiance of the whole Legislature'.

In the House of Lords, Sandwich moved into the attack. He had been grossly offended by Wilkes's assaults on Bute's ministry and according to his code, this was evidence of despicable disloyalty, and an insult to the fraternity of the Friars. Any measures, however vile, were therefore justified in the name of vengeance. Solemnly he informed the peers and bishops that he held in his hand a salacious work which attacked the Bishop of Gloucester and which was a venal abuse of parliamentary privilege. The author, he claimed, was John Wilkes MP and the work was *Essay on Woman*. Sandwich then proceeded to a lip-smacking reading of this work before the House of Lords.

Essay on Woman was a satirical parody of Alexander Pope's *Essay on Man*, composed around 1755 by Thomas Potter with assistance from Wilkes. Nowadays, one would find it quite witty in parts but otherwise dull rather than shocking:

> Awake, my Fanny, leave all meaner things
> This morn shall prove what rapture swiving brings.
> Let us (since life can little more supply
> Than just a few good fucks and then we die)
> Expiate free o'er the loved scene of Man;
> A mighty Maze, for mighty Pricks to scan . . .

Then, although few really believed in Christianity, we have seen that everybody paid lip service to it as a binding social cement. In consequence, everybody in the House of Lords that day pretended to be horrified.

It was unfortunate for Wilkes that this book fell into the hands of Sandwich. How did it happen? It seems that after the death of Potter, Wilkes made moves to have some copies bound and privately printed for circulation among the Friars, who had relished Potter's private readings. The papers relating to this matter were seized by the officers of the law who had raided Wilkes's house. In addition there is the matter of the Reverend John Kidgell.

Kidgell was chaplain to the Medmenhamite, the Earl of March. Why on earth that rake 'Old Q' would have wanted a chaplain is not quite clear until one inspects the matter further. Kidgell was a classic Christian hypocrite. He toadied to rich old ladies, he fondled the buttocks and genitals of choirboys, he dabbled in pornography – and he fulminated against sexual sin in his sermons. It was not a problem for this extremely unpleasant man to seek out the printer of *Essay on Woman* as an agent of the Earl of March and to buy the proof sheets for £233. These were then passed to March.

March shared the view of Sandwich that the acid critique of Bute's ministry by Wilkes had severely breached all rules of monkish hospitality and so he passed all papers on to him. There are still texts available at the Home Office, where Sandwich lodged copies. Wilkes may have played only a minor part in the matter but it didn't matter to Sandwich. It was all grist to his mill.

Wilkes really had gone too far for most people's taste in this printed edition. The indecent commentary which he had himself probably composed was attributed to Dr William Warburton, Bishop of Gloucester, thus leaving Wilkes open to a charge of seditious libel. The title page went further:

> An Essay on Woman, by Pego Borewell, Esq. with notes by Rogerus Cunaeus, Vigerus Muntoniatus, etc. and a Commentary by the Rev. Dr. Warburton, inscribed to Miss Fanny Murray.

Fanny Murray, as has been observed, was one of the most celebrated courtesans of the time, and also a mistress of Lord Sandwich. Worse was to come. On the same page, there was an engraving of a stiff penis with the words 'Saviour of the World' in Greek and there was sinister Latin at the bottom: 'From the original frequently in the crutch of the Most Reverend George Stone, Primate of Ireland, more frequently in the anus of the intrepid hero George Sackville.' Dr George Stone, Archbishop of Armagh, was a noted sexual deviant, and Lord George Sackville had been rightly criticised for cowardice in the face of the enemy at the Battle of Minden. These censures are true and just, but no establishment welcomes truth and justice.

Sandwich gloated as he read out the verses to the House of Lords:

> Say first, of Woman's latent charms below,
> What can we reason, but from what we know?
> . . . Presumptuous Prick! the reason wouldst thou find,
> Why formed so weak, so little, and so blind?

'But he can't (if the phrase may be pardoned) keep it up,' Ashe comments wryly. He adds that the information in the verses, which state that Lord Bute gave Princess Augusta advice on the architecture of the pagoda erected in Kew Gardens, was passed to the public and the building was promptly known as 'Bute's Erection'.

The majority of lords and bishops pretended to be shocked as Sandwich read with obvious relish the verses which had delighted him in the company of the Friars. He condemned without reserve the obscenities and blasphemies of the poem despite the fact that the Beefsteak Club was about to expel him for obscenity and blasphemy. Dashwood couldn't stand it. 'I never thought to hear the Devil preach,' he remarked loudly.

Lord Lyttleton, who had abandoned the consolations of being a rake for the rigours of Christianity, implored the House of Lords to hear no more; but when they insisted on further salacious verses, he failed to leave. The Bishop of Gloucester indignantly declared that 'the blackest fiend in Hell would not keep company with Wilkes'. No doubt he had also rubbed his hands with joy and felt a frisson of illicit pleasure as Sandwich read:

> The grasp divine, th'emphatic, thrilling squeeze,
> The throbbing, panting breasts and trembling knees,
> The tickling motion, the enlivening flow,
> The rapturous shiver and dissolving, oh!

Lord Temple made a lukewarm endeavour to defend Wilkes. After all, he had roared with laughter when listening to these verses at his dinner table. He condemned the methods of the government in obtaining *Essay on Woman* but that was about all. The House of Lords resolved that *Essay on Woman* was 'a most scandalous, obscene and impious libel'. The next question concerned the matter of the author. Sandwich claimed that it was Wilkes. Lord Mansfield moved for the right to hear Wilkes in his own defence and the motion was carried.

Wilkes had two days to prepare his case but these were spoiled by duels. After all, it would be most convenient for the establishment if he were shot. To this end, he was challenged by one Mr Talbot, whom he had insulted in his paper. Talbot was so angry that he couldn't shoot straight and Wilkes was short-sighted and missed. Instantly this was followed by another duel. Mr Martin, Secretary of the Treasury and friend of Talbot, had been called 'treacherous, base, selfish, mean, abject, low-lived and dirty' in *The North Briton*. He had responded in the House of Commons by saying of Wilkes: 'A man capable of writing in that manner without putting his name to it, and thereby stabbing another man in the dark, is a cowardly, malignant and scandalous scoundrel.' Wilkes answered by sending Martin a note which acknowledged the authorship of the assault and challenged him to a duel. They met in Hyde Park. On the first shot they both missed. Their seconds begged them to desist but Martin insisted on a second round. Here Wilkes missed and Martin hit. Fortunately the lead ball was deflected by a button on the coat of Wilkes, but it passed into his groin.

As Wilkes lay in hospital, Parliament debated his fate. There was some hope, perhaps, in his former associate, William Pitt, now Earl of Chatham. If Wilkes had high hopes of him, they were soon enough dashed on this occasion. After a promising start, in which Pitt argued vehemently for the right of Members to be protected from government harassment under the protection of parliamentary privilege, he proceeded to state that Wilkes 'did not deserve to be ranked among the human species – he was the blasphemer of his God and the libeller of his King'. Pitt denied that he had ever entertained the slightest dealings with Wilkes and left the House before the vote.

The machinery of the establishment continued to grind along in its slow but relentless way. After his period in hospital, he went to France but the wound still affected him and he was taken ill once again. Mr Speaker was quite scathing, informing the House of Commons that he had received

a letter, by the General Post, from Mr Wilkes, dated Paris, the 11th instant, enclosing a Paper in the French language, purporting to be a Certificate of one of the French King's Physicians, and of a Surgeon of the said King's Army, relating to the State of Mr Wilkes' health, subscribed with Two Names, but not authenticated before a Notary Public, nor the Signature thereof verified in any Manner whatsoever.

On 20 January 1764 the House of Commons passed the motion 'That the said John Wilkes Esquire be, for the said Offence, expelled this House.' This said offence was, of course, 'a false, scandalous and seditious libel'. The resolution robbed Wilkes of the protection of parliamentary privilege. This enabled his enemies to have him tried in his absence before Lord Mansfield in February 1764, whereby he was found guilty of seditious libel against King George III in *The North Briton* and the Bishop of Gloucester in *Essay on Woman*. Imprisonment awaited Wilkes should he ever have the courage to return to England.

Lord Chesterfield, the celebrated epistolarian, was his usual sardonic self over the matter. 'Thank heavens, gentlemen,' he declared over a pinch of snuff, 'that we have a Wilkes to protect our liberties and a Sandwich to safeguard our morals.'

One can easily comprehend the anger of Wilkes as he recovered from his gunshot wound in Paris. One can also understand both the outrage of his fellow Monks and the fury of the establishment that he had both ridiculed and threatened.

'Sir!' Lord Sandwich had fulminated, 'you will die either on the gallows or of the pox!'

'That, sir,' Wilkes replied coolly, 'depends on whether I embrace your principles or your mistress.'

11

West Wycombe

Grenville became Prime Minister in 1763. Sandwich continued to feather his own nest, working away with his customary vigour at the Admiralty and making enemies whom he treated with his usual scorn and disdain. Dashwood, now Lord Le Despenser and aged fifty-six in 1764, had to reconsider his own position. Frederick, Prince of Wales, Thomas Potter, Bubb Dodington and Charles Churchill were all dead. Bute had taken an early retirement and Wilkes had been forced into exile. Moreover, there were publications which abused the Monks of Medmenham.

Principal among them was Johnstone's *Chrysal: The Adventures of a Guinea*, published in four volumes between 1760 and 1765. As we have seen, its account of the Vansittart baboon released in the temple as a practical joke by Wilkes as Sandwich invoked Satan is simply not true and is drawn from an urban myth in Ned Ward's *The Secret History of Clubs* of 1708. Nevertheless, this made Medmenham Abbey the focus of unwelcome and unfavourable publicity. As usual, Horace Walpole commented upon the matter acidly in his *Memoirs*:

Yet their follies would have escaped the eye of the public if Lord Bute, from this seminary of piety and wisdom, had not selected a Chancellor of the Exchequer. But politics had no sooner infused themselves amongst these rosy anchorites than dissensions were kindled and a false brother arose, who divulged the arcane and exposed the good Prior in order to ridicule him as Minister of the Finances.

The 'Chancellor', the 'Prior' and the 'Minister of Finances' is Dashwood; the 'false brother' is Wilkes. Walpole added of Wilkes:

Mr Wilkes is sent to the Tower for the last *North Briton*...It said Lord Bute had made the King utter a great falsehood in his last speech. This hero is as bad a fellow as ever hero was, abominable in private life, dull in Parliament, but, they say, very entertaining in a room and certainly no bad writer, besides having had the honour of contributing a great deal to Lord Bute's fall.

Walpole made his uninvited visit to Medmenham in 1763, finding it all 'very ruinous and bad'. As has been observed, John Tucker was amazed to find the chapter-room 'stripped naked' in 1766. Although it appears that occasional meetings of the Monks still took place at the Abbey, the balance of evidence is that the principal seat of operations had been transferred to Dashwood's estate at West Wycombe.

'I never could get a set speech by heart,' Dashwood had lamented during his dismal days as Chancellor. He was not a man who could operate effectively unless he could write his own part. This he had proceeded to do in his own inimitable fashion at West Wycombe Park. There are four buildings which concern us here: the house; the church; the mausoleum; and the caves.

Dashwood had made himself popular in the locality by providing employment in having a road built to his house between 1748 and 1752, using the chalk from a nearby cave. The house was intended to be a representation of all he loved in a sermon delivered in stone, with marble and plasterwork, supplemented by all the arts of the painter and interior designer. He worked feverishly to have the house his father had left him remoulded after his own design.

The original house had been built by his father in the Queen

Anne style around 1710. It was 'exactly the sort of house a wealthy businessman turned squire might have been expected to build', Eric Towers writes, adding: 'It was commodious, comfortable, and, above all, solidly English. It lacked the imagination and the touch of magnificence, perhaps even eccentricity, which was the characteristic of its new owner.'

Some critics have deplored as a curious compound the varying styles deployed by Dashwood. The present writer cannot agree with them and admires the harmonious synthesis of the contrasting styles. The north front is standard enough for the time, with two stone lions, Ionic columns and stone steps to the main door. Towers terms it 'polite English classicism'. However, the south front is somewhat more exotic and influenced by Italy. Here one sees a beautiful view of a lawn and a lake from beneath a double colonnade. The centrepiece consisted of a stone sarcophagus around which carved dophins swam. There were busts of gods, emperors and philosophers. The central section of the ceiling was decorated by a fresco featuring Bacchus and Ariadne, painted by Giuseppe Borgnis and completed after his untimely death in 1761 by his son Giovanni. This Greco-Roman theme was repeated in the interior. The main drawing room is adorned by a picture of Psyche being admitted to Olympus, after an original by Raphael. The ceiling of the dining room is after Caracci and reiterates the theme of Bacchus and Ariadne. Bacchus clearly represents drinking, fornication, and the male probing lust after truth; and Ariadne represents its thread.

The east wing, built in 1754, is after the manner of an Ancient Greek temple. The west wing was built under the supervision of the architect Nicholas Revett: it is a reconstruction of the temple of Bacchus which Dashwood had seen in Smyrna, Turkey. Again and again we find the theme of Dionysus-Bacchus, a wild male to be mated with the Goddess of Truth.

Around the house there were further delights. There were woods. There was a menagerie. The lake contained four sailing vessels, including a full-rigged sixty-tonner. There was a greenhouse which housed exotic plants standing before a circular pond which was home to the golden and silver fish of India.

This was only the start of a series of remarkable buildings. Down the hill, Dashwood erected the church of St Lawrence. There is no church quite like this one. The ceiling is a copy of that in the ruined Temple of the Sun at Palmyna. Flowers abound; these are, of course, a symbol of female sexuality. There are four portholes at north, south, east and west. One can then climb the stone steps to a golden globe above the church; this globe once more symbolises the sun and can seat a maximum of four people. Wikes said that from there one could look out on to a garden deliberately planted in the shape of the female form. This sounds like an utterly enchanting idea and assuming that this tale is true, it is a pity that this garden is no longer visible.

Next to the church, Dashwood erected a mausoleum. This had six sides, as in Rabelais, and as we shall see, six is the number of the sun. Dodington was buried there in 1762 and Dashwood's wife was laid to rest in 1769. The contemporary visitor finds it to be gratifyingly bereft of tourist trappings and silent and beautiful to behold.

Now we come to the caves. These were built by Cornish miners: it is curious that Dashwood did not use local labour. The entrance leads us two hundred feet into the centre of the hill. High on the right wall 'XXII-F' is inscribed. 'F' has to be Dashwood as Francis. 'XXII' can be subjected to analysis by Qabalah (see Chapter 14). Jesse Lasky Jnr and Pat Silver are most interesting guides here, for they discern a pattern.

The Lasky-Silver thesis is that Dashwood's labyrinth was laid out according to a precise design so as to represent the Tantric World Egg 'bisected twice through the centre', a symbol dating from 2000 BC. We shall be examining Tantricism in Chapter 13. After the figure XXXIV, a tunnel then leads to a cellar chamber forty feet in diameter, with four alcoves precisely positioned at north, south, east and west just like Dashwood's church. Beyond that, there are passages laid out to the left and the right so as to form a triangle which, Lasky and Silver argue convincingly, is the Tantric symbol for the sacred vulva. This symbolism is reinforced when one comes to an artificial river which the Friars knew as 'the Styx', the river of death in Greek mythology – and comes to the 'Inner Temple' on crossing that river to find, carved into the wall and half-hidden by pebbles at foot level, an ovoid representation of a vulva. One also finds a bas-relief key roughly five and a half inches long, probably the average length of an erect male penis at that time.

These caves are hardly a good place for holding an orgy. They are cold, draughty, hard and uncomfortable. In fact, there would be absolutely no point in holding an orgy in these caves if one had a delightful and luxurious house just up a nearby hill which would be ideal for the purpose. The caves were built with a markedly different intention, and here we shall have to investigate the nature of the 'Eleusinian Mysteries' noted by Wilkes. It will be discovered that there was rather more to Dashwood and his friend Sandwich than the words cruelly composed by Charles Churchill to satirise the latter:

> Nature design'd him, in a rage,
> To be the Wharton of his age,
> But having given all the sin,
> Forgot to put the virtues in.

The few hundred Whig families, who had run England for over half a century, wanted to carry on doing so. King George III wanted to curb their powers and favoured a return to the days of the divine right of kings, in which he was supported by the Tories. The King wanted a regime based on benevolent paternalism with curbs on freedom of speech. The third combatant was the emerging movement of democracy, personified by John Wilkes 'That Devil Wilkes' would return to upset the King, and also the Whig oligarchy.

A fourth factor was represented by Dashwood and other Independents. They did not owe anything to anybody and did whatever they chose. It is appropriate at this juncture to summarise what we know so far about Dashwood's vision:

- Britain should be ruled by a wise elite.
- This elite should represent true aristocracy rather than mere oligarchy and its purposes are best served if there is a patriot king on the throne.
- This elite should practise a religion based upon the truths of Nature.
- It should be done in the most exquisitely aesthetic surroundings and preceded and followed by the finest wines and feasting and sexual satisfaction.
- Women should be admitted on equal terms.
- This religion, essentially pagan in nature, is based upon the worship of the male and female principles in life and upon their union, which is sacred, not sinful.
- This includes practices designed to enhance intelligence and human evolution.
- If the political objectives could not be achieved overtly, they could perhaps be achieved underground and covertly.

As we shall see, Dashwood made contact with one of the principal architects of the American Revolution, Benjamin Franklin, in 1764. He was also in touch with that extraordinary transvestite French secret agent, the Chevalier D'Eon.

12

The Pagan Influence

Under the temple lay a cave
Made by some guilty coward slave
Whose actions feared rebuke, a maze
Of intricate and winding ways
Not to be found without a clue
One passage only known to few
In paths direct led to a cell
Where fraud in secret loved to dwell
With all her tools and slaves around her
Nor feared less honesty should rout her.

Thus wrote Charles Churchill and we shall certainly find that we
are entering deeper caverns of an underground maze. Here every
symbol can have multi-levelled meanings. For example, let us take
the word 'egregious' as written about Dashwood by John Hall
Stevenson. *Collins Dictionary* defines it as 'outstandingly bad;
flagrant' and gives the example of 'an egregious lie'. But it also
observes that there is an 'archaic' meaning as 'distinguished,
eminent', which derives from the Latin *egregius*, 'outstanding,
(literally: standing out from the herd)' and this comes from e –
'out' – and – 'goat flock, herd'.

The *OED* broadly concurs:

Egregious, towering above the flock.

1. Prominent, projecting.
2. Remarkable in a good sense.
   1. of persons & personal qualities; distinguished, eminent, excellent, renowned.
   2. of things; remarkable good or great; of events and utterances; striking; significant.
3. Remarkable in a bad sense; gross, flagrant, outrageous.
   1. of persons and personal attributes.
   2. of things, actions, etc.
4. Nonce-use; wandering from the flock.

Certainly, therefore, the Theseus who enters this labyrinth will require the assistance of Ariadne – but who was she? After all, the theme of Bacchus and Ariadne is reiterated in Dashwood's mansion at West Wycombe. According to Manfred Lurker in *Dictionary of Gods and Goddesses, Devils and Demons*:

Originally a Minoan goddess; her Cretan name Aridela means: 'She who shines in splendour'. Her death as described in Homer suggests a goddess of vegetation. In the myth, Ariadne is the daughter of the Cretan King Minos and of Pasiphae.

'Ariadne, daughter of King Minos, fell in love with the handsome Theseus the moment she saw him disembark from the boat that had brought the pitiful group of Athenian youths and maidens for the Minotaur', as Joseph Campbell takes up the story in his *The Hero With a Thousand Faces*:

She found a way to talk with him, and declared that she would supply a means to help him back out of the labyrinth if he would promise to take her away from Crete and make her his wife. The pledge was given. Ariadne turned for help, then, to the crafty Daedalus, by whose art the labyrinth had been constructed and Ariadne's mother enabled to give birth to its inhabitant. Daedalus simply presented her with a skein of linen thread, which the visiting hero might fix to the entrance and unwind as he went into the maze. It is, indeed, very little that we need! But lacking that, the adventure into the labyrinth is without hope.

As is generally known, Theseus found his way to the centre of the labyrinth and slew the Minotaur, who was half man, half beast. Michael Page and Robert Ingpen continue the story in *Encyclopaedia of Things That Never Were*:

Theseus found his way back into the open with the help of Ariadne's thread. The young Athenians rejoiced at the victory of their young prince, and the story ended happily for them but not for Ariadne...Theseus proved himself a singularly ungrateful lover. He enjoyed Ariadne's favours until the ship reached the island of Naxos on the homeward journey, but when Ariadne fell asleep on the beach he quickly set sail again and left her there.

What appalling sexual manners!

Clearly Theseus was a rather ungrateful swine, in spite of his undoubted bravery, and ultimately, as Greek mythology relates, he disgraced himself and went to Hades. Ariadne enjoyed rather a better fate, for her commitment to honesty and heroism had earned her the attention of the god Dionysus. When she died and went to Hades, as all mortals allegedly did at that time, Dionysus came and led her out of there to the heights of Olympus, where he introduced her as his wife. Zeus, king of the gods, was charmed by the sincerity of Ariadne, and crowned her as a princess: this crown would sparkle in the heavens as the Aurora Borealis.

We find Ariadne pictured twice with Dionysus as Bacchus at West Wycombe House, with Dionysus, grown or aged into Bacchus, as her husband. We also note Dashwood's observed worship of *Bona Dea* – the Great Goddess. One recalls the statues at Medmenham Abbey: Venus bending over to pluck a thorn from her foot; and Angerona. Nor can one ignore the Lasky-Silver thesis concerning the homage paid to the vagina in the layout of the West Wycombe caves.

Where did Goddess worship come from? After all, there is no doubt that human beings have worshipped the divine in female form in various cultures throughout history. One school of thought attributes the origin of this to 10,000 BC when humanity was just emerging from the Ice Age. Archaeologists are still puzzling to explain the fact that around this time, figurines of females can be found all over the globe. There are two characteristics which one invariably finds: the face lacks features and the buttocks are exaggerated, as if to suggest healthy possibilities of bearing a child. The most simple and rational explanation is that these figurines were made to invoke the fertility of the earth, which, since it gave birth, was conceived as being female.

This has led some, most notably feminist historians, to declare that humanity passed through a period of matriarchy. Males were apparently so dense that they could not discern the connection between sexual intercourse and the birth of a child nine months later; this secret of childbirth was, it has been said, jealously guarded by the high priestesses of the various tribes. Religion, it has been argued, was then based upon the worship of the Goddess in one form or another. Some tribes worshipped the goddess of the stars; others worshipped the goddess of the moon; and others, the goddess of the earth. This hypothesis is perfectly plausible; the only trouble is that no one has yet come up with any concrete evidence so as to establish that position.

Moreover, one should not be too simplistic in the ascription of sexual symbolism. The sun is usually attributed to the male and the moon to the female; but in Ancient Egyptian mythology, one finds Sekhmet, the lioness-headed sun goddess, and Khonsu, the moon god; and the deity of Earth, customarily thought of as female, is sometimes in Ancient Egyptian iconography described as Seb or Geb, lying on his back with a huge erect penis directed towards the stars symbolised by the Goddess Nuit.

The world may or may not have been dominated by worship of the Goddess in the pre-Christian era, but it cannot be doubted that this survived well into the latter days of the Roman Empire, usually under the name of Isis. One only has to read *The Golden Ass* by Apuleius, preferably (if not in the original Latin) in the translation of the late English poet and classicist, Robert Graves, also author of *The White Goddess*. In this entertaining tale, as we have seen, a man who inadvertently insults the goddess Isis is changed into an ass by her; he undergoes various trials, tribulations and sundry adventures and then, in a celebration of the sacred Mysteries of Isis, he is transformed by her from a beast-man into a god-man via a mystical experience.

Mediterranean paintings, statues, statuettes, mosaics and writings, dated with reasonable accuracy, inform one that a shift in religious values came over that part of the globe in the several hundred years which preceded the rule of Christianity. There is more and more art which features the divinity of the male. Although Goddess worship continued, attention shifted to deities who were solar-phallic in nature. It is easy to comprehend the connection between the sun and the phallus: they both rise, travel, come down and go up again, and they both give life upon Earth.

Some feminist historians have argued that herein lies the origin of the suppression of women. Other historians think that the switch to a worship of solar-phallic divinities was an essential step forward in human evolution and, with the exception of the Judeo-Christian tradition, did not involve or imply the suppression of women at all. In any event, one finds a profusion of Mediterranean solar-phallic deities, all of whose myths declared them to have died and risen again.

The subject was thoroughly explored in the later years of the nineteenth century by Sir James G. Frazer in *The Golden Bough*. As Joseph Campbell summarises the matter: 'Throughout the ancient world such myths and legends abounded: the deaths and resurrections of Tammuz, Adonis, Mithra, Virbius, Attis, and Osiris, and of their various animal representatives (goats and sheep, bulls, pigs, horses, fish and birds) are known to every student of comparative religion...'

The cult of Attis certainly wasn't suppressive of the female, for the priests used to castrate themselves in honour of the goddess. Nothing like this happened (obviously) in the cult of Priapus, which involved orgies, but women flocked to join them. The nature of these cults varied but they were all centred on a solar-phallic deity. For our present purposes, the most interesting one is Dionysus-Bacchus, who stands for drink, a free flow of sex, inspired creativity and divine intoxication. This was the god who most inspired Dashwood.

It can easily be argued that Jesus Christ is a composite figure, based upon a relatively obscure Jewish radical prophet, on to whom the entire corpus of Mediterranean deist legend has been unloaded. A virgin birth, or at least a birth by divine intervention, is usually present in the myths of the solar-phallic gods. The iconography of the Madonna and Child had at least two thousand years of precedent in Ancient Egyptian depictions of the Great Mother Isis with the infant Horus. There is an astonishing similarity between the trial of Dionysus before King Pentheus in *The Bacchae* of Euripides and the trial of Jesus Christ before Pontius Pilate. In common with the other solar-phallic deities, Jesus Christ rose froln the dead and came to be their judge, just like Osiris some thousands of years before him. It is possible that Christianity was cobbled together by competing groups of priests whose throats were getting cut by competition and who saw a new money market in the slaves. One can't help feeling rather sorry for Jesus, son of Joseph and Mary, who said some excellent things, albeit said many times before by religious and ethical teachers, who died an agonising death by crucifixion, and who then had the myth of Dionysus nailed upon him as the repeated atrocities he would have damned were done in his name in succeeding centuries.

There were tensions in religion long prior to the arrival of Christianity. In *A History of Western Philosophy*, Bertrand Russell explored the dichotomy between religious reason and religious rapture which runs through Ancient Greek culture, the same dichotomy also examined earlier by Nietzsche, as we have seen earlier. Ancient Athens, like eighteenth-century London, had its philosophers and literary artists, its insistence upon cultured and civilised values and its men and women of Reason. There was a commitment to harmonious classicism; Nietzsche would later term this 'Apollo' and contrast it with the cult of Dionysus.

The religion of Olympus tended to be formal and comforting, endorsing a civilised social order; this could not be said for the Dionysian cult and certainly not of its Bacchic frenzies. In addition there were the Eleusinian Mysteries, most succinctly described by Godfrey Brangham in the journal *Avallaunius*:

> In Ancient Greece, these mysteries were celebrated annually at Eleusis, the second most important centre in Attica after Athens. The secret and precise nature of these rites were so successfully guarded, that even today, an enigma surrounds them. The Mysteries formed a devotional cult, totally distinct from the then prevailing worship of the anthropomorphic Olympian family presided over by Zeus and Hera. The original simple, agrarian rites of death and rebirth of the cornfields, came to acquire at Eleusis an exalted meaning. Only the selected initiates, the *Mystae*, were allowed to witness the secret ceremony, which was thought to consist of a ritual marriage followed by some form of *revelation*. It has been theorised that the initiate, elaborately preconditioned by instruction and ceremony, drank a potion prepared from the liquor of barley, wheat and rye, prior to the revelation. Rather prosaically, Science has demonstrated that a fungus, Ergot, is present as a parasite on cereals and would thus be present and concentrated, in the final liquor. In large doses Ergot is known to produce hallucinogenic experiences. The cult at Eleusis was eventually suppressed by the Christian church around the 4th century AD.

The Eleusinian Mysteries were celebrated in caves, as were the mysteries enacted at West Wycombe. Sex was present as in the 'ritual marriage' Brangham mentions and so was death in the 'exalted . . . agrarian rites of death and rebirth in the cornfields'. One recalls also the River Styx at the West Wycombe caves and wonders if there was similar symbolism at the caves of Eleusis. Ergot is in fact the fungus from which LSD was developed.

It is extremely unlikely that the beverages quaffed in huge quantities by the Friars of St Francis were laced with ergot. One also doubts whether a drink made from 'barley, wheat and rye' was necessarily anything other than a very strong and spirited beer, though it is possible. Certainly, strong drink is sacred to Dionysus-Bacchus and leads sometimes to invocatory outbursts, such as Aleister Crowley's cry in *Magick in Theory and Practice*:

> Come, Bacchus, come thou hither, come out of the East; come out of the East, astride the Ass of Priapus! Come with thy revel of dancers and singers! Who followeth thee, forbearing to laugh and to leap? Come, in thy name Dionysus, that maidens be mated to God-head! Come, in thy name Iacchus, with thy mystical fan to winnow the air, each gust of thy Spirit inspiring our Soul, that we bear to thee Sons in Thine Image!

Given this, it is hardly surprising that initiates of both the Eleusinian Mysteries and those of Medmenham and West Wycombe were sworn to the strictest secrecy. No member of Dashwood's inner circle ever violated this oath.

At Medmenham Abbey the vows of secrecy and silence were enjoined by the statues of Angerona and Harpocrates. Harpocrates, which is the Ancient Greek pronunciation of the Ancient Egyptian Hoor-pear-krast, was customarily pictured as a baby, sometimes as a babe in the egg of the world, and said to be the twin brother of the hawk-headed Horus. Once again, we find that oaths are commanded by deities both male and female.

Before we return to the intriguing subject of sexual polarity, it may well be asked why birds, mammals and reptiles play such a significant part in pagan religious symbolism. This appears to come from an instinctive notion, anticipating Darwin's theory of evolution by thousands of years, that humanity shares much in common with these creatures. The ancients appeared to have recognised that *Homo sapiens* is midway between the beast and the god. The pagans did not deny or repress their beastly characteristics, for they thought it necessary for us to realise ourselves as animals before we can realise ourselves as gods. After all, the most intelligent of contemporary human beings has a reptile brain at the back of their head which will react instinctively to stimuli.

The use of bird symbolism is definitely curious, though. The student of mythology will recall that Leda was impregnated by Zeus in the form of a swan; and Mary, mother of Jesus, became pregnant on account of a visit from a dove. Birds seem to belong to a separate branch of evolution from humanity; one modern hypothesis holds that they are the ultimate descendants of the dinosaurs, dating from the days when our ancestors looked like rats; but certainly they have played a part in the religions of the world.

We find the eagle to be the national symbol of the United States of America. The dollar bill bears the symbol of an eye surmounting a pyramid, a symbol also found in Freemasonry, and it is the eye of the hawk. In Ancient Egypt, the hawk-headed deity was Horus, god of war, and (again) solar-phallic. The cock is another bird sacred to the sexual expression of the human male, and it appears to have played a part in the rites of Medmenham.

The reader will recall Wilkes's description of what was inscribed on the pedestal of Priapus at Medmenham: beneath the motto one can translate from the Latin as 'Everyone is sad after sexual intercourse', there was a monk laughing and a cock crowing. A further statue, copied from one in the Vatican, showed a man's body with a cock's head crowned by a phallus. 'Cock' is still slang for the penis. Obviously the cock is yet another solar-phallic symbol, that hailed by the pagans as 'The Saviour of the World'. To repeat the words of Sir Richard Payne-Knight in *A Discourse on the Worship of Priapus*: 'The figure represents the generative powers of Eros, Osiris, Mithras and Bacchus, whose centre is the sun incarnate in men.'

Dashwood's visit to Pompeii in 1748 to view the brothel art with Whitehead clearly influenced his choices of visual imagery. Not for nothing did Wilkes refer to 'the English Eleusinian mysteries' at Medmenham where 'the more secret rites were performed and libations poured forth in much pomp to the *Bona Dea*'. The idea, then, is that a man should embody a solar-phallic divine being so as to worship the Goddess personified as a woman, the ideal of the Eleusinian 'ritual marriage'.

One should not forget that despite his devotion to Dionysus, Dashwood did not neglect the opposite aspect of solar-phallic godliness. Here I refer to the representation of the cave of Trophonius on the pedestal of Priapus on Medmenham island. Trophonius, as we may recall, was reputedly the builder of Apollo's temple at Delphi and from his cave he inspired the priestesses. Apollo is (once more) a solar-phallic deity, but he stands for the reasoning powers of the civilised male. In honouring Trophonius, Dashwood was surely endeavouring to suggest that a man is at his best when balancing the Apollonian and Dionysian aspects of his nature in equilibrium.

Dashwood's love of the sun can be seen clearly in the church of St Lawrence at West Wycombe, which he had erected. As we have seen, a copy of the ceiling in the Temple of the Sun, Palmyna, graces this ceiling too. Nor can one forget the golden globe which tops the church.

Essentially, what one finds in paganism is exactly what one finds in Dashwood: emphasis upon the necessary sexual polarity between the Great Goddess and the solar-phallic God, out of whose union all created things proceed. Once this basic truth is perceived, we have the five-and-a-half-inch key, carved into the cave at West Wycombe, to the locked door of the chapter-room at Medmenham. We can discern why the statue of Priapus with red-tipped erect phallus at Medmenham leads on directly to the statue of Venus bending over, with its warning not to enter by the wrong way. We can discern also the connection between sex and death, remembering that the French call the orgasm *le petit mort*. We find, perhaps to our surprise, that the Friars were behaving in accordance with the injunction of the mind-hating, sex-loathing St Augustine when he wrote: 'Love, and do as ye will.'

13

Tantra

Much nonsense has been written about the subject known variously as Tantra, Tantrika or Tantricism. The essence of the matter is simplicity itself. It is held by those of the Tantric persuasion that all created things come out of the sexual union between the male, acting as a god, and the female, incarnating the Goddess. The sexual act can therefore be a deeply religious ritual which is capable of expanding consciousness and enhancing evolution.

Few Western pagans would have disagreed with this although most Christians would. How is the matter relevant to our study of Dashwood and his fellow Friars? It is insofar as one can discern parallels between Western and Eastern pagan religious practices and the influence of the East upon the West. As the reader will recall, Dashwood and Sandwich visited Turkey, which brought them into contact with Middle Eastern culture; and let us not forget that Sir Henry Vansittart brought back from Bengal a copy of the *Kama Sutra* which he inscribed 'To the Founder'.

There are not very many reliable guides here. One can find Tantric practice in *The Shiva Sanhita* but (perhaps mercifully) not much coherent theory. Very good work has been done by 'Arthur Avalon', the pseudonym of Sir John Woodruffe, in *The Serpent Power*. Sir Richard Burton did one and all a service by translating the *Kama Sutra*, a Hindu manual of Tantra, and *The Perfumed Garden*, an Islamic manual laid out on similar lines. Probably the most succinct summary of Tantric teachings is contained in a slim, contemporary volume, *Tantra for Westerners* by Francis King. To this one would add the remarks made by Ernest Wood in his book called simply *Yoga*, and the writings on the subject by Dr Benjamin Walker.

As King points out, Tantra is a way which we find expressed in both Hinduism and Buddhism. There is, however, a fundamental difference. Hindus believe that there is a soul (*atman*) within us which is the spirit of the divine. Buddhists believe that there isn't (*anatta*). There is a firm distinction too between the Hindu and Buddhist manifestations of Tantra, as King rightly discerns. The Buddhist tradition, influenced by the Bon religion of Tibet, sees the female as the active force and the male as the passive form. The Hindu version has it the other way around.

It is unlikely that Dashwood encountered the Buddhist rescension of Tantricism. He would have been influenced by Bengal, which is Hindu, and Turkey, which is Muslim. Since the books were not translated into English in his time, it is unlikely that he read those delightful Hindu Tantric sacred scriptures in which the married god and goddess debate the nature of man and woman all day, tell delightful stories to illustrate their points and go to bed and make love at night.

Hinduism holds that the energies of Brahman (the All) manifest in Maya (the universe of illusion) in the forces and forms of gods and goddesses. At this point, Hinduism becomes virtually indistinguishable from paganism. The initial manifestation in a universe of illusion is normally portrayed by a trinity of gods – Brahma the Creator, Vishnu the Preserver and Shiva the Destroyer, all three of whom have goddesses with whom they consort so as to create, maintain and destroy life in the universe. The coupling results in a more dense manifestation of gods and goddesses and these in turn manifest yet more densely, so in consequence we find roughly three hundred and twenty million deities, all of whom were begotten by Brahma, Vishnu and/or Shiva with their wives, mistresses, consorts, and hence are part of Brahman.

Hindu Tantricism affirms that whether we are worshipping the creative, preservative or destructive powers of the universe, all these come about via its interaction between the male and the female energies in life. We must therefore do what the gods and goddesses do, which is to love one another with burning hearts. In the course of doing so, if we have the right techniques, we can advance our own evolution. The *Kama Sutra* gives both technical instruction and advice on attitude. Here sex is superb if genuine lust is combined with exquisite technique; and better still if there is love in one's heart.

It was Islam that brought civilisation to the West during the Dark Ages of Christianity, and its accompanying barbarism. Islam spawned some curious sects. One was the Sufis, although it has been claimed that they antedated Islam and simply adapted to it. Another was the Assassins or *Hashishi* under Hasan Al-Sabad, who would in time make contact with the Christian Knights Templar in the course of the Crusades.

In these heresies we continue to find the symbols of sex and death. Either there is the male and the female creating and sustaining, or there is destruction. The wisdom of the East and of the Middle East passed into the West via the Crusades. Essentially the Christians were barbarian marauders endeavouring to suppress a recrudescence of civilisation. The only good that came out of these pointless and stupid wars was a transmission of information.

The worshippers of Shiva in India tend to venerate the lingam. The devotees of Vishnu tend to worship the yoni. Those who adore the goddess Kali, mainly in Bengal, equate sex and death.

As usual, Francis King puts the matter succinctly in his *Tantra: A Practical Guide to the Way of Action*:

It is perfectly correct to describe Tantra as 'an unorthodox religious tendency to be found in Jainism, Hinduism and Buddhism'.

It is equally correct to describe it as 'a mystical system concerned with polarity in general and sexuality in particular'.

But both descriptions are incomplete. While Tantra has mystical, philosophical, and religious aspects it is, above all, a technique of *action* – a physical, mental, and spiritual discipline which incorporates meditation, yoga, and sacramental worship in the very widest sense of that phrase.

All the actions undertaken by a practitioner of Tantra are performed with one purpose only; they are all means to the same end. That end is the transformation of the individual, his or her rebirth to a new existence on every level of consciousness.

There is no 'tantric faith', to be accepted or rejected on the basis of thought and emotion; the philosophy, cosmology, and psychology of Tantra certainly exist – but they are no more than hypotheses which explain, reasonably satisfactorily, the results which are achieved by the performance of certain processes.

'Tantra makes precisely the same claim as that made by ritual magic,' King continues. 'If you follow a certain course of action with dedication and persistence you will be led back to the roots of your own identity, you will learn the truth about yourself and the universe which you inhabit, and the nature of your existence will be transformed.'

This is precisely what Dashwood was trying to do.

14

A Magical Mystery Tour

The reader may he puzzled by the use of the words 'magick' and 'magic'. The former term denotes the science and art of the Magi, who developed a technology for maximising the use of the brain and nervous system; the latter refers to conjuring tricks or is used to describe a blasphemous parody, as in 'black magic'.

We are about to take an overview of three exponents of magick who built a corpus of wisdom during the Renaissance which would influence many, including Dashwood. I refer to Henry Comelius Agrippa, Paracelsus and Dr John Dee.

The Renaissance or rebirth from the hell-hole of Church suppression, was originally brought about by the flight of scholars carrying Greco-Roman learning from Constantinople to Italy in the wake of the Ottoman conquest. This new learning revived the pagan tradition, as we have observed in Rabelais, and spread north to German-speaking states and ultimately to England. Some men were moved to investigate the religious techniques of the pagans.

Agrippa endeavoured to pursue truth via a union of magick and science. The Church denounced him and some priests declared him to be a devil-worshipper, although he had no interest in anything so silly. He undertook experiments in telepathy. He also wrote three volumes called *The Occult Philosophy*, copies of which were later purchased by Dashwood in Venice. He made rather grandiose claims for himself:

No one has such powers but he who has cohabited with the elements, vanquished nature, mounted higher than the heavens, elevating himself above the angels.

Agrippa's *Occult Philosophy* proclaims that man should live in harmony with nature, and gives methods for so doing. It is notable too for its theory of correspondences. This is the idea that everything in the universe is connected to everything else and that tables can be made to expound particular connections. These connections are based upon the Jewish Qabalah.

What is Qabalah? That admirable scholar, the late Dame Frances Yates, attributes the origins of Renaissance hermetic philosophy to the work of Ramon Lull of Moorish Spain. The writings of Lull give full credit to his teachers, the Sufis. According to Yates and other scholars, this 'Renaissance, hermetic or occult philosophy' can be summarised in the following nine propositions:

1. All is a unity, created and sustained by God through His Laws.
2. These Laws are predicated upon number.
3. There is an art of combining Hebrew letters and equating them with number so as to perceive profound truths concerning the nature of God and His dealings with man.
4. Man is of divine origin. Far from being created out of dust, as in the Genesis account, he is in essence a star daemon.
5. As such, he has come from God and must return to Him.
6. It is essential to regenerate the divine essence within man, and this can be done by the powers of his divine intellect.
7. According to the Qabalah, God manifests Himself by means of ten progressively more dense emanations and man, by dedicating his mind to the study of divine wisdom, by refining his whole being and by eventual communion with the angels themselves, may at last enter into the presence of God.
8. An accurate understanding of natural processes, visible and invisible, enables man to manipulate these processes through the powers of his will, intellect and imagination.

9. The universe is an ordered pattern of correspondences; or as John Dee put it: 'Whatever is in the Universe possesses order, agreement and similar form with something else.'

'The Word means "tradition"', Dame Frances Yates wrote of Qabalah in *The Occult Philosophy in the Elizabethan Age*. 'It was believed that when God gave the Law to Moses He gave also a second revelation as to the secret meaning of the Law. The esoteric tradition was said to have been passed down the ages orally by initiates. It was a mysticism and a cult but rooted in the text of the Scriptures, in the Hebrew language, the holy language in which God had spoken to man.'

In an appendix to his *777 Revised Vel Prolecomena Symbolica Symbolica Ad Systemam Sceptico-Mysticae Viae Explicandae, Fundamentum Hieroglyphicum Sanctissimorum Scientie Summae,* Aleister Crowley gives a succinct summary of the use of Qabalah during the Renaissance and after:
Qabalah is:

1. A language fitted to describe certain classes of phenomena and to express certain classes of ideas which escape regular phraseology. You might as well object to the technical terminology of chemistry.
2. An unsectarian and elastic terminology by means of which it is possible to equate the mental processes of people apparently diverse owing to the constraint imposed upon them by the peculiarities of their literary expression. You might as well object to a lexicon or a treatise on comparative religion.
3. A system of symbolism which enables thinkers to formulate their ideas with complete precision and to find simple expression for complex thoughts, especially such as include previously disconnected orders of conception. You might as well object to algebraic symbols.
4. An instrument for interpreting symbols whose meaning has been obscure, forgotten or misunderstood by establishing a necessary connection between the essence of forms, sounds,

simple ideas (such as number) and their spiritual, moral or intellectual equivalents. You might as well object to interpreting ancient art by consideration of beauty as determined by physiological facts.

5. A system of omniform ideas so as to enable the mind to increase its vocabulary of thoughts and facts through organising and correlating them. You might as well object to the mnemonic value of Arabic modifications of roots.

6. An instrument for proceeding from the known to the unknown on similar principles to those of mathematics. You might as well object to the use of $\sqrt{-1}$, x^4 etc.

7. A system of criteria by which the truth of correspondences may be tested with a view to criticising new discoveries in the light of their coherence with the whole body of truth. You might as well object to judging character and status by educational and social convention.

The formalised basis of this system is a diagram known as the Tree of Life. This is a multi-purpose map. It can be used to classify states of consciousness, numbers, letters, colours, deities of every mythology, plants, jewels, the physical body and anything else in the universe. It is a unifying symbol, like the Yin-Yang of the Chinese, which embodies the entire cosmos.

Many are initially baffled by the qabalistic equations but the matter is simple enough. One begins by recalling Crowley's point that 'when a Japanese thinks of Hachiman, and a Boer of the Lord of Hosts, they are not two thoughts, but one'.

It is held in Qabalah that numbers and letters equate so as to reveal Truth. A very good exposition is given by the late Dr Israel Regardie in *A Garden of Pomegranates*. 'Its method of procedure,' Regardie writes of this qabalistic usage, 'depends on the fact that each Hebrew letter has a definite numerical value and may actually be used in place of a number. When the total of the numbers of the letters of any one word were identical with that of another word, no matter how different its meaning and translation, a close correspondence and analogy was seen.'

Regardie offers an interesting example. If by Qabalah we change the word 'Messiah' into Hebrew and then change these Hebrew letters into the formally attributed numbers, we get 358. Bafflingly enough, the identical result occurs if we do the same with 'Serpent'. This matter is not particularly baffling to Regardie, however, for as he puts it: 'The Serpent is a symbol of the Kundalini, the spiritual creative force in each man which, when aroused by means of a trained will, recreates the entire individual, making him a God-Man.' The Messiah is a God-Man.

Furthermore, if we add up the digits 3, 5 and 8 of 358, we obtain 16, and if we look up the correspondences in Crowley's *777* we find Dionysus the Redeemer, and Parsifal who performs the messianic miracle of redemption. As Regardie rightly remarks: 'We thus see the specific analogy between the words "Serpent" and "Messiah" which the Qabalah has been able to reveal.'

It is an interesting exercise to apply Qabalah to the *Gargantua and Pantagruel* of Rabelais, who must have been familiar with the system. His description of the Abbey of Thelema states that there are six sides, six storeys of rooms and six storeys of books. '666' is of course the number of the Beast in the Bible's Book of Revelation. In the qabalistic Tree of Life, 6 is the number of the Son of God and also of the sun. In Renaissance magick, the sign of the hexagram symbolised the union of two triangles, the male and the female; the microcosm and the macrocosm. Rabelais states that 9,332 men and women were monks and nuns at the Abbey of Thelema. If one divides this figure twice by 2, one obtains 2,333, which is a prime number. Adding up its digits produces 11. That intensely beautiful prose-poem, *The Book of the Law* (Cairo, 1904), dictated to Aleister Crowley by a being he called 'a praeter-human intelligence' and which declares that 'The Word of the Law is THELEMA', also contains interesting verses concerning the number 11. In the first of its three chapters, Nuit, the goddess of infinite space and the infinite stars thereof, cries out:

My number is 11, as all their numbers who are of us. The Five

Pointed Star, with a Circle in the Middle, & the circle is Red. My colour is black to the blind, but the blue & gold are seen of the seeing. Also I have a secret glory for them that love me.

In the second, there is the utterance of Hadit, the infinitely small force within the atom and the point from which the Big Bang came that made the universe manifest:

I am the Empress & the Hierophant. Thus eleven as my bride is eleven.

To a Renaissance qabalist, this is hardly an enigmatic matter. Five – 5 – is the number of the Pentagram, the five-pointed star. If a man stands with his arms out and his legs extended, he will fit into a well-drawn pentagram. The six-pointed star, known as the hexagram, has been called the Star of Woman and of God and so it is greater than man. Its number is 6. If we put 5 and 6 together – as in *Homo sapiens* plus God or Goddess – we get 11. A qabalist would therefore state that Rabelais, having boiled down 2,333 to 11, proceeded to multiply the original 233 twice to symbolise both women and men and arrive at an Abbey of Thelema population of 9,332, the numbers of woman being 2 and 6.

As Regardie would state in this instance, we thus see the specific analogy between various formulations of Rabelais's Abbey of Thelema which the Qabalah has been able to reveal. Dashwood's reading of Agrippa would have familiarised him with notions of number. In the West Wycombe caves, one finds 'XXII–F' carved into the white chalk high on the right wall of a small circular alcove. 'F' probably stands for Francis or Founder. XXII is 22 and the number of paths between the various spheres of divine emanation in the qabalistic Tree of Life. It is the number of letters in the Hebrew alphabet.

The number XXXIV – 34 – is found carved before the entrance of the tunnel which leads to the main chapter-room. By Qabalah, 34 = 2 x 17. 17 is the number of masculine energy, made up of the trinity enunciated by the Hebrew letters of Aleph, Vau and

Yod. This is therefore a doubling of masculine energy. Aleph is man as a wild, Dionysian Fool, Vau is man as a Hierophant of the mysteries of life and death; and Yod is man as a Hermit. Again, 2 is, of course, woman. As *The Book of the Law* states:

> Behold! these be grave mysteries; for there are also of my friends who be hermits. Now think not to find them in the forest or on the mountain; but in beds of purple, caressed by magnificent beasts of women with large limbs, and fire and light in their eyes, and masses of flaming hair about them; there shall ye find them. Ye shall see them at rule, at victorious armies, at all the joy; and there shall be in them a joy a million times greater than this. Beware lest any force another, King against King! Love one another with burning hearts; on the low men trample in the fierce lust of your pride, in the day of your wrath!

Although this was written in 1904, it could have been describing the vision and doings of Dashwood and the Friars.

Paracelsus is the second member of a remarkable Renaissance trinity. Agrippa upset so many because he was so acute; Paracelsus often upset people simply because he was usually intoxicated. Nevertheless, he was a brilliant man. He healed people and was a pioneer of homeopathic medicine. He studied the causes and cures of syphilis and epilepsy. His chemical experiments gave us zinc. He synthesised laudanum, a solution of opium in alcohol, which was the best painkiller of its time. In common with Agrippa, though separately from him, he sought out a harmony with the law of Nature. Again in common with Agrippa, he wrote a book called *Occult Philosophy*, which declared:

> Magic has the power to experience and fathom things which are inaccessible to human reason. For magic is a great secret wisdom, just as reason is a great public folly.

Some of the cures of Paracelsus were done with magnets, a practice pursued by Mesmer in the eighteenth century. Paracelsus

William Hogarth's *Charity in the Cellar.* Dashwood holds the map, Sandwich stares.

◀ Sir Francis Dashwood (later Premier Baron of England as Lord Le Despenser).

▶ Dashwood as head of the Divan Club.

Francois Rabelais, author of the great *Gargantua and Pantagruel*. His vision of an 'Abbey of Thelema' inspired Dashwood and later Aleister Crowley.

▲George Selwyn (left) with
George Williams and
standing, Richard Edge
Combe.
THE BRIDGEMAN ART LIBRARY

▶ William Hogarth, greatest
artist of the eighteenth
century, who portrayed so
many of the friars.
THE BRIDGEMAN ART LIBRARY

Frederick, Prince of Wales, on white horse in typical hunting pose.

Dashwood's church at
West Wycombe (below)
and the Golden Globe
which could seat five
people (right).

Medmenham Abbey: A perfect place to realise Dashwood's vision.

was also an alchemist who spoke of the elixir of immortality, the transmutation of base metals into gold, the existence of astral bodies within us which can move beyond the physical, and of man as the microcosm of all mysteries in the macrocosm.

Agrippa and Paracelsus both influenced Dr John Dee, who became the most learned man of his time. Dee was extraordinarily accomplished and in common with many pleasant and highly intelligent men, somewhat naïve. His skills were nevertheless remarkable. Having been created one of the original Fellows of Trinity College, Cambridge in 1546, he went on to lecture on Euclid in Paris at the tender age of twenty-three, which as he said was 'a thing never done publiquely in any University in Christendome'. Subsequently he became a principal adviser to Queen Elizabeth I. Dame Frances Yates discerned Dee as being the prime mover of the English Renaissance and a moving spirit in European developments.

His *Supplication to Queen Mary* contains the first proposal for a British Library at a period when, in 1552, there were merely 451 books and manuscripts at the Cambridge University Library, and Dee in 1583 had 'in all neere 4,000: the fourth part of which were written bookes'. He was England's greatest astrologer at a time when this activity was synonymous with astronomy, on account of which he was invited to choose the best date for the coronation of Queen Bess. *The Monas Hieroglyphica* (1564), dedicated to the Emperor Mamilian II, endeavours to resolve all things under one unifying symbol. The *Mathematical Preface* to Euclid's *Elements of Geometrie* (1570) was considered to be such a fine work that it was reprinted twice, almost a century later. *General and Rare Memorials Pertaining to the Perfect Art of Navigation* (1577) saw the first mention of the phrase 'The British Empire' and the first call for an officially recognised merchant navy. Dee encouraged exploration, tutored seafaring adventurers and insisted upon the Queen's rights in America, newly discovered, which he termed 'Atlantis'.

However, and perhaps unfortunately, he is better known for his involvement in magick, even though Professor E.G.R. Taylor gave him 'an honoured place in the history of Geography' in her *Tudor Geography* (1930). He thought that it might be possible for human beings to obtain evolutionary information from extra-human intelligences whom he called 'spirits'. Being unable to see these with his own eyes, he employed a proven rogue, Edward Kelley, to stare into a crystal, communicate what the spirits saw and tell him about the words heard. The result was an utterly extraordinary series of documents, published finally in London in 1659 with Meric Casaubon as editor under the title *A True and Faithful Relation of what Passed for Many Years Between Dr John Dee . . . And Some Spirits*. Dame Frances Yates argued convincingly that in *The Tempest* by William Shakespeare, the character of Prospero is based upon Dr John Dee.

Agrippa, Paracelsus and Dee are the three prime movers of Renaissance magick, and each one in his own way epitomises the legend of Faust. The twentieth-century American author, Norman Mailer, has seen Faust as being the essential myth for Western man. The basic legend is that Faust was a scholar who sold his soul to the Devil in exchange for power, love and wisdom. After enjoying a wonderful time, he had to pay the bill and the Devil dragged him away to an eternity of damnation in hell. This somewhat primitive legend was dramatised unforgettably in Christopher Marlowe's play, *Dr Faustus*. The matter was probed and expounded in a less guilty fashion by Goethe in *Faust Part One* and *Faust Part Two*, roughly two centuries later. Here Faust saves his soul, after many adventures, by his sheer audacity of aspiration in willing to evolve, and by the power of love for the Goddess. Faust became a cultural icon of the West even though historians have claimed either that he never existed or else that if he did, he was no more than a grubby little sorcerer. Even if this is the case, artists have turned the base metal of the tale into the gleaming gold of opera, drama and the novel. *Doctor Faustus* by Thomas Mann is probably the most notable twentieth-century rescension of the story.

There is, then, the figure of a man who is sufficiently courageous to dare all things and undertake even the method of magick in a headstrong pursuit of wisdom, power and love. In order to realise these laudable aims, the man might require some companions, which brings one to the subject of secret societies. Analysis of esoteric symbols and the history and cultural context of these sodalities is essential if there is to be comprehension of the aims, motives and practices of Dashwood's inner circle.

15

Freemasonry and Rosicrucianism

There were various groupings of individuals who rejected the Christian doctrine of original sin and consequent submission to the Church in favour of further development of human intelligence. One of the groupings which endeavoured to advance human evolution is these days known as Freemasonry.

No one has managed to prove decisively where Freemasonry comes from. There are quite a number of theories. The ancient civilisations of China, Egypt, Greece and Israel/Palestine have all been suggested, along with Ireland and outer space. Rationalists argue that it originated with the guilds of medieval stonemasons and that the modern rituals developed from these in the seventeenth century. Metaphysicians have argued that architecture is sacred, that it comes from the Temple of Solomon, that the medieval stonemasons, knowing that, made their sermons in stone, and that Freemasonry grew out of the truths thus enshrined. Presently, there are roughly six million men all over the globe who are Freemasons, with 800,000 in Great Britain, 312,000 under the United Grand Lodge; this is divided into 8,488 lodges of which 1,6721 are in London.

One could well ask why the Roman Catholic Church became so hostile to Freemasonry. What its adherents saw was a network of sodalities and individuals who opposed Christian teachings without embracing satanism (which is merely inverted Christianity). They were dedicated to far finer ideals than original sin, shame, fear and guilt. This was a developing network which sought ways of advancing human evolution through enlightened methods of reason, intelligence, perception, tolerance, science, art, enquiry, veneration of the noble nature of the human spirit, and respect between men and women.

There were two ways of reacting to Christian cruelty and the insane behaviour of its proponents. Intelligent men (and women) might well want to band together in order to do things better. They might possibly share the reverence for the divine persistently expressed by their persecutors, but they would want it expressed in a different way for the lasting benefit of humanity.

Freemasonry in England appears to have been born from a mating between idealism and practicality. Although liberated from the heavy hand of the Catholic Church, there were plenty of areas in the life of the country where the Church of England interfered with the free flow of reason. The United Grand Lodge of England was founded in 1717 and Philip, Duke of Wharton, the original 'Hell-Fire Duke', became for a time its Grand Master. The Madrid Lodge of Freemasons was established in 1728, two years after Wharton's visit, though it was soon suppressed by the Inquisition with its customary cruelty. In 1731 a Lodge of Freemasons was established in Philadelphia, Pennsylvania, by Benjamin Franklin, a future Friar. Freemasonry was established in France in 1732. One year later, the first known German Lodge was founded in Hamburg and this flourished until the Nazis annihilated it in 1933. Other Lodges were established in Portugal (1735), Holland (1735) – thus moving into both Catholic and Protestant territory – in Scotland (1736), Switzerland (1740), Italy (1763), Belgium (1765), Russia (1771) and Sweden (1773).

Descriptions of the rites of Freemasonry are freely available today in bookshops along London's Charing Cross Road. Their essence can be easily discerned in the first three rituals of initiation. The first is about birth, the second about life and the third about death. Anyone who undertakes these becomes a Master Mason. All the rituals emphasise the importance of building a temple. This does not only refer to the creation of an excellent building displaying man's place in the universe. It refers also to the temple of the planet Earth we inhabit, and to the temple of the individual human spirit each one of us must build within ourselves.

The key figure of Masonic ritual is Hiram Abiff, who was said to be the architect of King Solomon's Temple. He was betrayed and murdered. Subsequent Freemasonic rituals honour him as this crime is re-enacted. In *The Secret Rituals of the O.T.O.*, a work about an early twentieth-century Masonically derived semi-secret society which still exists in various forms today, Francis King, the editor, suggested reasonably that in its rituals the murdered Hiram, architect of King Solomon's Temple, 'was really Jacques de Molay, the martyred Grand Master of the Templars. Of course the Knights Templar, one of the crusading military orders, took their name from the temple in Jerusalem.

No historian has yet solved the problem of where the unarrested Templars went and what became of their treasure. It has been alleged by some unorthodox historians that a number of Templars escaped to Scotland where they allied with the future king, Robert the Bruce, against his enemy, King Edward II, who had confiscated Templar property. Apparently the Templars played a vital part in winning the battle of Bannockburn, which secured Scottish independence. Then, it is argued, the Templars founded the Ancient and Accepted Rite of Scottish Freemasonry. This may seem unlikely but it is possible. However, it is hard to believe historians who allege that the Templars became the Scots Guards of the French Bourbon monarchy in cementing 'the auld alliance' between Scotland and France. One can't see why they would wish to guard the family which for its own ends had tortured and murdered their Grand Master, Jacques de Molay, and robbed them of their power, position and pecuniary advantage.

Freemasonry spread. In 1736 Great Britain's Parliament, consisting as it did largely of worldly wise men, repealed the evil statutes against 'witchcraft' on the grounds that it did not exist. In the very same year, and perhaps on account of this, Pope Clement XII condemned Freemasonry. The position of the Catholic

Church, that it was heresy to doubt the matter of witchcraft, was stoutly maintained. In 1738 the papal bull, *In Emenenti,* anathematised Freemasonry.

The development of Freemasonry and its schisms must next be traced. In the early eighteenth century there was a schism between the Hanoverian Grand Lodge (Grand Lodge of England) and the Jacobite Lodge (Ancient and Accepted Scottish Rite), although they would eventually make peace in 1813. The Grand Lodge of England – these days known as United Grand Lodge – demanded a recognition of deism, i.e. belief in a Supreme Being. The Scottish Freemasons of the Ancient and Accepted Rite preserved 'the auld alliance' with France, where its Grand Orient Lodge demanded atheism. Although the Scots agreed with the English on a belief in 'the Great Architect of the Universe', the Grand Orient Lodge did not. This is why, to this day, the United Grand Lodge of England does not recognise either the Grand Orient or Grand Lodge of France, but does recognise that country's National Grand Lodge.

The activities of the Grand Orient Lodge led the Roman Catholic Church to stigmatise Freemasons as atheists or even as 'satanists'. Nevertheless, the growth of Freemasonry in France surprised even its adherents. By 1775 it was claimed that there was a Masonic Lodge in every major town of the nation.

One must here take note of the work done by Voltaire, Rousseau and Diderot, all of whom were Freemasons. Freemasons such as Mirabeau and Lafayette would play a major part in influencing the revolutionary course of events in France. There we also find Jean Baptiste Willermooz, Grand Master of the Lyons Masonic Lodge; there was Pasqually, who, in common with Willermooz, practised ceremonial magick. There was Pasqually's student, Louis Claude de Saint Martin, a pale and elegant magician turned mystic, whose Martinist Lodges would spread to Russia, as we find in Tolstoy's *War and Peace*, a movement which still continues quietly today. There was the visit to Paris by Mozart of Vienna, some of whose operas enshrine Masonic truths, for he was a Freemason too. So was Mesmer of Vienna, who created a sensation in Paris with his techniques of healing.

There were many other remarkable men around at that time, including Casanova, who knew most of them and who also studied the occult; he met with those mysterious figures, the Count of St Germain and Cagliostro. Any probing of France, then the centre of Western civilisation, leads to an encounter with the endeavours of the Encyclopedists to essay an eruption of Enlightenment, not merely among an elite but to move the masses. The state of the country was leading inexorably towards revolution. Only intelligent government by a wise elite could have prevented that, and most of the ruling class were incapable.

England, as usual, was not in a revolutionary mood. Yet in 1723 the first documented Freemasonic Constitution appeared. This espoused the ideals of liberty, equality, fraternity; the Rights of Man; pursuit of the arts and sciences – in fact, everything that could benefit human evolution. Therefore one wonders just why the Church hated it. At its heart was the contention that the architecture of King Solomon's Temple enshrined certain immortal principles concerning man and his place in nature. *Pagan Wisdom* by John Carey, present Fellow of Gonville & Caius College, Cambridge, offers probably the best contemporary exposition of these ideals.

Dr Carey's is a twentieth-century viewpoint and so varies a little in detail from the ideals of over two hundred years before. One wonders, however, whether Dr Carey would seriously disagree with the values then enshrined by the Freemasonic symbol of the eye on the pyramid, a symbol President Franklin D. Roosevelt, during his presidency from 1932 to 1945 ordered to be stamped on every dollar bill so as to grace the Great Seal of the American nation. Let us not forget also that the Statue of Liberty, purchased by the United States of America, was conceived and designed by French Freemasons. The original eighteenth-century values can be summarised as follows:

1. That human evolution should advance.
2. That this can be done best in terms of free human intelligence.

3. That every man should practise a code of ethical honour.
4. That the principal enemies of human evolution are the oppressive powers of priest and king.
5. That these evil powers, which suppress human evolution, should be overthrown.
6. That humanity has become sufficiently responsible to practise democracy.
7. That the facts of nature should be celebrated in due ceremonial and religious form.
8. That times must change.

Two results of the attempt to practise these values would be the American and the French Revolutions.

'From research I made when Eric Towers was writing his book on Dashwood I know that there is no documentary evidence of Sir Francis having been a Freemason,' John Hammil, librarian and curator at the Library and Museum of United Grand Lodge of England, wrote to me on 9 December 1992. 'That is not to say that he was not, simply that central registers were not kept until the mid-18th century and that for the early period we have to rely on extant lodge minutes books, press reports of meetings etc. for details of who the members were.

'HRH Frederick, Prince of Wales,' Hammil continued, 'John Wilkes, the Chevalier D'Eon and Sir Joseph Banks I know were members.'

Dashwood may or may not have been a Freemason but he was certainly in contact with these men; and equally certainly, he would have agreed with most of the Masonic ideals enunciated above.

Were there ever any real Rosicrucians? Did they have 'an Invisible College'? Whether there was a formal grouping or not, Dame Frances Yates was sure that Cornelius Agrippa, Paracelsus and Dr John Dee formed part of a 'hermetic', pagan and magical tradition which was the mainspring of Renaissance thought and sensibility. In *The Rosicrucian Enlightenment* she argued convincingly that there was a serious endeavour to essay this in the Palatinate of 1617, an endeavour which triggered off the horrendous Thirty Years War. She holds that the *Rosicrucian Manifestos* were in fact a hoax written by a brilliant man, Andrea, inspired the ideals of its new King Frederick and his charming Queen Elizabeth, daughter of King James I of England, and encapsulated the Renaissance vision. 'The German Rosicrucian manifestos reflect the philosophy of John Dee which he had spread abroad in his missionary venture of his second, or continental, period,' she writes.

Unfortunately it all turned out to be a complete disaster. Frederick misguidedly accepted the crown of Bohemia. The Catholics went to war and chased him out of the Palatinate as his father-in-law, King James I of England, stood by and did nothing. As the Thirty Years War wore on, the Protestant response would be no less virulent than the Catholic atrocities.

Meanwhile, back in England, professed Rosicrucians such as Robert Fludd and Elias Ashmole (the latter was also a Freemason), obviously believed in the legend of Christian Rosenkreuz and of his elite of wise men who illuminate humanity. One result was the founding of an 'Invisible College' in brick and concrete, later known in Great Britain as the Royal Society.

The primary symbol of the Rosicrucian societies, or at least those which alleged direct derivation, was the visual image of a cross upon a rose. One may easily discern that the cross is phallic and the rose is vaginal and so that what is being signifled here is the energetic union of the male and the female for productive purposes. As we saw earlier, Lasky and Silver state that at the George & Vulture by St Michael's Alley where the Friars were originally founded, there was a 'Rosicrucian Lamp':

But perhaps it was no accident that this ancient pub had been the home of Wharton's original Hell-Fire Club – and that the landlord was suspected of practising Black Magic. He owned a collection of metaphysical curios, one of which still exists: an Everlasting Lamp.

This large crystal globe was encircled by a tail-biting serpent carved in pure gold; the twin symbol of eternity and cosmic energy. Twisted snake chains hung from the globe and a silver winged dove perched on the top. Dashwood, who seemed to have overlooked nothing of the exotic, had studied Rosicrucianism, and no doubt borrowed from these teachings in building his personal philosophy.

Lasky and Silver proceed to assert, regarding the main chapter-room of the West Wycombe caves: 'In the centre of the chamber hung the Rosicrucian lamp.'

It would make one's enquiry much easier if there were some proof of this assertion, for this intriguing lamp is not there now. Did this delightful object ever exist physically? If so, where is it? One finds it drawn and painted by many artists in numerous books and prints and the initial meaning is obvious. The snake and the egg are the sperm and the ovum. Lasky and Silver claim that Dashwood's West Wycombe caves are 'laid out in the precise design of the Tantric fertilised world-egg.'

Normally the eighteenth century is called 'The Age of Reason'. Then other historians point out how brutal and barbaric life could be at that time and indicate 'a revolt of irrationality' which climaxed in what are commonly termed the Gothic and Romantic revivals. Nevertheless, the possibility remains that we may be considering not irrationality, but supra-rationality.

The Rosicrucian lamp of truth may not have existed physically but it's certainly a metaphorical truth among many of the men under discussion. Aleister Crowley, dedicated exponent of 'Do what thou wilt', gave instructions on how to make one on the last page of his *Magick: In Theory and Practice* (1929). 'Dominus Liminis' means simply 'Lord of the Threshold'.

THE LAMP

Let the Dominus Liminis take pure lead, tin, and quicksilver, with platinum, and, if need be, glass.

Let him by his understanding and ingenium devise a Magick

Lamp that shall burn without wick or oil, being fed by the Aethyr.

This shall be accomplished secretly and apart, without asking the advice or approval of his Adeptus Minor.

Let the Dominus Liminis keep it when consecrated in the secret chamber of Art.

This then is that which is written: 'Being furnished with complete armour and armed, he is similar to the goddess.'

And again, 'I am armed, I am armed'.

The practices we are inspecting have nothing to do with the cheap and vulgar satanism practised at the Court of Louis XIV by the Abbé Gibourg and the procuress and poisoner, La Voisine, in the closing years of the seventeenth century. We are not looking here at degenerates, though we may well be regarding eccentrics.

One such was Baron von Hund (1722–76),who established an order of esoteric practices between 1751 and 1754. He claimed that he had received his instructions from 'unknown superiors', a claim he maintained until his death; and also that he possessed secret Templar documents dating back to the fourteenth century. Unknown superiors? What a crazy notion! It sounds like aliens from Venus or Mars. Even so, highly intelligent and influential individuals such as the Count of St Germain and Cagliostro claimed to have made the acquaintance of these strange and mysterious beings. Baron von Hund called them: 'irresponsible themselves but claiming absolute jurisdiction and obedience without question'.

Mirabeau, a prime mover in the initial events of the French Revolution, did not disagree. In his *History of the Prussian Monarchy* he wrote: 'In about 1756 there appeared, as if they had sprung out of the earth, men sent, so they said, by Unknown Superiors and armed with power to reform the Order and re-establish it in its ancient purity.'

This claim was in fact made on 1 May 1776 when Adam Weishaupt, Professor of Law at Bavaria's University of Ingoldstadt, established the Illuminati, a group of men and women committed to the advancement of individual consciousness and collective human evolution. These laudable aims were portrayed by a symbol we have already seen – the eye on the pyramid.

On 4 July 1776, sixty-five days later, the Founding Fathers of the United States of America, including Dashwood's friend, Benjamin Franklin, signed the Declaration of Independence. This declaration, that certain rights of the individual are 'inalienable', principally the rights to 'life, liberty and the pursuit of happiness', is summarised by the visual image of the eye on the pyramid. As has been noted, this is a Freemasonic symbol and according to a consensus of a variety of sources, between fifty and fifty-three of the fifty-six signatories, including George Washington and Benjamin Franklin, were Freemasons. In addition, for qabalists, 56 is the number of the goddess of the stars.

Connections extend to the French Revolution, including that between the Chevalier D'Eon and Sir Francis Dashwood. Martine de Pasqually, sometime teacher of Saint Martin, is a mysterious figure too. He may have been Portuguese; he might equally well have been Jewish; yet he was at least nominally a Catholic if one judges by the record of his son's baptism. No one knows for certain. What we do know is that he founded the Order of the Elect Cohens at Bordeaux in 1760; that its grades were extremely similar to, if no precisely identical with, the Ancient and Accepted Rite of Scottish Freemasonry; and that according to René La Forestier in *La France: Macconerie Occultiste au XVIII Siècle et l'Ordre de Elus Coens* and Auguste Viatta's *Les Sources Occulte du Romantise* (both books: Paris,1928), this order practised ceremonial magick. We also know that the ranks of Girondins and Jacobins were packed with Freemasons, and that in 1795, Robespierre ordered the public feast of the Supreme Being.

The complex subject of the Illuminati obviously requires a separate book. Here the facts can only be summarised:

1. It was, as we have noted, founded on 1 May 1776 by Adam Weishaupt, Professor of Law at Bavaria's University of Ingoldstadt.

2. It included women members, which does not occur in Freemasonry.

3. Its symbol was the eye in the triangle, which does occur in Freemasonry.

4. It was praised by the century's greatest thinker, Goethe.

5. It was soon suppressed by Bavarian Catholic authorities.

6. Very little is known about Adam Weishaupt. There are no certain details regarding the date of his birth or the date of his death. It is known that he fled from Bavaria after the suppression of the Illuminati – but where did he go? Accounts vary. The most amusing one has him escaping to America and changing his identity in becoming George Washington.

7. Although the accounts we have of the Illuminati's ideals have been presented by their enemies, these are in accord with the aims of the American and French revolutionaries.

8. The Declaration of Independence was signed sixty-five days after the foundation of the Illuminati, as noted. The fall of the Bastille took place in 1789, the year when the first American Congress met to elect a Freemason, George Washington, as the first President of the United States, and an impassioned libertarian, Thomas Jefferson, as the Secretary of State.

Coincidence, or connections, one wonders.

To what extent, therefore, was there a conscious and concerted endeavour to accelerate human evolution involving strange individuals and a stranger series of groupings? One finds a common thread in the ideals of 'Liberty! Equality! Fraternity!' and in the idea of human evolution based upon increasing intelligence. Dashwood was a keen student of these matters if one judges by the number of occult books in his library. But it is surely time to go from the metaphysical back to the physical world, to the return of John Wilkes and its cataclysmic consequences, to the sizzling discontent of America and Benjamin Franklin's influence on Dashwood, and to the connections between the Friar and the Chevalier D'Eon of France.

One cannot forget, however, Dashwood's vast expenditure on

the West Wycombe caves, nor the fact that 22 is the number of
letters in the Hebrew alphabet, the basis of the Qabalah, as one
contemplates the following folk-rhyme of West Wycombe village:

> Take twenty steps and rest awhile
> Then take a pick and find the style
> Where once I did my love beguile
> T'was twenty-two in Dashwood's time
> Perhaps to hide this cell divine
> Where lay my love in peace sublime.

16

The Return of Wilkes

It is astonishing that a movie has not been made about John Wilkes, of whom the *Encyclopaedia Britannica* states that he 'came to be regarded as a victim of persecution and as a champion of liberty... His widespread popular support may have been the beginning of English Radicalism'. During his enforced exile in Paris, as one wit put it, 'he hoped for Constitution, Restitution and Prostitution – sorry, Prosperity'. His approaches as an outlaw to the successive ministries of William Pitt the Elder, now Earl of Chatham, and of Lord Rockingham were dismissed. So was his endeavour to curry favour with Rockingham's successor, the vain and idle Duke of Grafton; Wilkes wrote a public *Letter to the Duke of Grafton* which was a savage attack upon Chatham, and it was dismissed. Meanwhile, his debts piled up in Paris. Wilkes gambled all he had on a return to England.

When he finally arrived, the London mob welcomed him with joyous cries of 'Wilkes and Liberty!' Unfortunately for Wilkes, they didn't have the vote and so his endeavour to be elected as a London MP was a failure. The government moved cautiously, fearing the wrath of the mob, and Wilkes was not arrested. He was elected MP for Middlesex by a large majority only to be expelled by the House of Commons. This raised a vital constitutional point. Did the House of Commons have the right to expel a Member duly elected?

The London mob rioted. Wilkes promptly pulled another move. He surrendered to the authorities, fought them in court and in June had his conviction for outlawry quashed on a technical point. Then, in countering the two charges of which he had been convicted in 1764, he waived his privileges as an MP at that time and accepted a sentence of two years' imprisonment and a fine of £1,000. The London mob rioted once again.

Wilkes had not only aroused the mob: he had activated the middle classes, who had no love for the Whig oligarchy, and who desired a more powerful political presence. In early 1769 they formed the Society of the Bill of Rights to pay the debts of Wilkes and further the values for which he was their most powerful spokesman. In the following year, this would become his principal political machine. Meanwhile he slogged on relentlessly, demanding a full pardon and restoration to his former position. It was a war which Wilkes relished.

He published savage attacks on the government for its use of the military against rioters. A petition to the Commons complained of the illegality of the proceedings undertaken against him. Having been expelled from the Commons on 3 February 1769, Wilkes promptly won re-election for Middlesex on 16 February, provoking deliberately a resolution that he was ineligible to be elected to serve in the present parliament. The reply of Wilkes was to win another election as MP for Middlesex on 16 March, and once again the House expelled him.

The next election of a Member for Middlesex, undertaken on 13 April 1769, rendered these proceedings even more farcical. Wilkes easily defeated his opponent, Colonel Henry Luttrell. The House of Commons answered democracy by expelling Wilkes once more and declaring Colonel Luttrell to be the duly elected Member. The precedents of expulsion for a Member elected four times were spurious and relied upon the right of parliamentary privilege over the choice of the electors. Naturally the London mob enjoyed another riot.

Wilkes hit back, as usual, and he did so through building on his power base in London. Having become an alderman in 1769, he was made a sheriff in 1771 and Lord Mayor in 1774. That was the year in which he was once again re-elected as MP for Middlesex. This time the House of Commons did not dare to expel him, even though he was standing for a radical programme. The Bill of Rights, proposed and embraced by him in 1771, in concert with his supporters, called for shorter parliaments, more votes for more people and the abolition of boroughs controlled by the pockets of the oligarchy. This was also the year in which he established the freedom of printers in their reporting of parliamentary debates and secured them from arrest by invoking the judicial privileges of the City. As *Encyclopaedia Britannica* observes: 'As a magistrate of the city, he frequently showed himself to be conscientious and enlightened, though he remained characteristically irresponsible in financial matters.'

Having established the right of a democratically elected Member to take his seat in the House of Commons, no matter how much the oligarchy might dislike him, Wilkes spoke in favour of parliamentary reform in 1776 and consistently defended the rights of the Americans. His enormous popularity with the common people had made him a man of respect. It is hardly surprising that he stated: 'Sir, I consider the voice of the people to be the voice of God.'

There is much to like in the character of this man. Certainly he had wit, even though his friends worried that his drinking habits might lead to his drowning, like the Duke of Clarence in Shakespeare's *King Richard III*, in a butt of malmsey. 'I'll be your butt no longer!' an associate snapped at him in a fit of temper. 'With all my heart,' Wilkes retorted, 'I never like an empty one.' When King George III was calling him 'that Devil Wilkes', and some men who had heard the epithet invited him to play cards, he replied: 'Don't ask me, for I can't tell the difference between a king and a knave.' When his foe, the King, was forcibly hospitalised and a regency declared, Wilkes did not care for the Prince Regent, the future King George IV, who was waiting to step into a dead man's shoes.

'Long life to His Majesty!' Wilkes declared at a dinner party where the Prince Regent was present. 'And,' he added sweetly, 'I am sure His Royal Highness, the Prince of Wales, will join me in drinking this toast.'

'Since when did you become so solicitous of the King's health, John Wilkes?' the Prince Regent enquired.

'Ever since I had the honour of knowing your Royal Highness,' Wilkes shot back scathingly.

No lover of Boswell's *Life of Johnson* can possibly forget the meeting between Wilkes and Johnson which Boswell dextrously engineered. Johnson detested the reputation of Wilkes as a rake and a dissident radical. Boswell managed to bring the men together, after much diplomatic manoeuvring, at the table of one Mr Dilly. As Boswell states:

> Two men more different could perhaps not be selected out of all mankind. They had even attacked one another with some asperity in their writings; yet I lived in habits of friendship with both, I could fully relish the excellence of each; for I have ever delighted in that intellectual chemistry, which can separate good qualities from evil in the same person . . .

'I was persuaded,' Boswell continues, 'that if I had come upon him with a direct proposal, "Sir, will you dine in company with Jack Wilkes?" he would have flown into a passion, and would probably have answered: "Dine with Jack Wilkes, Sir! I'd as soon dine with Jack Ketch."'

Jack Ketch was a thief, rogue and highwayman who was hanged for his crimes, though Boswell does add a footnote: 'This has been circulated as if actually said by Johnson; when the truth is, it was only *supposed* by me.'

After a number of difficulties, Boswell finally managed to inveigle Johnson to Mr Dilly's dinner where Wilkes was present.

> Mr Wilkes placed himself next to Dr Johnson, and behaved to him with so much attention and politeness, that he gained upon him insensibly. No man ate more heartily than Johnson, or

loved better what was nice and delicate. Mr Wilkes was very assiduous in helping him to some fine veal. 'Pray give me leave, Sir – It is better here – A little of the brown – some fat, Sir – A little of the stuffing – Some gravy – Let me have the pleasure of giving you some butter – Allow me to recommend a squeeze of this orange; – or the lemon, perhaps, may have more zest.' – 'Sir, Sir, I am obliged to you, Sir,' cried Johnson, bowing, and turning his head to him with a look for some time of 'surly virtue', but, in a short while, of complacency.

'Did we not hear so much said of Jack Wilkes, we should think more highly of his conversation,' Johnson said to Boswell a year later. 'Jack has great variety of talk, Jack is a scholar, and Jack has the manners of a gentleman. But after hearing his name sounded from pole to pole, as the phoenix of convivial felicity, we are disappointed in his company. He has always been at me: but I would do Jack a kindness, rather than not. The contest is now over.'

Here Johnson exhibited even more than his customary prescience, for Wilkes would shortly fall within the fold of the establishment he had fought and become its tool during the Gordon Riots of 1780; Boswell records that on Tuesday 8 May 1781, 'Mr Wilkes paid Dr Johnson a visit, was courteously received and sat with him a long time.'

Boswell goes on in his inimitable manner:

I was struck with observing Dr Samuel Johnson and John Wilkes, Esq, literally *tête-a-tête*; for they were reclined upon their chairs, with their heads leaning almost close to each other, and talking earnestly, in a kind of confidential whisper, of the personal quarrel between George the Second and the King of Prussia. Such a scene of perfectly easy sociality between two such opponents in the war of political controversy, as that which I now behold, would have been an excellent subject for a picture. It presented to my mind the happy days which are foretold in Scripture, when the lion shall lie down with the kid.

Boswell adds in a footnote: 'When I mentioned this to the Bishop of Killalee, "With the *goat*", said his Lordship.'

Standing for a Bill of Rights, John Wilkes was again re-elected as MP for Middlesex in 1780. In 1782 he achieved an ambition in having the Commons resolution against him of 1769 expunged from the parliamentary record, thus vindicating the rights of those who vote and those who stand for them. He was elected once more in 1784. According to *Everyman's Encyclopaedia*:

Wilkes was a debauchee and a political adventurer, but his career was of constitutional importance in hastening the end of the much abused general warrants system, giving the Press recognised entry to parliamentary debates and establishing the right of an elected member to take his seat.

According to the *Encyclopaedia Britannica*:

As an opposition journalist and pamphleteer he was hard-hitting and incisive, but he lacked either voice or talent for debate in the House of Commons. His real achievement lay in extending the liberties of the press. His challenge led to the court findings that general warrants as hitherto used by government against the press were illegal, and he effectively destroyed the power of the Houses of Parliament to exact retribution for the reporting of parliamentary debates.

This is all perfectly true but there is more to it. The assaults of Wilkes upon the monarchy caused a decline in its credibility and a general loss of public respect. In his crusade for English civil liberties, Wilkes wielded the London mob as a potent political force whilst allying its concerns with those of the emergent middle classes, thus creating powerful pressure for parliamentary reform. This would not occur until the Great Reform Act of 1832, but it is in Wilkes that one finds the seeds. He advanced the cause of democracy and advocated meritocracy. He began the struggle of the House of Commons to liberate itself from the domination of the House of Lords, which would finally be achieved by the Parliament Act of 1911. His actions reminded people that public affairs are indeed public. He was definitely a demagogue but he brought wit to the business.

'And you, sir, can I count on your vote?' he cried out at the hustings.

'I'd rather vote for the Devil,' the man replied sullenly.

'Certainly,' Wilkes yelled back, 'but if your friend doesn't stand, can I count on your vote then . . . ?'

17

Doings of Dashwood

During the 1760s Dashwood was deprived of many men, women and activities which had hitherto given him much joy. Dodington was dead. Churchill had rejected his friendship in favour of opposing him politically and was dead too. Wilkes had caused a schism among the Friars and was busy pursuing his own vision. The dream of a 'patriot king', enshrined in Bute's ministry, had finished in fiasco. Even so, Dashwood continued in his independent ways and at least there was still his old and faithful friend, Paul Whitehead, although the latter was suffering from headaches and gout.

'Whom God loveth He Chastiseth,' Whitehead wrote to Dashwood:

I don't know whether I ought or no, to desire the Prayers of the Chapter for a sick and weak Brother, however if you are convinced that you are not too wicked to prevail, you may try their Efficacy...

This demonstrates that magical works of healing were sometimes done within the chapter-room of infamous secrecy. It also shows that the meetings of Medmenham continued. The few fragments remaining from the cellar-books show that the Abbey still witnessed meetings in 1764. There is further confirmation in John Tucker's letter to Dashwood, now Baron Le Despenser, in August of that year.

> My heart and inclinations will be with your Lordship and your
> friends at Medmenham at the next Chapter, but I am cruelly
> detained here by the sickness of my mother...If this should
> reach your Lordship at Medmenham, I pray you will present
> my filial duty to our Holy Father and fraternal love and respect
> to the pious brotherhood, to whom I wish all possible joy, spirit
> and vigour.

Tucker's mother may not have recovered, but Whitehead did.
The testimony of both Boswell and Johnson is interesting here. In
discussing Johnson's acceptance of ten guineas for a poem,
Boswell quotes Johnson as saying: 'I might, perhaps, have
accepted of less; but that Paul Whitehead had a little before got
ten guineas for a poem and I would not take less than Paul
Whitehead.' Boswell doesn't quite agree:

> I may here observe, that Johnson appeared to me to undervalue
> Paul Whitehead upon every occasion when he was mentioned,
> and, in my opinion, did not do him justice; but when it is
> considered that Paul Whitehead was a member of a riotous and
> profane club, we may account for Johnson's having a prejudice
> against him. Paul Whitehead was, indeed, unfortunate in being
> not only slighted by Johnson, but violently attacked by
> Churchill...yet I shall never be persuaded to think meanly of
> the author of so brilliant and pointed a satire as *Manners*.

Whitehead continued to assist Dashwood. There were still
occasional meetings at Medmenham. The final sheet from the
cellar-book demonstrates that the freeholder, Francis Duffield,
was there as a Friar in July 1770 and that John Clarke came in
September of that year. There is a letter of the same month and
year from Dashwood-King, which excuses his attendance and
mentions the 'Sisterhood'. As we have already noted, Francis
Duffield sold the Abbey in 1777; and there was an alternative

venue at West Wycombe.

Meanwhile, in his private life, Dashwood was devastated by the loss of his wife after a long illness. Seven weeks before, Whitehead had written to him about the death of his own wife, Anna, daughter of Sir Swinnerton Dyer:

> I imagine that I need not to aggravate my Distress, when I tell you the Death of Mrs Whitehead is the Cause of it – I strive to avail myself of your Lordship's Philosophy, but find by woeful experience what Humanity must feel – the tear that is now trickling down makes me almost ashamed of my weakness, and yet methinks I should be more ashamed of the want of that weakness. That your Lordship's final Trial upon the like occasion may long be put off is the fervent wish of . . .

On 19 January 1769 Sarah, Baroness Le Despenser, died. She was buried in the family vault at St Lawrence's Church. Her husband suffered considerable grief. Although marriage had never prevented him from fornicating promiscuously, he had genuinely liked his wife. On one occasion, he had even turned down an invitation from the Duke of Grafton to undertake the honour of seconding the Loyal Address in the House of Lords. 'I have long since been the constant attendant upon the afflictions and uncommon distress of a woman,' he wrote back in explanation, 'the worthiest and best friend any man ever had.'

To commemorate her, Dashwood had a stone canopy on four columns built at the centre of his mausoleum, with an urn on a tall plinth beneath it. One side of this plinth recorded his late wife's sufferings in her last days with the motto: MORS SOLAMEN MISERIS, which means: 'Death consoles the afflicted.' The other side reads:

> May this Cenotaph, sacred to the Virtues and Graces that constitute female Excellence, perpetuate the memory of Sarah, Baroness Le Despenser, who finished a most exemplary life January the 19th 1769.

His grief did not prevent his amorous activities from continuing unabated, even at the age of sixty-one. He sired two children by his last known mistress, Fanny Barry. He continued to dote on his illegitimate daughter, Fanny Rachel Antonina.

Eric Towers has to be right in stating his view of Dashwood's mentality in the wake of his wife's death:

> In this, the darkest period of his life, he stood in most need of the consolation of the belief in the indestructibility of life that he had expressed by building the six-sided mausoleum, a vast and permanent reminder of the sixth splendid light along that eternal path between God and man.

For despite his late wife's lingering illness and sad death, Dashwood had not been idle, nor would he be idle, in matters of politics and religion. Let us first consider the politics. Although after the fall of Bute's ministry, Dashwood could continue as an Independent in the House of Lords, he wanted to exercise real political influence. Under Grenville, he had an appointment in the Royal Household. Grenville had been recommended by Bute to King George III as the outstanding expert on finance in the nation but the King couldn't bear Grenville's lengthy lectures. 'When he has wearied me for two hours, he looks at his watch to see if he may not tire me for an hour more,' the King complained bitterly, and dismissed him.

The Marquis of Rockingham succeeded Grenville. Rockingham was an ally of Newcastle, Bute had brought about the fall of Newcastle, Dashwood had been an ally of Bute – and therefore Dashwood was dismissed. Lord Egmont signed the letter of 10 July 1765:

> I never till this day felt repugnance in the Execution of the King's commands; but His Majesty has now employed me to acquaint your Lordship that the circumstances of his Affairs have at length rendered it necessary for him to make a New Arrangement of his great Employments, and among the rest, of

that which you at present Hold – it is improper for me to make any Comment of my own upon this unpleasing Occasion, farther than to express my personal Concern to your Lordship in the strongest Manner; Nor can I presume to say more in his Majesty's Name than to assure your Lordship that notwithstanding this Event, you may depend on the Continuance of his Regard, as for one whose Services he knows to have been faithful and sincere and on whose future attachment to himself in all Situations he shall ever entirely rely.

Dashwood responded to being fired with good grace, adding in a postscript:

'Notwithstanding the afflicting state of Lady Le Despenser's health I shall pay my duty to the King tomorrow.' He continued to be a welcome guest of the King; meanwhile, William Pitt, Earl of Chatham, who had often exchanged hot words with Dashwood, was nevertheless outraged by Rockingham's action, declaring of Dashwood in the Commons: 'I see that his employment is taken from him. Had I been employed, he is one of the first persons I should have endeavoured to keep in.'

Soon enough, King George III informed Rockingham that he found himself 'unable to go on with him'. The succeeding government was arranged by Pitt with the Duke of Grafton as titular head, and Dashwood came back as joint Postmaster-General. He retained that post under the ministry of Lord North, in spite of his criticism of the latter's policies towards America.

Politically, Dashwood's principal concerns were to expedite swift transmission of communications as joint Postmaster-General; to develop diplomatic relationships with significant revolutionary groups in America and France; and to speak his mind on any matter that concerned him. Absolutely nobody could tell him to shut his mouth.

In religious terms, he does not appear to have lost his original vision. No doubt he continued to spend time in his library, perusing the occult books he had bought over the years. One was *Conjerecta Cabalistica* by Henry More, published in 1653. We have already looked at the nature of Qabalah.

Certainly Dashwood was one who venerated the sun and its qabalistic number, 6. He also stood for mutual worship between the male and the female, as earthly representatives of the God and the Goddess. As has been seen, his church of St Lawrence was surmounted by that glorious golden ball which symbolises the sun and his mausoleum had six sides. Clearly it made much more sense to a commonsensical man of his nature to worship the sun, which we can see and feel and which undeniably gives life on Earth, than to worship some gaseous invertebrate who seems to do one no good whatsoever.

The sexual activities of Lord Le Despenser remained the same as ever. Once he had recovered from the tragic death of his wife – and it was unusual for an eighteenth-century aristocrat to describe his wife as being his 'worthiest and best friend' – he returned to politics with vigour and his customary enthusiasm. Moreover, as we shall see, he reinvigorated religion.

18

Weird Scenes Inside the Gold Mine

Halfway up West Wycombe Hill, one encounters a flint arch constructed in the neo-Gothic style which leads to a low-vaulted tunnel of entry. This goes straight into the hill for about two hundred feet and then there is a slight turn to the left. Subsequent tunnels wind on for roughly a quarter of a mile. These join and rejoin in a pattern that has already been examined. Some of them lead to chambers to which names have been ascribed. The first chamber on the right after the left-hand turning in the entry tunnel has been called the Robing Room.

If one goes straight from there into the main tunnel, one finds oneself turning right and into a circular hall, which some call the Banqueting Hall, though it seems to be most uncomfortable for such an occasion. This measures forty feet horizontally and sixty feet vertically. According to Qabalah, $6 + 4 = 10$, which is the number of the Earth. Appropriately, there are four alcoves. These obviously symbolise the four elements which the pagan philosophers thought to constitute the world: fire, water, air and earth. According to legend, a lamp once hung in the centre of this room. If it did, it stood for Spirit, which crowns the five-pointed star of man, the pentagram.

As previously remarked, the tunnels are then laid out in the form of a triangle so as to symbolise the vagina, and they converge at its apex. After sex, there is death and so one arrives at the 'River Styx', a narrow strip of water. Although today it can be crossed by a bridge, it used to be crossed by a boat. In Greco-Roman mythology, the ferryman who rowed the dead to their destination was Charon. Page and Ingpen inform us.

> There is some uncertainty as to whether he actually rows the ferryboat, or whether he simply keeps the queues of ghosts in order and takes the fares. It may be that he is bad-tempered because of the endless work of rowing (or poling) the ferry to and fro across the dark waters of the river, or perhaps he is irritated by the jostling crowds of ghosts. He has no mercy on ghosts who try to board the ferry without paying the fare, and drives them away to join all the others who wail eternally at their fate. The ferry fare is one vail or obulus, which relatives of the deceased person must place within the tongue so that he or she will be able to pay the ferryman.

The Coin is the symbol of Earth.

We have already considered the 'revelation' of Horace Walpole that the Friars wore clothes becoming to a waterman.

After the passage over the Styx, one finds an inner temple. These days it is disfigured by badly made wax figures enacting some crass tavern scene for the presumed edification of tourists from Kansas. What did Dashwood and the Friars actually do in these caves constructed at vast expense?

First let us return to the poem of John Hall Stevenson, the founder of the Demoniacks:

> Where can I find a cave to muse
> Upon his lordship's envied glory,
> Which of the Nine dare to refuse
> To tell the strange and recent story?
> Mounting I saw the egregious lord
> O'er all impediments and bars;
> I saw him at Jove's council board
> And saw him stuck among the stars.

Analysis of this poem gives one much information. The 'cave' clearly refers to West Wycombe. 'Muse' is a pun on Dashwood's and the poet's worship of the Goddess. ' ... his lordship's envied glory' refers both to the elevation of Dashwood to the position of premier baron of England and to his position of leadership among the Friars. ' ... the Nine' were the members present at this ceremony. 'Mounting' probably refers to a sexual act done to honour the God and Goddess. The word 'egregious' has already been examined: essentially it means either very good or very bad. 'Mounting' could also refer to Dashwood's ability to forge ahead 'o'er all impediments and bars'; 'Jove's council board' indicates that Dashwood was in consultation with the highest in the land.

'Stars' has a variety of meanings, and perhaps the pun is intended. The word was eighteenth-century slang for courtesans. It can refer also to the most prominent people of the kingdom, with whom he is 'stuck'. A third meaning is that Dashwood was bringing stellar glory and worship into the hearts of men and women.

There are intriguing parallels in *The Golden Ass* by Apuleius. He is obviously familiar with the assertions of his classical predecessors that initiation involves a sex rite in an underground chamber with the priest and priestess playing the parts of god and goddess. At the climax of his novel, the ass-headed narrator is finally initiated into the Mysteries of Isis. He has to begin his journey from a temple of the goddess, he has to put on appropriate clothes and then he has to walk underground to an especial temple. There he 'set one foot on Proserpine's threshold', indicating that he is in the underworld of Hades, but having crossed the River Styx, he 'saw the sun shining at midnight and entered the presence of the gods of the under-world and the gods of the upper-world'.

This underground theme was reiterated more openly for the religious services in Dashwood's overground scheme of his church. Here one sees once again his notion of an inner and an outer circle. The caves were for the few. The church was for the many. He had spent £6,000 – roughly £300,000 in today's values

– on the organ alone. Charles Churchill growled that this church had been created for show rather than prayer but one wonders when Churchill actually prayed himself. Even so, Churchill was not the only one to be disconcerted by Dashwood's restoration and erection.

'[As] striking as a fine *concert* or *ball* room', one lady wrote, and continued: ''Tis indeed an Egyptian hall and certainly gives one not the least idea of a place sacred to religious worship.' In fact, this church was not intended to be either 'a *concert* or *ball* room'. It was intended to restore what had originally been built.

Originally there had been a pagan temple upon the site. In the Middle Ages the Church conquered the place, and took it over. According to local legend, this church was plagued by demons and 'little, crooked men'. Anyway, it fell into rack and ruin. In restoring it, Dashwood was restoring paganism. He was taking back from the Christians what they had stolen.

The design of the church is quite extraordinary. Instead of hard, uncomfortable pews, there are comfy armchairs. The font's design is based upon the spirit of the legendary Rosicrucian lamp. The ceiling portrays the Last Supper and was executed by Borgnis and son. The dominant figure is Judas Iscariot. His eyes follow you everywhere. This is a visual trick that Borgnis learned from studying Leonardo da Vinci, but it works.

No one doubts that betrayal is a despicable action but it has been argued convincingly that Judas Iscariot was simply a scapegoat for anti-semitism. After all, the Gospel According to Saint Judas Iscariot was burned by the Church. One version of the story is that for Jesus to fulfil his function as prophesied in the Old Testament and antedated by the dying gods of Mediterranean myth and legend, Judas had to be then playing his part.

The globe at the top of the church is absolutely delightful. From eighty feet above the ground, one can survey a most beautiful landscape, and as the sun gleams upon its gold, there is a true sensibility of holiness.

The same is true of the mausoleum. As already noted, this is six-sided and it is wonderful to witness. It has enchanting columns and urns and arches, and its six-sided shape recalls the sun worship celebrated by the golden globe of the church which overlooks it. Dodington was the first to be laid to rest there. As we have seen, Dashwood's friend, that fat and genial fixer, was joined by Dashwood's wife.

Lord Le Despenser did not feel that he had anything to hide from anybody. In September 1771 he opened his gardens to the general public. Here, anyone could see a statue of Bacchus in his temple. The event of opening was marked by a procession of Bacchanals who were all wearing animal skins and vine leaves and were led by the high priest. There was music, there were prayers to God and Goddess, there were more songs, there was booze and food in the marquee by the lake, and then everybody cheered as the procession was welcomed aboard a boat, fittingly decked out for its reception, and a cannon fired as it disembarked.

It is plain that Dashwood was celebrating the energy which obtains between the male and the female, preferably portrayed as the God and the Goddess.

Which god and which goddess? The art and sculpture at Medmenham and West Wycombe shows the repeated motif of Bacchus and/or members of his entourage such as Priapus. Again and again one encounters symbols which venerate the sun. This is a very easy puzzle to solve. But the curious may question: Which Goddess?

Wilkes called her *Bona Dea*. She is known by many names. When Aleister Crowley endeavoured to classify all known Western deities using the schema of the Qabalah based upon thirty-two numbers, he discovered the following difficulty:

But a goddess like Isis might be given to Zero as coterminous with Nature, to 3 as Mother, to 4 as Venus, to 6 as Harmony, to 7 as Love, to 9 as the Moon, to 10 as Virgin, to 13 again as the Moon, to 14 as Venus, to 15 as connected with the letter Hé, to 16 as the Sacred Cow, to 18 as Goddess of Water, to 24 as Draco, to 25 as Giver of Rain, to 29 as the Moon, and to 32 as Lady of the Mysteries (Saturn, Binah). In such cases one must be content with a more or less arbitrary selection, and make an independent investigation in each particular case in reference to the matter immediately under consideration.

As Crowley indeed pointed out, a greater simplification can be achieved by a classification based upon the Virgin, the Wife and Mother, and the Crone. The inspirational function of the Virgin is represented by the huntress Diana, or Artemis in Greek mythology; and in the myths and legends of Atalanta, Endymion, Persephone, Hebe and Pallas Athena. We find the Wife and Mother primarily in Aphrodite-Venus, Ceres, Demeter, Cybele, Sekhmet, Hathor, Kali, Durga, Astarte and Ashtoreth, among many others. Hecate or Kali in her most malignant aspect are principal representatives of the Crone.

At the same time, there is another aspect. So many men and women and boys and girls are grateful to their grandmothers. This shows the golden heart of the Crone.

However, all the available evidence shows that Dashwood was not especially concerned by what name he adored the *Bona Dea*. He adored her in all her aspects just as the poets have hymned her; though the Hogarth portrayal makes it clear that he adored her most in her aspect as Venus. Few who have seen Botticelli's *Venus Arising from the Waves* in the Uffizi Gallery, Florence, can ever forget it.

19

Twin-Sexed

One of the most extraordinary of Dashwood's acquaintances during this time was called 'Charlotte Genevieve D'Eon Beaumont' and also known as the Chevalier D'Eon. No one knew at the time whether this person was a man or a woman and many claims made about him or her remain in doubt.

This strange personage was born in 1728, baptised as a male, and died in 1810. Although 'his' baptismal name was Charles, 'he' was also called Genevieve and dressed in girls' clothing from the age of three to seven. After that, 'he' received a male education. This led to 'his' joining the French secret service under Louis XV. D'Eon went on a mission to St Petersburg disguised as a woman, and this disguise persuaded the Empress of Russia that 'she' was a lady. Returning to France in 1758, 'he' became a captain in the Dragoons. 'She' donned petticoats and went to England on a mission in 1762 yet proceeded to give expert lessons in fencing.

Was D'Eon a man or a woman, a transvestite, transsexual or hermaphrodite? The question fascinated London society. A transvestite is a man who likes to wear the clothing of women and most transvestites are heterosexual. A transsexual is a man or woman who feels that he or she has been born into the wrong body in terms of gender; the eighteenth century lacked the surgical remedies of the twenty-first. A hermaphrodite has the genitalia of both sexes, though contemporary medical science is sceptical about this possibility.

In any event, the Chevalier was an able diplomat who became friendly with the Dashwood circle and contributed to the Peace of Paris, which ended the Seven Years War in 1762. The Earl of Sandwich took a liking to 'her' and gave his protection against a threat of murder. Meanwhile, there was fierce betting on the sex of this individual, and the punters included John Wilkes.

The total sum of bets laid on the Chevalier's sex came to the colossal amount of £120,000, roughly £6 million in today's terms. The question was made more intriguing by the fact that the Chevalier appeared to have no interest in either heterosexual or homosexual activities. There was an endeavour to settle the debate at Medmenham Abbey on 24 May 1771. It was agreed that the matter should be decided by a committee of aristocratic ladies. A contemporary artist drew a picture of the Chevalier sitting on a table wearing a towel, a cocked hat and a French decoration for meritorious service. The ladies are inspecting this person with lorgnettes, magnifying glasses and telescopes. They declared that they had made 'a most thorough investigation' but all bets were off since they returned a verdict of 'doubtful'.

In 1777 a French jury ruled that D'Eon was a woman and 'she' was commanded to wear the clothes of 'her' gender for the rest of 'her' life. 'She' returned to England to spend 'her' old age with the companionship of a certain Mrs Cole. The 1810 post-mortem made it clear that the Chevalier was in fact a man.

20

A Freeman

'Franklin' means 'Free man'. Throughout his long and eminent life, Benjamin Franklin, friend and associate of Dashwood, exemplified this notion. He wanted freedom for himself and for everybody else too. The general details of his life are too well known to bear repetition. He was a man of many talents, as is known, yet curiously enough he first came to Dashwood's attention when the latter was Chancellor of the Exchequer. A Mr William Denny informed Dashwood that Mr Franklin, agent for Pennsylvania in London, had detailed information on the American cod fishing trade. Denny was in a position to know, having been a former Governor of Pennsylvania.

Franklin paid his second visit to England in 1757 and stayed for five years as the London representative of Pennsylvania and the deputy Postmaster-General for the American colonies, a position to which he had been appointed in 1753. His earlier experiments with a kite concerning the effects of lightning and the resulting advance in comprehending the application of electricity had granted him a justly earned reputation among men of science in both America and Europe.

Franklin came from a very different background to that of Dashwood, to put it mildly. He was the tenth of seventeen children, sired from a poor immigrant to America who had settled in Boston, Massachusetts. He left school at the age of twelve and became an apprentice to his brother James, a printer. After a quarrel, Franklin left for Philadelphia and established his own small business. In time, and by dint of sheer hard work, he proceeded to prosper, becoming a noted publisher, proprietor of newspapers and the printer of Pennsylvania's money. As we have seen, he also established America's first Freemasonic Lodge.

Although these two men came from such sharply contrasting backgrounds, nevertheless they had much in common. Both were good-natured and shared a similar sense of humour. Both men were sociable and shared a love of sex, politics and religion.

Franklin had been sent to England to negotiate a difficult and complex business concerning the status of Pennsylvania. In exchange for writing off a debt of £16,000, King Charles II had granted this American land to the father of William Penn. The Penn family therefore governed Pennsylvania, and could see no reason why they should be taxed. The land was theirs by royal grant; it was not a Crown colony. Franklin's diplomatic skills were so exquisite that he managed to arrange a compromise acceptable to both sides.

After the end of the Seven Years War and the Peace of Paris, the Pennsylvania Assembly resolved that it would be in the best interests of the state to become a Crown colony and Franklin was instructed to negotiate the terms. Of course, these became engulfed in the general discontent of the thirteen colonies and their justifiable demand for 'no taxation without representation'. Franklin became the unofficial ambassador for an emerging United States of America.

Despite the differences of upbringing, Franklin soon found common ground with Dashwood. They might have met briefly at the Royal Society on the occasion of Franklin's first visit to England; Dashwood had been elected in 1746 and Franklin was elected in 1757. They had much in common as ministers for the post. Agriculture was another interest that they shared. Dashwood gave Franklin samples of barley and oats to plant in America. Meanwhile Franklin gave Dashwood a better comprehension of the American political position.

To begin with, Dashwood was his usual patriotic self,

straightforward and blunt-spoken and crashing wildly into complex issues. In the mid-1760s Lord Le Despenser spoke in the House of Lords to defend Grenville's Stamp Act and went on to vote against its repeal. At the time, he did not appear to realise just how and why the American colonists hated that tax; it was Franklin who changed his mind.

One issue between Great Britain and the American colonists caused much misunderstanding. Although the Peace of Paris had seen the French surrender every claim to Canadian territory and to all lands between the thirteen American colonies and the Mississippi River, it was thought that the French might rise and fight again. Consequently there should be troops to protect the colonies and the colonists should be taxed to pay for them: that was the thinking in London. It was not the thinking in the American States; Dashwood came to grasp that.

In 1770 King George III appointed Lord North as his First Lord of the Treasury and therefore Prime Minister. These men are not guilty of malice, but they are guilty of stupidity. In fact, North was not a terrible man any more than the King. He had fifteen years of experience in the House of Commons. Family connections assisted his rise. He was the son of the first Earl of Guildford, a friend of Frederick, Prince of Wales. Within five years of his appointment as the Member for Banbury – it would be misleading to call the affair an election – he was appointed a junior Lord of the Treasury by the Duke of Newcastle, a relative. In domestic affairs, he proved himself to be reasonably able and was thought to have some talent for managing the finances of the nation, for in 1766 Pitt made North joint Paymaster-General and promoted him to the post of Chancellor of the Exchequer just one year later. The trouble with North and the King was that they had no understanding at all of the American situation.

The matter could have been summarised for them as follows:

1. The Southern plantationers owe £2 million to London bankers and are looking for any easy way of clearing these debts.
2. Northern land grabbers want territory beyond the

Appalachian mountains and resent the interdict on the matter pronounced by London.
3. America is an extraordinary and expanding land with vast and virtually unlimited potential.
4. The American colonists don't want to pay taxes unless their views can be represented properly in Parliament, especially if they discern no particular benefit.
5. There are many idealists in America who would like to make the world a better place, starting with the land on which they live.
6. With the threat of French domination gone, the American States don't really need England any more, save possibly as a friend.

The unfortunate truth is that North and the King weren't up to comprehending these relatively simple propositions. Their thinking was narrowly provincial; they could only think of the New World in the outdated terms of the Old. Small wonder, then, that they took a silk purse and made a sow's ear of it.

Franklin persuaded Dashwood to change his mind and speak in Parliament on behalf of the rights of the Americans. Dashwood responded by arranging a meeting between North and Franklin at West Wycombe, but this did no good. North, unlike Dashwood, could add up a tavern bill and reckon out a balance sheet; but he was incapable of understanding a land which had become a foreign nation. North thought that the only answer was a show of strength backed up by repression.

The Americans responded to British intransigence with a boycott of English exports. The British government, rather than make endeavours to calm the situation, blundered further by imposing a tax of threepence a pound upon tea. Rather unsurprisingly, this provoked the Boston Tea Party.

Franklin argued sensibly that this misguided attitude would in the end lead to an irrecoverable breach between the States of America and Great Britain. Dashwood saw his point and proposed a plan of peace in 1770. Unfortunately it has not survived, even though Franklin warmly welcomed it.

'I heartily wish your Lordship would urge the Plan of Reconciliation between the two countries which you did me the honour to mention to me this morning,' he wrote to Dashwood. 'I am persuaded that so far as the Consent of America is requisite, it must succeed. I am sure I should do everything in my Power there to promote it.' It has been suggested that Lord North's proposals of reconciliation were based upon those of Dashwood but by then it was too little, too late.

By 1773 Dashwood and Franklin were getting on so well that the former invited the latter to West Wycombe. '. . . the exquisite sense of classical design, charmingly reproduced by the Lord Le Despenser at West Wycombe.' Franklin wrote, 'whimsical and puzzling as it may sometimes be in its imagery, is as evident below the earth as above it'.

Another endeavour was made by the two men to bring about an accord between Great Britain and the American States. In July 1773 they went to Oxford together to witness the ceremonial confirmation of the appointment of Lord North as the Chancellor of the University. Afterwards, Dashwood invited Lord North and his wife back to his place at West Wycombe in the hope that there might be a better acquaintanceship with Franklin. Although Lady North behaved with the utmost courtesy, Lord North conducted himself boorishly and pointedly ignored Franklin, who did not hold this crass behaviour as a mark against Dashwood.

'But a pleasanter thing is the kind Countenance, the facetious and very intelligent Conversation of mine Host, who having seen all Parts of Europe and kept the best Company in the World, is himself the best existing,' he wrote to his son William. 'I am in this House as much at my Ease as if it was my own, and the Gardens are a Paradise.'

This did not stop Franklin from playing a practical joke upon Dashwood. This tale is told well by Lasky and Silver:

Some 300 feet below the top of the hill, on a level with the floor of the valley, flows an underground river. Today it is no more than a glassy pool, but in Dashwood's time it must have been much larger and with a strong current, for Paul Whitehead related the following story about it: 'Ben Franklin, a great practical joker, offered to bring peace to its stormy waters. While Dashwood and his brothers watched by torchlight, Franklin waved his walking stick above the agitated cauldron. It became strangely calm. Franklin's "miracle" was performed by pouring oil from a secret vial in his walking stick on to the waters Dashwood had named the River Styx.'

During the summer of 1773 Franklin and Dashwood worked together on a revised edition of the Book of Common Prayer. What were these most unchristian men doing in their rewriting of a classic of Christianity?

21

The Franklin-Dashwood Book of Common Prayer

We have already explored organised religion in eighteenth-century England. It was largely a matter of social conformity. No one was worried about what one actually believed as long as one did the right thing and went to church every Sunday. Here the service was governed by the Book of Common Prayer. The advantage was Thomas Cranmer's exceptionally beautiful sixteenth-century English prose. The disadvantage was that an unscrupulous and egotistical parson could make the service insufferably long.

Even an atheist would surely admit that there are moments in life which embody the appellation 'sacred' and that this word could apply to a ceremony involving beautiful language and marvellous music, possibly accompanied by incense and exquisite visual images in perfectly proportioned stained glass. One might not agree with the theology involved, but if it is done well, it will give one a sense of divine dignity, whether or not it is within one or without one.

Unless one is irredeemably hostile to the Christian faith, this can be done by intelligent use of the Book of Common Prayer. Unfortunately, it was rarely being done in the time of Dashwood and Franklin. In the seventeenth century, some parsons had had the nerve to weary the congregation with a four-hour sermon, and that was just a minor part of the programme. In the eighteenth century, most respectable citizens went to church, but the weekly occasion which should have given them a true refreshment of spirit, left them bored out of their minds. It was to this end that Dashwood collaborated with Franklin on a revised version of the Book of Common Prayer. As the former wrote in its preface:

> It has often been observed and complained of that the Morning and Evening Services, as practised in the Church of England and elsewhere, are so long and filled with so many repetitions that the continued attention to such serious duty becomes impracticable, the mind wanders and the fervency of devotion is slackened. Moreover, many pious and devout persons whose age and infirmity will not suffer them to remain for hours in a Cold Church, more especially in the Winter season, are obliged to forgo the comfort and Edification they would receive by their attendance on divine Service. These, by shortening the time, would be relieved.

It would be wrong to see this worthy endeavour as the product of two repentant rakes: neither of them ever repented of anything. What it does demonstrate is Dashwood's continuing conviction that there should be an inner and an outer circle, that the pagan religion he practised was not for the masses. For them, he clearly thought, there should be a short and decent ceremony to remind ordinary people that there is more to life than merely 'birth, copulation and death'. He hoped that the younger and more giddy sort, along with well-disposed tradesmen, shopkeepers, artificers and others who were pressed for time, would be attracted to church on Sunday.

To this purpose, Dashwood shortened the Order for the Burial of the Dead, stating in his preface that although the original version was 'very solemn and moving' it needed to be done 'to preserve the health and lives of the living, this Service ought particularly to be shortened, being very long. Numbers standing in the open air with their Hats off, often in tempestuous weather, must render it dangerous to the attendants.'

Dashwood wanted to cut into the core of the matter, extract the juice and distil its essence. 'He professes himself to be a Protestant of the Church of England and holds in the highest veneration the doctrines of Jesus Christ,' Dashwood wrote about himself. A cynic would state that he had to do so in order to get the book published. As for the Church of England, he was 'deeply sensible of its usefulness to society'.

He had little patience with the Old Testament, having told Lady Mary Wortley Montagu that its God was merely 'an angry old man in a blue cloak'. Dashwood went further in his preface: 'The Old Testament is allowed to be an accurate and concise history and, as such, may and ought to be read at home...It is a Jewish book, very curious, perhaps more fit for the perusal of the learned rather than suited to the capacities of the general illiterate part of Mankind.'

'[It does] imprecate, in the most bitter terms,' Franklin concurred in his commentary upon the Psalms, 'the vengeance of God on our Adversaries, contrary to the spirit of Christianity, which commands us to love our enemies and to pray for those who hate us.'

The collaboration worked well. The Preface and Services were written by Dashwood and edited by Franklin. The Catechism, the Psalms and the Commentary were the work of Franklin, edited by Dashwood, who went on to pay for the printing. There is an interesting note at the top of the first page of Dashwood's first draft to Franklin, of summer 1773. 'Doctor Franklin is desired to add, alter or diminish as he shall think proper anything herein contained. LLD is by no means tenacious. He is a sincere lover of Social Worship, deeply sensible of its usefulness to society, and he aims at doing some service to religion...' LLD is obviously Lord Le Despenser.

The Athanasian and Nicene Creeds were cut from the Dashwood-Franklin version of the Book of Common Prayer. The creed of the Apostles was boiled down to its essentials as: 'I believe in God the Father Almighty, Maker of Heaven and Earth; And in Jesus Christ his Son, our Lord. I believe in the Holy Ghost; the Forgiveness of Sins; and the Life everlasting. Amen.'

This version of the Book of Common Prayer came to be used widely in American churches, most notably those of Episcopalian persuasion – essentially Anglican in terms of doctrine – though all the credit was given to Franklin and none to Dashwood. However, anyone who sees this genial move to refresh organised religion as a gesture of Christian repentance should consider the eyewitness account of the opening of Dashwood's west wing at West Wycombe House, dedicated as a Temple of Bacchus 1771:

> Bacchantes, Priests, Priestesses, Pan, Fauns, Satyrs, Silenus, etc, all in proper habits and skins, wreathed with vine leaves. On the arrival of the procession in the portico the High Priest addressed the Statue in an Invocation, which was succeeded by several hymns and other pieces of music, vocal and instrumental, suitable to the occasion, and having finished the sacrifice, proceeded through the groves to a Tent pitched among several others at the head of the lake, where the Paens and libations were repeated – then ferrying to a vessel adorned with colours and streamers, again performed various ceremonies, with discharges of cannon and bursts of acclamation from the populace. The ceremony was finished by a congratulatory address or ode to the Deity of the place. Several of the company wore masques on this occasion.

It is ironic that Dashwood and Franklin gave birth to a Book of Common Prayer which is still used today in the United States of America, for the Founding Fathers of the nation were hardly committed Christians. 'The United States is in no sense founded upon Christian doctrine,' said George Washington. 'I do not find in orthodox Christianity one redeeming feature,' Thomas Jefferson stated, continuing: 'It does me no injury for my neighbour to say there are twenty gods or no god. It neither picks my pocket nor breaks my leg.'

The creed of the Founding Fathers was also that of Dashwood and was probably best enunciated by Thomas Paine:

'I do not believe in the creed professed by the Jewish church, by the Roman church, by the Greek church, by the Turkish church, by the Protestant church, nor by any church that I know of. My own mind is my own church.'

22

The Diplomacy of Franklin and Dashwood

It is easy to see why, despite the differences in background, Dashwood and Franklin became friends. Among their many common interests, both men loved good poetry and had endured the bullying of their fathers. 'Verse-makers were always beggars,' Franklin's father had told him.

Even so, by 1757 Franklin's printing had made him moderately prosperous and he had established his name as the author of *Poor Richard's Almanac*, American founder of Freemasonry, spokesman for the rights of the American colonies and leading technologist. The stove he invented gave more warmth at less expense than open fires. He gave humanity the lightning rod and bifocal spectacles; and he introduced a public library system, a fire brigade, an insurance company, an academy and a hospital, institutions previously unknown in North America.

Poor Richard's Almanac, written under the pseudonym of 'Richard Saunders' was a self-help manual which probably inspired the nineteenth-century bestseller, *Self-Help* by Samuel Smiles, and the twentieth-century mega-seller, *How to Win Friends and Influence People* by Dale Carnegie. This aroused the ire of Max Weber, the nineteenth-century German sociologist, who thought that Franklin's embodiment of the Protestant work ethic had contributed much to the degeneracy of capitalism. In the twentieth century, D.H. Lawrence savaged Franklin as a materialist hypocrite who personified the worst traits of America.

In later life, Franklin admitted that his youth had been disfigured by a number of errors. Perhaps he was trying to excuse himself in *A Dissertation on Liberty and Necessity, Pleasure and Pain* (1725): its thesis is that since man is conditioned by genetics and environment, which give him no freedom of choice, there is no such thing as moral responsibility for one's actions.

By the time Franklin met Dashwood, he was older, wiser and richer, and had no need to defer to Lord Le Despenser. His call in 1743 for a 'constant correspondence' among men of science had led to a gradually growing reputation and the 1744 foundation of the American Philosophical Society. He had also founded what we would nowadays term a neighbourhood watch scheme to deter crime. His prestige had enabled him to found the Academy of Philadelphia in 1751 and this became the University of Pennsylvania.

As has been noted, Franklin established a formidable scientific reputation for himself through his pioneering work on electricity. He commenced a major period of experimentation in 1746–7. The results were passed to London's Royal Society or else to *The Gentleman's Magazine*, then collected and printed as *Experiments and Observations on Electricity* (1751). This was a stunning success. The first French translation was published in 1752. By 1769 there had been two more French editions and four more in English, plus one in German (1758); and there would soon enough be one in Italian (1774).

He was also one of the most sensible statesmen of his time, proving the point that 'A statesman thinks in terms of the next generation; a politician thinks in terms of the next election.' Having been clerk of the Pennsylvania legislature from 1736 to 1751, he also organised a militia to defend the territory against the possibility of French or Spanish invasion and made the business popular among his fellow citizens with *Plain Truth; Or: Serious Considerations on the Present State of the City of Philadelphia and Province of Pennsylvania* (1747).

He hoped for closer union between the various colonies. In 1754 the Albany Congress adopted his 'Plan of Union', which would have established a general council for the States of America, but this was brought to nothing by a coalition of British interests and varieties of colonial factionalism. As we have seen, he was sent to Britain to negotiate on behalf of Pennsylvania and became firm friends with Dashwood. In common with the latter, Franklin was clubbable, having founded the Junto or Leather Apron Club in 1727 to discuss politics, morals and natural philosophy in addition to exchanging commercial information. Dashwood's rakishness would hardly have disconcerted Franklin, who had a strong sexual drive he called 'that hard-to-be-governed Passion of Youth'. Both men were in fact very fond of their wives. Franklin married his common-law wife, Deborah Reed, on 1 September 1730 and the relationship lasted until her death in 1774. But this did not stop him, like Dashwood, from being drawn to those he called 'low Women'.

As we have also seen, Franklin negotiated an acceptable compromise between Great Britain and the Penn family in 1762. Essentially, the Penns agreed to the taxation of any lands they had improved and the British agreed not to tax any land which had not yet been surveyed. Franklin had continued to argue for intelligent peace in *The Interest of Great Britain Considered with Regard to her Colonies and the Acquisitions of Canada and Guadeloupe* (1760). Here he argued that Great Britain should annex Canada. His opponents wanted to leave Canada to the French as a counterbalance to the growing strength of the thirteen American colonies. Even so, by the 1763 Treaty of Paris, Great Britain took Canada.

The crisis of the Stamp Act gave him many headaches and forced many twists and turns. The year was 1765 and the affair is described best in *English History: A Survey* by Sir George Clark.

The Seven Years War had been victorious for the Americans, and for them the gains were near at home. They had done their share of fighting, and the British exchequer had contributed, not ungenerously, to their expenses. For Great Britain however this war, again more expensive than the last, had added so much to the national debt that the country needed some new source of revenue. Hitherto the Americans had never contributed anything to the overhead expenses of their local wars, the services of the navy in keeping the seas open, and the services of the armies on the European continent. It seemed reasonable that they should do so, and it seemed inoffensive to pass an Act of parliament in 1765 extending to America the familiar system of stamp-duties, which the British had copied from the Dutch. Certain classes of legal documents were not to be valid unless they bore inexpensive stamps bought from the government. This was the first tax other than customs duties ever imposed on the colonies by Great Britain. It was greeted with arguments that it was illegal and with perorations about Brutus and Cromwell, also with riots. There was a change of government in England, and the new liberally minded ministry of Rockingham repealed the Act in 1766. They also passed a Declaratory Act, affirming that the British parliament had the right to tax America. The Americans did not demand the repeal of this Act, nor did the British ever take any action under it.

Clark endeavours to show that the British government was in fact being quite reasonable by the standards of the time. He is probably right; but what he fails to see is what the British government failed to see, and that was the growing sense of independence in America.

Franklin tried hard to put his point of view to the British government and Dashwood came to see its validity. Even so, Franklin found that the Stamp Act drove him into a maze of contradictions. At first, he had asserted in his 'Plan of Union' that taxation was the responsibility of each separate State. Now he went back on that view, endeavoured to appease Great Britain and appointed a friend as Stamp Officer in Philadelphia. The Americans hovered on the verge of violence and seethed with indignant outrage. So he swiftly reversed his previously held view, and campaigned for the repeal of the Stamp Act.

In his appearance before the House of Commons, Benjamin

Franklin did himself genuine credit. He proceeded to answer 174 questions, some of which were deliberately hostile. During this interrogation he returned to his original insistence upon the rights of the colonies to tax themselves by their own laws.

Georgia (1768), New Jersey (1769) and Massachusetts (1770) joined Pennsylvania in supporting Franklin as their representative in Great Britain. Dashwood wasn't Franklin's only friend: the latter gained the support of British mercantile interests and middle-class groupings in favour of philanthropy and parliamentary reform. He did not want a war, he did not want a secession; what he did want was a union of American States allied with the British Empire in the form of a Commonwealth.

He tried so hard to put his point of view, writing 126 articles on the matter betwen 1765 and 1775. As time went by, he grew increasingly cynical about the prospects for the realisation of his vision. Lord Le Despenser spoke repeatedly in the House of Lords for the rights of the American colonists and for the need to negotiate a peaceful solution. It did no good.

Franklin endeavoured to establish sensible diplomatic dialogue. Dashwood tried to assist him. John Wilkes spoke for the rights of the Americans. It was quite useless. King George III and Lord North simply couldn't see the American point of view. Franklin had tried but now he gave up, leaving England in March 1775, when war broke out, eventually to liaise with the French.

In spite of the clash between England and the American States, Franklin endeavoured to stay on friendly terms with Dashwood, writing to him in 1775:

I hope my dear Friend continues well and happy, with good Mrs Barry and the little ones. I had a short Passage hither, arrived safe, was made very welcome by my old Friends and Country folks, and have constantly enjoyed my usual Health and Spirits. As I flatter myself you still retain your former Regard for me, I suppose this small News concerning me will not be unpleasing to you.

...We have here a little musical Club, at which Catches are

sometimes sung and heard with great Pleasure. But the Performers have only a few old Ones. May I take the Liberty of requesting your Lordship to send me half a Dozen of those you think best among the modern? It would add to the happiness of a Set of very honest fellows.

What did he mean? Given the name of Set, lord of the mysteries of sex and death in Ancient Egypt, the question is as easy as the answer is obvious. Franklin wants Dashwood to send some nice-looking young tarts to America where they will be well looked after. 'Whenever you write to Dr Franklin assure him of my Sincere good will and Esteem,' Dashwood wrote to one John Foxcroft, deputy Postmaster-General in New York.

The warm friendship between these two men and the genuine endeavour of both to bring about a peaceable accord between Great Britain and America should nevertheless not blind us to the fact that Dashwood was an elitist and Franklin, like Wilkes, was a democrat. One wonders what Dashwood felt as he read the opening lines of that most noble document of the human spirit, the American Declaration of Independence:

We hold these Truths to be self-evident, that all men are created equal, that they are endowed by their Creator with certain inalienable Rights, that among these are Life, Liberty and the Pursuit of Happiness...

23

'Liberty!'

Dashwood was an elitist, albeit a benevolent one; as opposed to Franklin and Wilkes, who were democrats. Dashwood believed in treating one's servants well, but he would have been appalled by the notion that those servants should be his political equals. Franklin and Wilkes declared that they should be. Dashwood agreed with the ideal of 'life, liberty and the pursuit of happiness...' but thought that this could be best secured by the rule of an intelligent elite.

Nowadays, 'democracy' has become a buzz-word. Without any consideration, it is automatically considered to be a Good Thing. In the eighteenth century, the aristocracy and gentry tended, without any consideration, to think of it as a Bad Thing, as rule by *demos* – the mob – and open to bribery and manipulation. Franklin discerned the divine within even the humblest of human beings; Dashwood believed that one should be kind and considerate to the lowly in the same sort of way that many think we should be kind and considerate to animals.

It would have surprised Franklin, who thought that a universal franchise and education for all would lead to a better world. To recapitulate, the reader will recall that on 1 May 1776, Adam Weishaupt established the Illuminati, a body of men and women committed to the advancement of individual consciousness and collective human evolution. Sixty-five days later, on 4 July 1776, the Founding Fathers of the United States of America signed the

Declaration of Independence. The only certain connection between these two events is that both the Illuminati and the Founding Fathers portrayed their aims by using the visual symbol of the eye on the pyramid. This, as we have seen, was also a symbol of Freemasonry.

The new Congress of the United States needed economic and military aid and wisely chose to send Franklin to Paris as one of three commissioners. Franklin was the *de facto* American ambassador to France from 1776 to 1785. In 1778 he became an influential member of a notable Parisian Masonic Lodge – *Neuf Soeurs* or *Nine Sisters*, members of which included Voltaire and the leading American exponent of naval warfare, John Paul Jones. Franklin was elected Master on 21 May 1779.

He made it his business to know everyone of note. He spent much time in discussions with the Count of Vergennes, Minister of Foreign Affairs. He also dealt with rogues, charlatans, spies and informers. He became astoundingly popular in France, where he was perceived as being a cross between the noble savage of Rousseau and the newly evolved genius of the New World. According to T. Hor:

> His portrait was everywhere, on *objets d'art* from snuff boxes to chamber pots, his society sought after by diplomats, scientists, Freemasons, and fashionable ladies alike. The adulation developed into a Franklin cult, which was not without its ridiculous side. Franklin, however, with his fur hat and spectacles, rose to the occasion with wit and social grace.

Having blundered into an avoidable war with the American States, the government of Great Britain proceeded to bungle its conduct. Lord George Germain, formerly Sackville, the coward who had refused to order a charge at Dettingen, was inexplicably in charge at the War Office and once more proved himself to be utterly incapable. The use of Hessian mercenaries to suppress the American Revolution and their brutish behaviour to civilians made partisans of those formerly neutral or even pro-British.

George Washington surprised everyone, including himself, by turning out to be a fairly good general as his British opponents performed with uncharacteristic ineptitude. Two further factors contributed to the eventual American victory. The British were clad in red coats which made them highly visible targets against a background of terrain that was largely green and brown. Moreover, the American commanders knew the lie of the land whilst their British counterparts could not be bothered to study it.

The support of France, subtly engineered by Franklin, was a further decisive element, for the colonies were initially vastly outnumbered in terms of both men and munitions. It took until the American victory over Britain's General Johnny Burgoyne at Saratoga in February 1778 for France to sign the treaty of assistance that Franklin so desperately desired. France proceeded to give the colonists roughly 12,000 soldiers and 32,000 sailors, along with substantial loans and that intriguing general, the Marquis de Lafayette. He was a Freemason who played a substantial part in both the American and the French Revolutions. In 1784 he presented Madame de Lafayette's exquisitely embroidered Masonic apron to George Washington.

Spain had entered the war on the side of the colonists in 1779. The victory of the coalition at Yorktown in 1781 proved decisive for the American States. Franklin was just the right man to negotiate peace terms with Great Britain and the formal treaty was finally signed on 3 September 1783. He stayed in Paris for a further two years, making trade treaties, observing the first ascent by balloon and investigating the claims made for the alleged phenomenon of 'animal magnetism' made by Dr Franz Anton Mesmer, for a committee set up by King Louis XVI.

On his return to America, an aged and ailing Franklin nevertheless played a vital part in the Constitutional Convention of 1787. He lived to witness the fulfilment of at least part of his vision. On 4 February 1789 George Washington, a Freemason, was elected first President of the United States of America, with another Freemason, John Adams, as Vice-President. One must concur with Turgot's remark about Franklin: 'He snatched the lightning from the skies and the sceptre from the tyrants.'

The inauguration was held on 30 April. Five days after this event, the French Estates-General met at Versailles and on 17 June formed a National Assembly. The Bastille was stormed on 14 July and the French Revolution commenced.

Aged eighty-four, Franklin died on 17 April 1790, having outlived his old friend Dashwood by nine years. One strongly suspects that Dashwood would have disliked the American and French revolutions, in which his friend played so prominent a part; but that nevertheless he would have agreed that the noble words written by Dr Johnson and inscribed upon the tombstone of Oliver Goldsmith, could equally well be applied to Franklin: 'He touched nothing that he did not adorn.'

24

John Wilkes: Pillar of the Establishment

The traveller in the United States of America will find a number of towns named after John Wilkes. This is on account of his sterling support for the rights of the American colonists in both the spoken and the printed word. His ebullience and energy made him the Americans' chief English adviser, but Franklin felt that Wilkes was his own worst enemy, standing not just for Liberty but for libertinism.

Even so, Wilkes had a series of solid achievements to his credit after fighting for most of his life, mainly for himself but also for causes greater than himself in which he genuinely believed. He had broken the stale mould of eighteenth-century English politics almost single-handedly, aided by little other than his own courage and wit and ready ability to communicate with the mob. Issues of principle and ideology would now play a part in politics. The increasingly prosperous middle class had been woken up to the nature of the power it could actually wield. Legal precedents had been established to secure the freedom of the press and the liberty of the individual. Parliamentary reform had become a serious and prominent issue. 'Accident made me a patriot,' Wilkes said, but he had served his country well.

He had eventually served himself well too. By 1780 Wilkes was a Member of Parliament and a City alderman. He was doing very nicely, thank you. That was when the Gordon Riots broke out.

These riots were caused by ignorance and bigotry. In 1778 the government had passed the Catholic Relief Act to ease restrictions upon Roman Catholics. Lord George Gordon, a rabidly insane but charismatic young Scot, demanded the repeal of this civilised Act and inflamed the London mob with his demagoguery. The mob went crazy, destroying property and looting the contents, seizing gin distilleries, consuming their contents and then torching the buildings, and breaking into gaols to free the criminals. Troops were called in to quell the rioting that was spreading all over London. Wilkes, who had used the rioting of the London mob to advance the causes of both liberty and his own ambitions, could now see how the power of demagoguery could be corrupted to foul ends. He had added the post of City magistrate to his collection of offices and when the mob endeavoured to storm the Bank of England, Wilkes turned upon his former supporters by commanding the militia to open fire.

This action quelled the riots, gained Wilkes renewed advantage with the ruling establishment and lost him his base of popular support. As has been noted, in 1782 the House of Commons expunged from its *Journal* the resolution of expulsion of 1769, implicitly vindicating his long struggle to ensure the rights of parliamentary electors. The mob dismissed him as a traitor to its cause: in contemporary vernacular, he had sold out. A younger generation of middle-class, idealistic political activists found his cynicism hard to stomach and deplored his apparent opportunism. Wilkes found himself to be more and more prosperous yet less and less relevant to the growing movement for political and administrative reform.

By 1790 Wilkes found the support in his own constituency of Middlesex to be so tepid that he retired from parliamentary life. His last seven years were passed in quiet retirement with the company of his adoring daughter Polly. He had started as a man on the make and by the end of his life, he had made it. He had even returned to some degree of favour in the eyes of royalty. One wonders how he felt, therefore, when Richard Brinsley Sheridan flung his gibe at him:

Johnny Wilkes, Johnny Wilkes
Thou greatest of bilks,
How changed are the notes that you sing!
Your famed Forty-Five
Is Prerogative
And your blasphemy,
God Save the King.

It was just tbe sort of gibe he would have gleefully flung at a hypocrite in his heyday. This man embodies so many of the contradictions of the century in which he lived. In common with most people, he often acted from mixed motives. It will not do either to praise him to the skies as a brave warrior in the cause of liberty or to damn him as a perfidious brother and vicious rake who cynically exploited popular discontent in order to advance his own interests.

The truth appears to be that he was a clever, rash, hot-tempered and warm-hearted man with a cutting wit, a hatred of hypocrisy, a passion for pooh-poohing pretension, a vaunting ambition, a love of drink and dames and an eventual desire for a safe haven in the cruel and hostile world in which he had been so strenuously embroiled. He had tremendous charm whenever he chose to exercise it and his nature was most kindly disposed towards anyone, man or woman, whom he genuinely happened to like. He was merciless towards his enemies and thoroughly relished the joys of assailing them in print, identifying their weaknesses and then subjecting these to cruel ridicule and exposure. He was not above making scathing jokes about his friends if he thought this might evoke laughter.

His careless spending on the good life usually far outstripped his income, thus putting him in debt to those who could demand political favours, though he was no more corrupt than any other eighteenth-century politician, and often less so. He had begun simply as an upstart and ambitious individual with few principles other than a desire to maintain his dignity and an intention to try and do more good than harm. It is difficult to detect a strong religious sensibility in Wilkes.

Four men played a principal part in his evolution. Thomas Potter expanded all the rakish tendencies already present in Wilkes, and aroused his ambition by showing him a world of carefree and cultured aristocratic sensibilities, which could co-exist cheerfully with a taste for the plain, blunt, cheerful and common. Charles Churchill impressed upon Wilkes his clumsy integrity, his love of the truth, his hatred of lies and his impassioned conviction that more democracy and reform would make the country a better place. Dashwood baffled Wilkes. He liked Dashwood as a man, respected his views despite disagreeing with him about elitism and, it seems, failed to comprehend the nature of any of his metaphysical or spiritual notions. The Earl of Sandwich aroused the ire of Wilkes so that what began as a personal battle against social snobbery became an impassioned crusade on far wider issues.

One wonders to what extent the religious convictions of Dashwood influenced John Wilkes and concludes, somewhat regretfully, that they didn't. From his writings it is clear that Wilkes saw the Friars as being little more than an enjoyable social joke, accompanied by some pseudo-religious mummery in the chapter-room to which he was never admitted, nevertheless he saw them as significant in political terms. He had joined the outer circle for social prestige, hedonistic enjoyments and political and economic advancement.

Sandwich, being a member of the inner circle, had discerned that motivation from the beginning and had never liked Wilkes. He regarded the latter's attack on the Bute ministry as a shameful betrayal of the values for which, in his view, all the Friars stood, and therefore had no compunction about hitting Wilkes below the belt by indicting him with the *Essay on Woman* in the House of Lords.

Wilkes's voice aroused the outrage of an emerging movement for democracy. He found himself swept along in its current. He fought for its cause with wit, dignity and exceptional bravery. Eventually he won on almost every issue for which he had battled. By this time, he was tired of fighting and wanted to go home to a good woman so as to enjoy the comfortable life he had always craved. When the establishment at last proceeded to bestow money and rank upon him, he was glad to receive it, showing just where he stood when he commanded the militia to fire upon the mob.

Cheap sneers at Wilkes fail to take account of his genuine courage. He was often placed in decisive historical situations with consequences way beyond anything he may have originally envisaged for himself, but he always reacted with reason. Certainly he had his faults. But anyone who values a British tradition of freedom of speech, the rights of the press, the rule of law as opposed to oligarchical or monarchical whim, and the liberty of the subject, should appreciate the achievements of 'That Devil Wilkes'.

25

The Survivors

The sensibility of the Friars survived in some. One was George Selwyn MP. A subsequent generation was puzzled by an extraordinary fact. Selwyn and Horace Walpole were thought to be the greatest letter-writers of their time; yet whilst Walpole zealously ensured that his letters were copied and preserved for posterity, Selwyn left strict instructions that his works of epistolary art must be destroyed. One wonders why he did that. Could it have been on account of his obsession with necrophilia? After all, death interested him rather more than sex, for he never married. It was said that he was unduly fond of little girls. There is something very morbid about the man. Walpole wrote:

A footman of Lord Dacre has been hanged for murdering the butler. George Selwyn had a great hand in bringing him to confess it. That Selwyn should be a capital performer in a scene of that kind is not extraordinary: I tell it you for the strange coolness which the young fellow, who was but nineteen, expressed: as he was writing his confession, 'I murd—' he stopped and asked, 'How do you spell *murdered?*'

T.H. White makes the picture more grisly in his *The Age of Scandal* by quoting a letter to Selwyn:

Harrington's porter was condemned yesterday. Cadogan and I

have already bespoken places at the Brazier's, and I hope
Parson Digby will come time enough to be of the party. I
presume we will have your honour's company, if your stomach
is not too squeamish for a single swing.

Ugh! One would not want to witness the twentieth-century
British hangings, whereby the neck was broken in an instant. Why
would anyone other than a pervert wish to witness a slow and
agonising strangulation?

Selwyn's contemporaries left testimony that he wasn't the ghastly
rotter he sounds. Even so, he is a paedophile suspect. The girl in
question was named Mie-Mie. Investigation of the facts makes it
reasonably clear that she was the natural daughter of another Friar,
the Duke of Queensberry, by an Italian marchioness. He liked this
little girl so much that he claimed to be the father and battled in
court for her legal custody. When she went to boarding-school, he
bombarded the headmistress with obsessive letters.

'Mrs Terry presents her best compliments to Mr Selwyn,' he
replied, 'is very sorry to find he is so uneasy. The dear child's
spirits are *not* depressed. She is very lively: ate a good dinner: and
behaves just like any other children.'

Selwyn doted on the girl for the rest of his life and left her
£33,000. The Duke of Queensberry left her £150,000. She then
hooked Lord Yarmouth and left him, went around Europe with
some lover of hers, was rumoured to be the mother of Sir Richard
Wallace and was ultimately portrayed by William Thackeray as the
Marchioness of Steyne in his *Vanity Fair*.

The fabled wit of Selwyn, so celebrated by his contemporaries,
raises at best only the briefest of smiles in our own day. For
example, when one Mr Foley fled to France to escape his debts,
Selwyn was applauded for stating that it was a passover which
would not be relished by the Jews. He was asked if Princess
Amelia would have a guard. 'Now and then one, I suppose,' he
replied. The best explanation of the effect he exercised upon his
time is probably that of T.H. White:

Wraxall explained Selwyn's jokes by saying that 'the effect when falling from his lips became greatly augmented by the listless and drowsy manner in which he uttered them, for he always seemed half-asleep'. This was the clue to the enigma. He possessed the play-actor's flair which made a stupid remark seem funny for the time being: the 'business' which actors exhibit by raising their eyebrows, like George Robey, or by looking pained and grieved. Selwyn's drooping eye-lids and demure look, which Reynolds drew with care, helped him to look sleepy.

White appears to entertain a hearty detestation of Selwyn. One's respect for the latter is hardly enhanced by the testimony of Glenvervie.

Mie-Miw never went out to air in the coach, never ate, or did anything without Selwyn attending her. When she began to grow up, she used to treat him with offensive disrespect. She took the tone, which many of the young men of the time had done; of treating him, this great wit, this father of all the *bon mots* that were circulating in London, as tiresome, and what is called a bore . . . However, Mlle Fagniani's treatment of him did not in any degree diminish his sort of maternal fondness and partiality towards her. Looking at her one day, he said to Storer: 'What a pleasure it is to love that girl so tenderly without having had the trouble to get her . . . ' Storer says that Selwyn professed never to have had connection with a woman but seven times in the whole course of his life, and that the last time was with a maid at the Inn at Andover, when he was 29. Yet he was a stout, healthy man, and never had any less natural taste or appetite imputed to him. But he undoubtedly had a fondness for the Duke of Queensberry. . . and Lord Carlisle, which had all the extravagance and blindness of passion. His attachment to them has been called a sort of sentimental sodomy. . . He had also latterly, as I have heard, fallen into the error of almost all men who love wit and anecdote when they become old, that of telling too many stories, and the same story too often.

White goes for the jugular:

> By some oversight, his own letters were not destroyed after all.
> They began to be published in 1897, by the Historical
> Manuscripts Commission, and the mystery of his character was
> cleared at once.
>   . . . To put it bluntly, it turned out that the great wit of
> Almack's had been a shallow, complaining and ignorant
> valetudinarian. He had written in a mixture of poor English,
> bad French and worse Italian. After all the talk of the
> 'monstrous good things' which George had said, the letters
> which came to light were the ill-spelt and endless chatter of an
> empty-headed fellow – a laughing-stock even, who had suffered
> the indignity, not only of falling in love with a baby that called
> him Yan-Yan, but also of catching the whooping cough from it
> at the age of sixty-one.

It seems that Selwyn was completely overrated, though one still
has to ask how he managed to charm so many people of his time.
He might have died as a mediocrity but he was reborn as a legend.
French fictionists saw him as the paragon of the cool English
sadist. It is likely that the legend of Selwyn influenced that
extraordinary gathering of four writers in Switzerland during the
British Regency and a generation after his death. I refer to Byron,
Shelley, Mary Shelley and Dr John Polidori. The Romantic
Revolution and the Gothic Revival were still ablaze. The company
of four agreed that each one would write a Gothic story.
Surprisingly, Byron and Shelley did no work of note, though they
may well have inspired those who did. Mary Shelley wrote
Frankenstein. Dr Polidori wrote *The Vampyre*, announcing the first
appearance of this in English literature. The theme was taken up
by Sheridan Le Fanu, who put it in a lesbian perspective in his
classic tale, *Camilla*. However, it was Bram Stoker, who imprinted
the vampire upon public consciousness with his novel, *Dracula*.

The personality traits of Selwyn have much in common with those of *Dracula*, who lives on in books and films. Selwyn spent most of his life being fascinated by death and in legend arose from the grave.

Paul Whitehead arose from the grave after another fashion. Having spent three days painstakingly burning all the papers of the Friars, he dropped dead in December 1774. As we have seen, he left his heart and fifty pounds for remembrance in the mausoleum to Lord Le Despenser. This heart was duly embalmed and enshrined in an urn, upon which was inscribed the epitaph: 'A heart that knew no guile.' An opponent called that heart 'as black in death as it had been in life'. Was he a good-hearted, decent man of wit and sensibillty, or a beastly and dishonourable pervert?

Certainly Dashwood showed his affection and respect by the funeral he gave to his old friend and steward of the Friars. Upon entrance to the mausoleum, the choir sang:

> From Earth to Heaven, Whitehead's soul is fled,
> Immortal glories beam around his head . . .

The conductor of the choir was Luffham Atterbury, Musician-in-Ordinary to the King. On the following day, his composition, the oratorio *Goliath*, was performed in honour of Whitehead at St Lawrence's.

His *Collected Poems* were published two years later, accompanied by a memoir authored by Edward Thompson. The dedication is to Sir Francis Dashwood. Thompson endeavoured to present the Friars in the best possible light:

> Now all that can be drawn from the publication of these ceremonies is that a set of worthy, jolly fellows, happy disciples of Venus and Bacchus, got occasionally together, to celebrate Woman in wine; and, to give more zest to the festive meeting, they plucked every luxurious idea from the ancients, and

enriched their own modern pleasures with the addition of classic luxury.

They also generated a ghost story. The spirit of Paul Whitehead continued to haunt West Wycombe Park. As the neurotic William Cowper wrote:

> Nor is this all; to ascertain the fact, and to put it out of the power of Scepticism to argue away the reality of it, there are few if any of his numerous household who have not likewise seen him, sometimes in the park, sometimes in the garden, as well as in the house, by day and by night indifferently.

This had been reported to him by Sir Francis's sister, Lady Austen, and Dashwood himself had seen the ghost of Whitehead 'beckoning' to him in 1781, the year he died. It is not known whether this ghost has survived to the present day.

Sandwich certainly survived. He retained a senior position in successive governments, usually First Lord of the Admiralty, then died in 1792, reincarnating not as a vampire nor as a ghost but as the name of a snack.

Dr Benjamin Bates outlived the lot of them, telling tales in his old age of how innocuous it all was. His tales have lived in the accounts of historians but his name has not.

Dashwood enjoyed his twilight years. He had a good mistress in the ex-actress, Frances Barry, who bore him a daughter, Rachel Frances Antonina, in 1774. As was customary with Dashwood, there was a reason for every name. Two of these reasons were plain: Rachel was the name of Dashwood's sister and Frances (Fanny) was the name of the mother. The third had classical allusions. Antonina was the wife of Belisarius, the great general of the armies of the emperor Justinian during the days of the Byzantine Empire. Robert Graves gives outstanding credit to Antonina in his novel *Count Belisarius*. She played a leading part in the deserved deposition of Pope Sylverius in 537.

Dashwood's ideal, for there to be a patriot king governing wisely and well in the interests of all the nation, came to nothing. King George III proved to be increasingly incompetent. The war against the American States had been abominably conceived and execrably executed, contrary to every principle that Dashwood had ever advocated. A notable resolution was carried by the House of Commons in April 1780, John Dunning's motion that 'the influence of the Crown has increased, is increasing and ought to be diminished'.

This motion was carried by eighteen votes. It marked the end of a monarchist ideal. In due course, most of the monarch's remaining powers would be removed by the oligarchy. In the meantime, the Prime Minister, Lord North, tendered his resignation. The King refused to accept it. North continued in office and bumbled on his way. Dashwood remained on good terms with both, showing more of his customary honest and blunt character in a letter to Lord North about Lord Temple:

I have no connection in the least with Lord Temple. I have not received any civilities from him; but I cannot set my face to an apparent injustice – he has raised and added a tenth company to the Regiment in time of need; however my inclinations may be, I cannot deny the truth. If your Lordship pleases tomorrow to apply to the King, I am sure I shall not take it ill. I only desire that I may in honour and Conscience stand clear in this disagreeable dispute.

Lord North displayed his respect for Dashwood by passing on Dashwood's letter to the King, fully endorsing the subsequent meeting between the two and before that, giving the King some judicious advice: 'It would be well if some method could be devised which might satisfy Lord Chesterfield without pressing Lord Le Despenser to do what he considers as an injustice to Lord Temple.'

The ministry of North fell nevertheless. So did the King. Unknown to anyone at the time but diagnosed by succeeding generations, he was suffering from porphyria. This caused him to leave his carriage on one occasion and greet a tree as the King of Prussia. The oligarchy pounced upon it and the King was thrown into a mental asylum where he was brutally treated. A regency was set up under George, Prince of Wales, who cared for little other than pleasure. Unfortunately for this political conspiracy, George III abruptly recovered. Yet the status of the monarchy deteriorated rapidly in the hands of this selfish, discourteous and inconsiderate heir to the throne. His behaviour made the very idea of a patriot king look like idealism at its silliest. The man duly succeeded to the crown and reigned from 1820 to 1830 and as Walter Savage Landor wrote:

> When George the Fourth to heaven ascended
> Thank God! The reign of Georges ended.

As Dashwood lay on his deathbed in the autumn of 1781, he must have pondered to what extent his own life had been worthwhile. He had celebrated the mysteries of sex and death but now he was incapable of sex and about to meet his death. What was the reckoning? On a practical level, he had been surprisingly efficient, as his will of 1780 testifies. It leaves the entailed estates of Buckinghamshire and West Wycombe Park to his brother John, his successor as baronet. Sir Thomas Stapleton received the Le Despenser title, Mereworth Castle and some land in Kent, to which he was entitled. Dashwood's brother also received bequests of land which Dashwood had acquired in Lincolnshire, Middlesex and Oxfordshire. His sister, Lady Rachel Austen, was a wealthy woman and so was left £100 a year for life as a gesture of goodwill. His mistress, Frances Barry, received £400 a year for life. His two illegitimate daughters, Frances and Rachel, were given trust funds to ensure their future financial independence. A later codicil amended the details of this will while preserving its essence. Another final codicil states: 'Whereas I have purchased several Farms Messuages, etc, in the several parishes of West Wycombe, Bradenham, Halton and Bledfloe or elsewhere in the

County of Bucks, I hereby charge the same with payment of £12,000 to my son Francis Dashwood to be paid to him at the Age of 21 years.'

For his immediate family, Dashwood had certainly left a legacy worthy of appreciation. Otherwise? The ideal of a patriot king was a fiasco. The ideal of government by a wise and benevolent aristocracy had been thoroughly discredited, and America and France would overthrow it altogether. Politically, Dashwood had been a failure in terms of achieving his objectives. Such success as he had, consisted of his own proud maintenance of his inner strength and integrity and independence. His political effect upon the nation was as paradoxical to him as to its observers. Having set out to design a benevolent elitism, he found his group nourishing the democracy of Wilkes and Franklin and engendering the seeds which flowered in the form of two major revolutions, leading to the sort of mob rule he had always endeavoured to avert.

If he failed to realise his political vision, he had been a fine Postmaster-General and parliamentarian. He had moreover the compensation of succeeding sexually, which is rather more than can be said for most politicians. Dashwood genuinely liked women and they genuinely liked him.

In religious terms, as we shall see, he gave birth to a legend and perpetuated an ethic. The legend was 'Do what you want'. The ethic was 'Do what thou wilt'.

26

Dashwood's Daughter

There was nothing dull about Dashwood's bastard daughter, Rachel Fanny Antonina (1774–1829). A governess tutored her until her father's death, which left her with £45,000. Her subsequent period in a French convent school gave her an abiding hatred of Christianity.

She returned to London and at the age of nineteen married one Matthew Lee, but left him within a year. She also built for herself a formidable reputation as an intellectual bluestockings an expert in the classics and in Hebrew. Her looks were stunning too. Thomas De Quincey called her 'a magnificent Witch'. She was as plain-spoken and hot-tempered as her father. In common with him she was rash, courageous, irreverent and cantankerous. Whenever something upset her, which was quite often, she made a point of raising hell until something was done about it.

She publicised herself. Her ostentatious carriage had 'The Hon. Antonina Dashwood' painted upon it. The fact of her illegitimate birth became one of her many obsessions. She wanted to be recognised as the true heiress. She wrote pamphlets. One tried to prove that Dashwood had secretly married her mother, which would give Antonina the right to call herself Baroness Le Despenser. Another claimed that her brother's will was a forgery and that all the money was intended for her, not his wife and children. She had marked the copy of Cornelius Agrippa's *Occult Philosophy* left to her by her father with a bookplate inscribed:

'Rachel Frances Antonina, Baroness Le Despenser.'

She was quite right in stating that Dashwood's sister, Lady Austen, had no legal right to call herself Baroness Le Despenser. However, she could not prove her own claim in a court of law. Gradually she fell victim to a growing paranoia. She thought that people were spying on her and put every scrap of paper, no matter how trivial in a sealed envelope. She was always accusing other people of stealing her documents. She took the two sons of her former governess to court on a kidnapping charge, then behaved so absurdly in the witness box that the accused were acquitted.

Her enemies called her the Infidel. She tried to form a club of her own but this venture did not succeed. She moved to Gloucestershire, where she immersed herself in occult studies, especially among the books her father had left her. Eventually she developed a conviction that she was the victim of psychic attack and fled to London in 1808 where she wrote an *Essay on Government*. Wordsworth praised it. It sold quite well. The theme is eminently sensible.

The introduction preaches 'Do what thou wilt'. She praises the law of Nature insisting that it is divinely ordained, and declares for human rights to life, liberty and the pursuit of happiness. She argues strongly that any action which promotes human happiness is permissible.

This is all very well – but she was not happy. She hurled ludicrous allegations against the landlord of the hotel where she resided. According to her, this man was in league with the international conspiracy against her and wanted to torture her mentally. His methods allegedly consisted of putting a pig in the room next door to her, and hiring men to climb ladders so as to hold up cages containing parrots that would squawk naughty words outside her window.

Her next move was to West Wycombe House where she was welcomed by its new squire, the Friar Sir John Dashwood-King. During her stay she visited the mausoleum every day and also became convinced that there was Something in the caves. Of her father she said that he was 'much-beloved but misled', but never explained her statement.

Her last work, *An Invocation to the Jews*, written in Hebrew, has yet to be fully explored. The probability is that it consists of private obsessions enciphered in qabalistic phrasing and numerology but it might not be so. Perhaps it is a masterpiece just waiting to be decoded.

Rachel Fanny Antonina spent most of her declining years still studying the occult books which her father had left her. She tore pages out of some of them. She possessed the translation of the *Kama Sutra* inscribed by Henry Vansittart. Now she became convinced that her enemies were trying to poison her. Her death in 1829 was ruled as due to natural causes.

It is a pity for posterity that she never explained her words about West Wycombe: 'The clue to all my troubles can be found in the heart of the hill.'

27

Pale Imitations

John Hall Stevenson was born John Hall into a family of Yorkshire country gentlemen and educated at Jesus College, Cambridge. There he met his lifelong friend, the budding novelist, Laurence Sterne. He went on the Grand Tour, married a wealthy woman and added her name, Stevenson, to his own. An eccentric uncle left him Skelton Castle, a fifteenth-century erection near Middlesbrough, and Hall Stevenson took possession, renaming it Crazy Castle.

The name was entirely appropriate, for Hall Stevenson was, to put it charitably, a highly eccentric man. He was a hypochondriac who retired to bed, convinced that he was dying, whenever an east wind blew. He was rabidly anti-Catholic. He loved to collect and peruse pornography. Nevertheless he had sufficient social skills to cultivate a circle of friends, including Wilkes, Paul Whitehead and Dashwood. It is known that he visited Medmenham – which he called the shrine of St Francis in June 1762 – and it led him to set up his own club, the Demoniacks. Dashwood was appointed their 'Privy Councillor'. Hall Stevenson's debt to Dashwood is demonstrated in a letter dated 31 August 1761:

Mr Hall presents his compliments to Mr Wilkes and is still under the scourge of an invincible Cholick which has reduced him to such a state of Contrition that he is obliged to live by rules entirely opposite to those of St Francis, whose shrine he venerates, but dare not approach under his present Incapacity; he desires ye prayers of ye congregation and hopes their Devotion may be attended with the choicest blessings of their Patron, Health Wealth and never failing vigour...

Given the fact that this letter is to Wilkes rather than Dashwood, it is most probable that Hall Stevenson was only a member of the outer circle. This opinion is confirmed by regarding the actual activities of the Demoniacks. There does not appear to have been any religious aspect, pagan, satanic or otherwise. The members drank, gambled, fornicated and told dirty jokes. Whilst there is nothing wrong with that, it is a pity that they did not do more, for the setting was immaculately Gothic. Crazy Castle was genuinely medieval, with mouldering battlements and decaying stone terraces. There was no drawbridge and one had to cross the stagnant moat by ferry.

Even so, Sterne was the only notable member, the others being boozy country gentlemen and neighbours.

A book of the club's jottings was eventually published as *Crazy Tales*. The preface by an anonymous editor stated:

It may be thought, by some over delicate persons, that an apology would here not be ill-placed for some of the performances now republished, this the editor declines, as he concurs in opinion with his Author, as already observed that *Outcries against writings composed for any intention than to promote good humour and cheerfulness by fighting against the taedium vitae, were reserved for an age of refined hypocrisy ...*

It has been said that one of the *Crazy Tales* at least was composed by Laurence Sterne as a preliminary sketch for a chapter in *Tristram Shandy*. In any event, Sterne grew bored with the Demoniacks, whose members included Pantagruel or 'Panty' – the club name the Reverend Robert Lascelles had drawn from Rabelais – 'Paddy Andrew' and 'Don Pringello', and became inactive.

After Hall Stevenson's death, his *The Confessions of Sir Fr— of Medmenham and of the Lady Mary, His Wife* was published, as we have noted. This poem accuses Dashwood of enjoying sexual relations with his mother – unlikely, since she died before he was two – and with three of his sisters, one of whom was apparently a lesbian. One concurs with Ashe that this is merely 'nasty doggerel' and 'too muddled to be evidence of anything but its author's unpleasantness'. Hall Stevenson was considered even by most of his contemporaries to be demented.

The man had fancied himself as the successor of Rabelais but this claim could be made more justly of his friend Laurence Sterne, vicar of Sutton-on-the-Forest, Yorkshire. Sterne's splendid *Tristram Shandy* was published between 1759 and 1761 and earned its author richly deserved fame and fortune. Chapter 36, Part Five slightly misquotes Dashwood's representation of the Cave of Trophonius: *Omne animal post coitum est triste* – All animals are sad after sex.

A curious anonymous work called *The Fruit Shop* was sarcastically dedicated to Laurence Sterne, addressed as 'Revd'. This referred to

> ...a certain club that assemble in a house not far from the Thames and who have acquired to themselves an universal notoriety (we leave our readers to settle in what sense) for some late proceedings, wherein they let out their understandings, to be the venal and prostituted tools of a single man's ambitious machinations.

Most of Sterne's book is a melange of *double entendre* and anti-Christianity. Towards the end, however, he gives a twelve-page account of a 'sect of philogynists' – womanisers – holding frankly sexual meetings preceded by ritual. The sect is depicted as an underground movement which has been going on for centuries and, one gathers, is still in being. The impression is strong that this is fake history in the Masonic or Rosicrucian style, meant to supply a pedigree for a secret society in the author's own London.

He describes the ritual: a short talk from the leader; wine and fruit, music and dancing; a travesty-hymn beginning '*Veni Spiritus Amoris*' (we have a link here with the *Essay on Woman* fragment); and then the real business of the evening.

The successors of the Friars appear to have taken everything that is commonplace from their practices without including anything that was noble. There is not much to be said for the revival of the Dublin Hell-Fire Club, denounced on 12 March 1771 in *The Freeman's Journal*. This grouping was called 'The Holy Fathers' and their toasts were 'The Devil' and 'Damn us all'. It seems to have been little more than an excuse for eating, drinking and fornicating to excess accompanied by ribaldry and a ceremonial mocking of Christianity, though more research is required. Its leader, Thomas 'Buck' Whaley, was the son of 'Burn-Chapel' Whaley, allegedly a leader of the preceding Dublin Hell-Fire Club and a pyromaniac. 'Burn-Chapel' loved setting fire to Roman Catholic churches, and after pouring brandy over a servant, he torched him. His son was no less eccentric.

It is hard to credit the tales that are told about 'Buck' Whaley. These include the story that he spent his (then colossal) income of £10,000 a year on gambling in Paris; that he recovered his fortunes by winning bets that he would ride to Jerusalem and back in a year; that his meetings on Montpelier Hill, the old site of a Hell-Fire Club, consisted of devil-worshipping, homosexual, sado-masochistic orgies; and that he trapped, killed, cooked and ate a farmer's daughter, genially sharing chunks of her roasted flesh with his gloating and lustful companions. In a final act of absurdity, he converted to Christianity, moved to the Isle of Man and ended his days in a house he called 'Whaley's Folly'. One cannot tell whether or not the man was more preposterous than his critics.

Rumours persisted of clubs similar to the Friars operating at the Universities of Oxford and Cambridge. After Lord Byron left Trinity College, Cambridge, he held a house party at his home, Newstead Abbey, in 1809. Here his friends dressed up as monks in hired costumes, drank from his cup made of a human skull, teased his tame bear and wolf and indulged in drinking and horseplay into the small hours. Dashwood's fraternity was the likely inspiration behind this affair.

So just what was it that made the Friars unique?

Conclusions

Do What Thou Wilt

The above words were the creed of Rabelais in his *Gargantua* of the early sixteenth century, of Dashwood during the mid-eighteenth century and of Aleister Crowley during the first half of the twentieth century. As we have seen, these words do not mean anything as banal as 'Do what you want'. They mean find your true will with your soul and do it. For example, it was the will of Bubb-Dodington to be a political fixer just as much as it was the will of William Hogarth to be a painter or Sandwich to be the First Lord of the Admiralty.

But was there an inner circle practising magic? Certainly there were magical ceremonies. Unless he is mad, a man such as Dashwood does not spend ferocious sums of money creating an environment at Medmenham and following through with a fabulous expenditure upon the West Wycombe caves, the church and the mausoleum without a purpose, involving absolute belief in a mystery. All the evidence indicates that Dashwood, though impulsive and impetuous, was completely sane.

His possession of so many books on magic suggests the nature of the ceremonies. But was there something extra, connected with the Bengali Tantrics, brought as the *Kama Sutra* to the Friars by Sir Henry Vansittart?

This initially seems unlikely since no women are known to have entered either the chapter-room at Medmenham or the West Wycombe caves. Yet insofar as one can tell, the Medmenham

234

rituals were about life, followed by making love: the cave rituals were about death and resurrection, followed by making love.

There is also the matter of the context. Although the eighteenth century is normally regarded as the age of Reason, there was also irrationalism bubbling and boiling beneath its surface. Horace Walpole, a spiteful man, condemned the Friars, yet they were hardly the only ones to embrace magic. After all, Walpole himself had a neo-Gothic building erected and wrote the first work of Gothic fiction, *The Castle of Otranto*. In France, Freemasonry in various forms embraced ceremonial magic. In Germany, there was Adam Weishaupt and the Illuminati.

But what did the Friars add to the sum of human knowledge and experience? Much was suppressed and obscured by the Victorians. The emerging middle classes, who embraced Christianity, deplored what they regarded as being little more than aristocratic degeneracy. In consequence, the position of woman deteriorated. She was seen either as a saintly mother or else as a whore. Whereas the Friars had accepted women as they are, the Victorians forced them into a tight-laced corset of false morality.

We start with Sir Francis Dashwood, creator of the Friars, and there is much to be said in his favour. His was neither the life of a degenerate satanist as portrayed by Montague Summers nor that of an affable, well-meaning bore as portrayed by Dr Betty Kemp. The man did much more good than harm. His achievements should be listed.

1. He adorned in extraordinary style everything at Medmenham Abbey.
2. He improved upon a house at West Wycombe which is still admired by connoisseurs of architecture.
3. He encouraged exquisite landscape gardening.
4. He patronised good painters and supported them financially, encouraging them to do some of their finest works; he was also an art collector.
5. His Clubs, the Divan and the Dilettante (the latter still

presently in existence) genuinely nourished an English interest in Middle Eastern and classical arts and architecture.

6. As a squire, and in an era when the squire often oppressed the peasant, he devised schemes for employment in the locality, such as road-building, cave-digging, and interior decoration.

7. His designs improved spectacularly on both Medmenham Abbey and the buildings of West Wycombe (though Giuseppe Borgnis helped him to realise his vision).

8. In Parliament, he was always an Independent who could not be bought or sold. He defended the unpopular cause of Admiral Byng at considerable cost to his own popularity with the ruling Whig establishment. He also pressed for the establishment of a militia, a territorial army, which would give further employment in his locality. He did not stop his pressure until he had succeeded in his demands.

9. Although his period as Chancellor of the Exchequer was somewhat inglorious, he came back as an effective joint Postmaster-General and though his proposal for a penny post was then rejected, it was finally taken up in the 1840s by Sir Rowland Hill.

10. Although his views were benevolently elitist rather than democratic, he nevertheless befriended that democrat, Benjamin Franklin, pioneer of the American Revolution, and spoke strongly in favour of the American cause.

11. He was a sociable genial, honest and honourable gentleman who always said exactly what he thought. He looked after his family and his friends; he treated his enemies with scorn, disdained criticism and endeavoured to realise his vision.

12. In the course of this endeavour, he founded the Friars, all the while giving the nation a lifetime of service on parliamentary committees so as to increase the national bounty.

13. In his buildings, he has left us sermons in stone. The interior decoration, landscape gardening, paintings and sculpture with which Dashwood supplied his group, whether at Medmenham or at West Wycombe, add much more to the remaining, fragmentary written records.

14. It seems that Dashwood, in his celebration of 'the English Eleusinian Mysteries', was advocating the Tantric notion that the sexual union between man and woman can be a sacred act as worship unto the divine, regenerating the creative energy that has enabled humanity to evolve. (This notion would later be violently opposed by the recrudescence of Christianity in the language of Victorian middle-class morality.)

Was all this merely the work of Dashwood alone? The answer must be no. All the other Friars possessed a clubbability which included intelligent and independent women. They contributed substantially to the cultural life of England. They also showed that it was both possible and desirable for a grouping of extraordinary men and women to come together in exquisite surroundings in order to raise the consciousness of those present. Although their endeavour to have Great Britain governed well by a patriot king backed by a loyal elite turned out to be a failure, it inadvertently provoked the rise of democracy in England and thus spread to ignite the torches of revolution in America and France.

Historian John Brooke denies the entire tale of 'The Boot and the Petticoat' and indignantly declares that Bute never was the lover of Princess Augusta, mother of King George III. The allegation is dismissed as a lie, spread about to discredit an unpopular ministry. Brooke appears to be stating that Princess Augusta, after the death of her husband Prince Frederick, chose to embrace a life of chastity. The fact of the matter is that neither Brooke nor the present writer know whether or not Princess Augusta enjoyed an affair with handsome Lord Bute. Nevertheless, the London mob believed this to be the case. This belief possessed sufficient power to cause riots, a fact which demands explanation.

Dashwood's inner circle, the 'Unholy Twelve' in some accounts though the Nine in others, appear sexually to have preserved some holy tradition from the past: that sex between a man and a woman is holy, sacred, sacramental and religious, in addition to being jolly good fun. Restoring pagan worship and occult rites graced by fine art, they were an inspiration and created a legend for those who might come after them.

'Do what thou wilt', wrote Rabelais, Dashwood and Crowley, bidding us to follow the law of Nature and of our own individual natures. This law bids carpenters to make tables, sheep to eat grass, wolves to eat sheep and authors to write books. Given the present wretched state of the world, it is high time that each and every one of us proceeded to realise our inmost will.

Appendix

Membership

The issue of who actually was a member of the Medmenham Monks or Friars of St Francis of Wycombe has always been a bone of contention among those who have written upon the subject. Excellent pioneering work was done by Louis Jones in *The Clubs of the Georgian Rakes* (1942), but the issue can now be explored further.

Obviously no one doubts that Dashwood was the centre of a certain circle. No one doubts that Whitehead served as steward. No one doubts that John Wilkes was a member, although all sources state that he was never admitted to the inner circle. The matter is best approached by enumerating the sources and then tabulating them according to names.

1. Hall Stevenson–Wilkes correspondence, British Library MSS 30876.
2. Johnstone, *Chrysal or: The Adventures of a Guinea*.
3. Thompson, ed., *Whiteheads Works* (1777).
4. Walpole, *Journals of Visits to Country Seats*, pp. 50–1.
5. Whitehead, *Paul to the Medmenhamites* (Thompson, ed., p. xxxix).
6. Wilkes–Churchill correspondence, British Library Add.MSS 30878.
7. Almon, *New Foundling Hospital for Wit*, III, pp. 103 ff.
8. Wilkes, *History of the Late Ministry*, pp. 407–9 (marginalia),

British Library MSS 13453 – Wilkes's own copy.

9. Baker, *Introduction to Chrysall; or, The Adventures of a Guinea* (London: Routledge; New York: E.P. Dutton. N.d, p. xviii.
10. Bleackley, *Life of John Wilkes*, p. 49.
11. Bolton, *Journal of the Ex Libris Society XI* (190L), pp. 47–51.
12. Chambers, *Book of Days*, I, p. 608.
13. Chancellor, *Lives of the Rakes*, Vol. IV.
14. Cross, *Sterne*, p. 130.
15. Davis, *Folio of Biographical and Literary Anecdotes*.
16. *Dictionary of National Biography* (under *Dashwood*).
17. Fuller, *Hell-Fire Francis*, p. 93.
18. Lipscombe, *History... Buckinghamshire*.
19. Plaisted, *Manor... of Medmenham*, p. 219.
20. Powys, *Diary*, Clemenson, ed. p. 381.
21. *Victoria History of... Bucks*, III, p. 35.
22. Ashe, *Do What You Will* (1974).
23. Lasky and Silver, 'Hell-Fire Dashwood' (*Men of Mystery*, ed. Colin Wilson, 1977).
24. Mannix, *The Hell-Fire Club* (1961).
25. McCormick, *The Hell-Fire Club* (1958).
26. Rhodes, *The Satanic Mass* (1954).
27. Towers, *Dashwood, The Man & The Myth* (1986).
28. Dashwood, *The Dashwoods of West Wycombe* (1988).

The names of those suspected of membership are followed by the numbers of those sources in which they are identified as possible members.

Bates, Benjamin, Dr., 9, 10, 12, 13, 18, 19, 20, 22, 23, 27.
Churchill, Charles, 6, 9, 10, 11, 12, 13, 18, 19, 20, 22, 23, 24, 25, 27.
Clarke, Mr, 4, 17, 22, 27, 28.
Collins, Henry Lovibond, 9, 10, 13, 18, 19.
Dashwood-King, Sir John, 17, 18, 19, 20, 21, 22, 23, 27, 28.
D'Aubrey, Sir John, 13, 17, 18, 20.
Delaval, Sir Francis, 21.

Dodington, George Bubb, 2, 9, 10, 11, 12, 13, 14, 15, 16, 17, 18, 19, 20, 22, 23, 24, 25, 26, 27, 28.

Douglas, William, 3rd Earl of March, 4th Duke of Queensberry, 9, 16, 21, 22, 23.

Duffield, Francis, 9, 10,19, 22, 26, 27.

Fane, John, 7th Earl of Westmorland, 2, 15.

Fox, Henry, Lord Holland, 2, 9, 15.

Frederick, Prince of Wales, 16, 21, 22, 23, 24.

Hall Stevenson, John, 1, 10, 14, 22, 23, 27.

Hogarth, William, 17, 24.

Hopkins, Richard, 10, 18.

Lloyd, Robert, 9, 10, 11, 12, 13, 18, 19, 20, 22, 23, 24, 25, 26, 27, 28.

Luttrell, Simon, 1st Earl of Carhampton, 16.

Manners, John, Marquis of Granby, 4.

Montagu, John, 4th Earl of Sandwich, 2, 3, 9, 10, 11, 13, 14, 15, 16, 17, 19, 20, 22, 23, 24, 25, 26, 27, 28.

Pierrepont, Evelyn, Duke of Kingston, 4.

Potter, Thomas, 5, 10, 11, 16, 19, 22, 23, 24, 25, 26, 27, 28.

Selwyn, George, 13, 20, 22, 23, 24, 25, 26.

Stanhope, Sir William, 9, 10, 12, 13, 14, 18, 19, 20, 21.

Stapleton, Sir Thomas, 4, 5, 7, 1O, 13, 22, 23, 27.

Stuart, John, Earl of Bute, 1, 6, 21, 22, 23, 24, 25.

Thompson, Dr, 2, 9, 15, 22.

Vanhattan, Henry, 21.

Vansittart, Arthur, 4, 17, 21, 23, 24, 27.

Vansittart, Henry, 4, I7, 21, 22, 23, 24, 25, 26, 27, 28.

Walpole, George, 3rd Earl of Oxford, 11, 22.

One hopes that this information will be of assistance to future scholars and researchers.

Select Bibliography

Almon, J. (ed.), *The New Foundling Hospital for Wit*, London, 1771, 1789.

Ashe, Geoffrey, *Do What You Will: A History of Anti-Morality*, 1974.

Bolingbroke, Viscount, *Letters on the Spirit of Patriotism and the Idea of a Patriot King*, edited by A. Hassall, 1917.

Campbell, Joseph, *The Hero With a Thousand Faces*, 1988.

Carey, John, *Pagan Wisdom*, 1991.

Cavendish, Richard, *The Black Arts*, 1967.

Chancellor, Edwin B., *The Lives of the Rakes*, 1924–5.

Churchill, Charles, *Poems*, edited by James Laver, 1933.

Crowley, Aleister, *The Book of the Law*, 1904, 1912, 1938, 1993; *The Book of Lies*, 1913, 1980; *Magick*, 1973; *777 and Other Qabalistic Writings*, edited by I. Regardie, 1977; *Gems from the Equinox*, edited by I. Regardie, 1986.

Dobson, H. Austin, *William Hogarth*, 1907.

Dodington, George Bubb, *Political Journal*, edited by John Carswell and Lewis Arnold Dralle, 1965.

French, Peter, *John Dee*, 1972.

Fuller, Ronald, *Hell-Fire Francis*, 1939.

Hodgart, Matthew (ed.), *Horace Walpole: Memoirs and Portraits*, 1963.

Howe, Ellic, *The Magicians of the Golden Dawn*, 1972.

Johnstone, Charles, *Chrysal: or The Adventures of a Guinea*, 1760–5.

Jones, Louis, *The Clubs of the Georgian Rakes*, 1942.

Kemp, Betty, *Sir Francis Dashwood: An Eighteenth Century Independent*, 1967.

King, Francis (ed.), *The Secret Rituals of the O.T.O.*, 1973; *Tantra for Westerners: A Practical Guide to the Way of Action*, 1986; *Modern Ritual Magic: The Rise of Western Occultism*, 1989.

Lasky, Jesse Jnr, and Silver, Pat, 'Hell-Fire Dashwood', published in *Men of Mystery*, edited by Colin Wilson, 1977.

Mannix, Daniel, *The Hell-Fire Club*, 1961.

McCormick, Donald, *The Hell-Fire Club*, 1958.

Plumb, J.H., *The First Four Georges*, 1956.

Postgate, Raymond William, *That Devil Wilkes*, 1956.

Praz, Mario, *The Romantic Agony*, 1960.

Regardie, Israel (ed.), *The Golden Dawn*, 1937–40; *Ceremonial Magic*, 1980.

Rhodes, H.T.F., *The Satanic Mass*, 1954.

Russell, Jeffrey B., *A History of Witchcraft*, 1980.

Summers, Montague, *Witchcraft and Black Magic*, 1946.

Suster, Gerald (ed.), *John Dee: Essential Readings*, 1986; *The Legacy of the Beast: The Life, Work and Influence of Aleister Crowley*, 1988.

Towers, Eric, *Dashwood: The Man and The Myth*, 1986.

Ward, Ned, *The Secret History of Clubs*, 1709.

White, T.H., *The Age of Scandal*, 1950.

Wilkes, John, *The Correspondence of John Wilkes and Charles Churchill*, edited by Edward N. Weatherly, 1954.

Wraxall, Nathaniel W., *Historical Memoirs of My Own Time*, 1815.

Index

Adams, John 210
Adonis 138
Agrippa, Henry Cornelius 61,
  148–9, 153, 154, 155, 156, 163,
  226
Almon, J. 5, 239
Al-Sabad, Hasan 146
American Declaration of
  Independence 209
American Philosophical Society 203
Angerona 102, 141
Anne, Queen 15, 36, 38, 48
Aphrodite 101, 104, 188
Apollo 100, 103, 104, 140, 143
'Appalling Club' 52
Apuleius 100, 138, 185
Ariadne 130, 135–6
Artabel 61
Artemis 188
Ashbee, Henry Spencer 6
Ashe, Geoffrey 10, 47, 49, 62, 66,
  69, 71, 73, 74, 76, 84, 109, 124,
  231, 240
Ashmole, Elias 164
Assassins 146
Ashtoreth 188
Astarte 188
Atalanta 188
Atterbury, Luffham 221
Attis 138–9

Augusta of Saxe-Gotha, Princess 65,
  70, 76, 77, 109, 111, 114, 124,
  237
Augustine, St 143
Austen, Lady Rachel 222, 224, 227
'Avalon, Arthur' see Woodruffe, Sir
  John

Bacchus 100, 107, 130, 135, 141,
  142, 187, 200, 221; see also
  Dionysus
Banks, Joseph 63, 163
Barnard, Lord 65
Barry, Frances (Fanny) 180, 206,
  222, 224
Barry, Rachel Fanny Antonina see
  Dashwood, Antonina
Bates, Dr Benjamin 3–4, 63, 222, 240
Beckford, William 99
Bedford Head Inn 17
Beefsteak Club see Sublime Society
  of Beefsteaks
Berkeley, Lord 89
Bird symbolism 142
Bolingbroke, Henry St John,
  Viscount 38
Bona Dea 26, 101, 106, 136–8,143,
  187, 188
Book of Common Prayer, The 24–5,
  196, 197–201

Borgnis, Giovanni 130
Borgnis, Giuseppe 17, 63, 98–9, 103, 130, 186, 236
Boswell, James 173,174,178
Boyne, Lord 93
Brahma 145
Brangham, Godfrey 140
Briton, The 111, 118
Brooke, John 237
Browning, Robert 71
Buddhism 145, 146
Burgis, Colonel 17
Burgoyne, General Johnny 210
Burlington, Lord 95
Burton, Sir Richard 144
Bute, John Stuart, Earl of 20, 21, 63, 68, 77, 78, 80–1, 94, 108–9, 110–4, 118, 119, 120, 122, 123, 124–5, 128, 129, 177, 180, 215, 237, 241
Byng, Admiral George 18, 109–10, 113, 236
Byron, Lord George 220, 232

Cagliostro, Count Alessandro di 162, 166
Campbell, Joseph 135, 138
Carey, John 162
Carlisle, Lord 219
Carnegie, Dale 202
Carpentiers 25, 26,101
Carr, Professor E.H. 2
Carswell, John and Dralle, Lewis Arnold 69
Casanova, Giovanni 162
Casaubon, Meric 156
Catholic Relief Act 213
Ceres 188
Champion, The 75
Chancellor, E. Beresford 7, 29, 70, 86
Chandler, Richard 23
Charles I 42
Charles II 35, 42, 43, 65,192
Chatham, Earl of *see* Pitt, William

Chesterfield, Lord 28, 127, 223
Chesterton, G.K. 42
Cholmondeley, Earl of 89
Churchill, Charles 3, 4, 6, 29, 49, 63, 64, 71, 78, 79, 81, 82, 94–5, 114, 116–8, 121, 128, 132, 177, 178, 186, 215, 239, 240
Churchill, John 35
Churchill, Lady Sarah 36
Clark, Sir George 204–5
Clarke, John 178
Clarke, Mr 62, 240
Cleland, John 55
Clement XII, Pope 17,160
Clubs 46–7, 53
Cole, Mrs 190
Colley, Linda 29
Collins, Henry Lovibond 240
Commons Club 25
Congreve, William 88
Constable, John 96
Cook, Captain James 31
Coram, Captain Thomas 93
Corneille, Pierre 16
Cowper, William 222
Cranmer, Thomas 197
Crazy Castle Hall *see* Skelton Hall
Cromwell, Oliver 42
Crowley, Aleister 58, 141, 150, 151, 152, 165, 187, 188, 234, 238
Cybele 188

Daly's Club 51
Damiens, Robert 85
Dance, Nathaniel 25
Dashwood, Antonina (Rachel Fanny Antonina Barry) 24, 180, 222, 224, 226–8
Dashwood, Charles 15
Dashwood, Sir Francis 1, 2, 3, 4, 5, 6, 7, 8, 9, 10, 11, 12, 13, 14–27, 28, 29, 31, 32–4, 39, 45, 48, 52, 53, 55, 57, 60, 61, 62, 63, 64, 65, 68, 69, 72, 75, 77, 78, 79, 80, 81, 82, 84, 87, 88, 89, 90, 93, 94, 96,

97, 99, 100, 101, 104, 105, 106, 107, 109–10, 111, 112, 115, 116, 119, 120, 121, 125, 128, 129, 130, 131, 132, 133, 134, 135, 136, 139, 141, 142, 143, 144, 145, 147, 148, 153, 154, 157, 163, 165, 167, 168, 177–82, 184, 185, 186, 187, 188, 190, 191, 192, 193, 194, 195, 196, 197–201, 202–7, 208, 211, 215, 221, 222–5, 227, 229, 230, 231, 233, 234–8, 239

Dashwood, Sir Francis, Jr 225

Dashwood, Sir Francis Sr. 15

Dashwood, Sir Francis (present Baronet) 11, 26, 240

Dashwood, Alderman George 14–15

Dashwood, Henrietta 15

Dashwood, John *see* Dashwood-King, Sir John

Dashwood, Maria 15

Dashwood, Mary 15

Dashwood, Rachel 15

Dashwood, Sarah, Baroness Le Despenser 22–3, 179, 180, 181, 182

Dashwood, Samuel 15

Dashwood, Susannah 15

Dashwood-King, Sir John 15, 62, 178, 224, 227, 240

D'Aubrey, Sir John 240

Deacon, Richard *see* Donald McCormick

Dee, Dr John 90, 148, 150, 155–6, 163, 164

Delaney, Mrs 14

Delaval, Sir Francis 240

Demoniacks, The 4, 184, 229–31

D'Eon, Chevalier 63, 133, 163, 167, 168, 189–90

Demeter 188

Denny, William 191

De Quincey, Thomas 52, 226

Dermott, Laurence 102

Diana *see* Artemis

Dickens, Charles 35, 104

Dictionary of National Biography 6–7, 18, 29, 31, 240

Diderot, Denis 161

Dilettante Society 23, 25, 53, 64, 68, 75, 89, 100, 235

Dionysus 11, 94, 103, 104, 130, 136, 139, 140, 141, 143, 152

Divan Club 18, 25, 53, 64, 88, 235

Dodington, George Bubb 6, 7, 10, 62, 67, 68, 69, 70–8, 87, 88, 89, 94, 97, 109, 110, 113, 128, 131, 177, 187, 234, 241

Douglas, William, Earl of March *see* Queensberry, Duke of

Downman, J. 80

Dralle, Lewis Arnold *see* Carswell, John and Dralle, Lewis Arnold

Dryden, John 46, 65

'Dublin Blasters' 51

Duelling 55, 125–6

Duffield, Francis 62, 98, 178, 241

Duncannon, Lord 18

Dunning, John 223

Durga 188

Dyer, Anna 179

Eagle Tavern, Cork Hill 51

Edinburgh, Devil worship in 52

Edinburgh Review 5

Egmont, Lord 180

Egremony, Lord 88–9

Eleusinian Mysteries 140–1, 142–3, 237

Ellys, Lady Sarah *see* Dashwood, Sarah, Baroness Le Despenser

Encyclopedia Britannica 29, 31, 170, 172, 175

Endymion 188

Eros 100, 142

Euripides 103, 139

Fane, John, *see* Westmorland, Earl of

Fane, Lady Mary 15

Faust 156

Fielding, Henry 74, 75, 78

Fisher, Kitty 32
Fludd, Robert 164
Fonthill Abbey 99
Forbes, Lord 18
Fountain Inn, The Strand 17
Fox, Henry *see* Lord Holland
Foxcroft, John 207
'Francis of Cookham' 62
'Francis of Wycombe' 62
Franklin, Benjamin 1l, 21–2, 25, 63,
    75, 95, 133, 159, 167, 168, 191–6,
    197–201, 202–7, 208–11, 212, 236
Frazer, Sir James G. 138
Frederick, Prince of Wales 14, 38,
    39, 63, 64–70, 73, 74, 75, 79, 83,
    108, 109, 128, 163, 193, 237, 241
Freemasonry 45, 51, 65, 79, 158–63,
    168, 192, 202, 209, 210, 237
Friars of St Francis of Wycombe, The
    see Monks of Medmenham, The
Fuller, Ronald 8,12, 239

Gay, John 29
Geb *see* Seb
George I 36, 37, 44, 47, 72
George II 30, 37, 39, 64, 65, 67, 76,
    109, 110, 174
George III 63, 65, 73, 77, 108, 109,
    111, 132, 172, 180, 181, 193, 194,
    206, 223, 224, 237
George IV 172, 224
George Inn, Southwark 26, 52
George & Vulture Inn 26, 52, 66,164
Germain, Lady Betty 89–90
Germain, Lord George 209
Gibourg, Abbé 166
Gide, André 14
Goethe, Johann 156, 168
Goldsmith, Oliver 211
Goncourt, Edmond De 85
Gordon Riots 212–3
Gothicism 99
Grafton, Duke of 109, 170, 179, 181
Granby, Marquis of 63, 241
Graves, Robert 138, 225

Gray, Thomas 84
Greece 18
Grenville, Lord 84, 128, 180, 193
Guildford, Earl of 193
Gwynne, Nell 42–3

Hackman, James 32
Hadit 153
Hall Stevenson, John 3, 4, 63, 134,
    184, 229–30, 239, 241
Hamilton, Sir William 54, 88
Hammil, John 163
Harpocrates 102, 141
Hathor 188
Hawkins, Sir John 79
Hayes, Charlotte 87
Hebe 188
Hecate 188
Hell-Fire Club (Dublin) 51, 232
Hell–Fire Club(Limerick) 51
Hell–Fire Club (Wharton's) 26, 44,
    47–51, 56, 164
'Hell–Fire Club' *see* Monks of
    Medmenham, The
'Hell–Fire Ministry' 20–21, 91,
    111–4
Henry IV of France 42
Hey, Lord Charles 89
Hinduism 144, 145–6
Hiram Abiff 160
Hoadly, Benjamin 44
Hogarth, William 25, 26, 33, 52, 63,
    71, 83, 92–6, 101, 105, 111, 116,
    117, 188, 234, 241
Holderness, Lord 77, 110
Holland, Lord 85, 111, 241
Home, John 111
Homer 104
Hopkins, Richard 241
Hor, T. 209
Horus 139, 141
Howe, Lady 109
Hund, Baron von 166
Illuminati 166–7, 167–8, 208, 209,
    235

Iscariot, Judas 186
Isis 100, 101, 138, 139, 185, 187
Islam 146
Italy 17, 18, 23

Jainism 146
James I 42, 164
James II 35, 36, 43, 48
Jefferson, Thomas 168, 200
Jennings, Mary 15
Jerome, Jerome K. 7
Jesus Christ 139
'John of Checkers' 62
'John of Henley' 62
'John of London' 62, 109
'John of Magdalen' 62
'John of Melcombe' 62
Johnson, Dr Samuel 39, 54, 79, 103,
    111, 112, 173, 174, 178, 211
Johnstone, Charles 4–5, 6, 7, 8, 115,
    128, 239
Jolivet, Maurice-Louis 99
Jones, John Paul 209
Jones, Louis C. 8, 239
Jonson, Ben 118
Joyce, James 56
Junto or Leather Apron Club 204

Kali 146, 188
Kama Sutra 24, 104, 144, 145, 228,
    234
Kelley, Edward 156
Kemp, Dr Betty 10, 19–20, 235
Khonsu 137
Kidgell, John 52, 123
King, Francis 145, 146, 147, 160
King, Mary 15
Kingston, Duke of 63, 241
Kit–Kat Club 48, 87
Knapton, George 17, 25, 26, 93,
    101, 116–7
Knight, Richard Payne 100
'Knights, The' *see* Monks of
    Medmenhan, The
Knights Templar 146, 160, 166

Lafayette, Marquis De 161, 210
La Forestier, Rene 167
Landor, Walter Savage 224
Langley, Betty 99
Laxcelles, Reverend Robert 230
Lasky, Jesse Jnr. and Silver, Pat 10,
    72, 90, 131, 136, 164, 165, 195,
    240
Laud, Archbishop 42
Lawrence, D.H. 202
Leather Apron Club *see* Junto or
    Leather Apron Club
Le Despenser, Baron *see* Dashwood,
    Sir Francis
Lee, Matthew 226
Le Fanu, Sheridan 220
Lens, Peter 51
Livy 103
Lloyd, Robert 63, 79, 114, 116–7,
    241
Loftus, Lucy 48
Lovat, Lord 85
Lull, Ramon 149
Lurker, Manfred 135
Luttrell, Colonel Henry 171
Luttrell, Simon, Earl of Carhampton
    241
Lyttleton, Lord 125

Macclesfield, Baron 47, 49
McCormick, Donald 9, 240
Machen, Arthur 57, 104
Macpherson, James 111
Magick 157, 161, 167
Mailer, Norman 14
Mann, Thomas 156
Manners, John *see* Granby, Marquis of
Mannix, Dan P. 9, 21, 240
Mansfield, Lord 125, 127
Maple, Eric 9, 51
Mar, Earl of 37
March, Lord *see* Queensberry, Duke
    of
Marlowe, Christopher 156
Martin, Mr 126

Martin, St 167
Mary II 35, 36
Marx, Karl 43
Masham, Mrs Abigail 36
Medmenham Abbey 2, 3, 4, 5, 6, 11, 12, 23, 53, 62, 63, 87, 88, 97–107, 116, 128, 129, 136, 141, 142, 143, 177, 178, 187, 190, 229, 234, 235, 236
Melcombe, Lord *see* Dodington, George Bubb
Mesmer, Dr Franz Anton 155, 161, 210
Middlesex, Grace, Countess of 65
Middleton, Charles 31
Mie-Mie 218–9
Militia Act 20
Miller, Norman 156
Mirabeau, Comte De 161,166
Mithras 100, 138, 142
Mohocks 47
Molay De, Jacques 160
Moliere 16
Mollies 47
Monboddo Lord 5
Monks of Medmenham 25–7, 33, 61–91, 108, 109, 110–1, 117, 120, 122, 123, 128, 154, 177, 184, 215, 221, 233, 234, 237, 239–41
Montagu, Edward Wortley 114
Montagu, George 29
Montagu, Mary 108, 109
Montagu, Lady Mary Wortley 18, 50, 74, 87–8, 89, 108, 199
More, Henry 181
Mozart, Wolfgang 161
Murray, Fanny 83, 90,124
Namier, Sir Lewis 38
Nash, Beau 83
Newcastle, Duke of, 74, 193
New Foundling Hospital for Wits, The 5–6, 239
Nietzsche, Karl 11, 44,103–4, 139–40
North, Lord 193, 195, 206, 223

North Briton, The 49, 95, 118, 119, 120, 122, 126, 127, 129
Northcote, James 32
Nuit 137, 152–3

Oates, Titus 43
'Old Q' *see* Queensberry, Duke of
Order of the Elect Cohens 167
Orford, Earl of 63, 241
Osiris 100, 138, 139, 142
Ovid 106

Page and Ingpen 184
Paine, Thomas 200
Palladio, Andrea, 17
Pallas Athena 188
Palliser, Hugh 31
Paracelsus 61, 148, 154–5, 156, 163
Paris 16
Parliament Act 20
Pars, William 23
Parsifal 152
Parsons, Richard, Earl of Ross 51
Partridge, Burgo 9–10
Pasqually, Martine De 161,167
Payne–Knight, Sir Richard 142
Penn, William 192
Pentagram 153
Perfumed Garden, The 144
Persephone 188
Pierrepoint, Evelyn *see* Kingston, Duke of
Pitt, William 24, 67, 76, 77, 78, 109, 110, 113, 115, 116, 118, 126, 170, 181, 193, 194
Polidori, Dr John 220
Political Register, The 106
Pollard, Arthur Frederick 6–7
Poor Richard's Almanac 202
Pope, Alexander 50, 87, 122
Postgate, Raymond 8–9, 63, 64, 80, 82–3, 117
Potter, Thomas 62, 82–4, 85, 90, 94, 115–6, 118, 122, 128, 215, 241
Powys, John Cowper 58

Praz, Professor Mario 85
Priapus 99–100, 103, 104, 139, 141, 142, 143, 187
Prostitution 54
Public Advertiser, The 81, 106

Qabalah 131, 149–54, 168, 182, 185, 187
Queensberry, Duke of 63, 64, 111, 123, 218, 219, 241
Querouaille, Louise de 42
Quiller-Couch, Sir Arthur 52

Rabelais, François 11, 16, 23, 56–60, 97, 98, 102, 103, 104, 131, 148, 152, 153, 231, 234, 238
Racine, Jean 16
Radcliffe, Ann 45
Ralph, James 75
Ray, Martha 32
Reed, Deborah 204
Regardie, Dr Israel 151–2, 153
Revett, Nicholas 23, 130; *see also* Stuart, James and Revett, Nicholas
Reynolds, Sir Joshua 17
Rhodes, H.T.F. 8, 14, 29, 63, 71, 80, 84, 115, 117, 240
Richardson, Samuel 49
Robespierre, Maximilien 167
Rockingham, Lord 170, 180, 181
Rodger, N.A.M. 29, 31
Roosevelt, President Franklin D. 162
Rosicrucianism 33, 45, 163–9
Rousseau, Jean–Jacques 161, 209
Royal Academy of Art 17
Royal Society 164, 192, 203
Russell, Bertrand 2, 139
Russell, Professor Jeffrey 10–11

Sackville, Lord George 124, 209
'Saint Agnes' 90
St Germain, Count of 162, 166
St Leger, Colonel Jack 51
Saint Martin, Louis Claude de 161
St Petersburg 18

Sandwich, John Montagu, Earl of 1, 2, 4, 5, 6, 18, 26, 28–34, 53, 62, 69, 75, 83, 86, 90, 93, 96, 111, 119, 122–5, 127, 128, 132, 144, 190, 215, 222, 234, 241
'Saunders, Richard' *see* Franklin, Benjamin
Sawyer, Robert 107
Schemers' Club 87
Seb 137
Sekhmet 137, 188
Selwyn, George 5, 7, 63, 84–7, 217–21, 241
Set 207
Seven Years War 109, 110, 192, 204
Sexual mores 53–5
Sheahan, James Joseph 6
Shelley, Mary 220
Shelley, Percy Bysshe 220
Sheridan, Richard Brinsley 213
Shirley, Sewallis 89
Shiva 145, 146
Shiva Sanhita, The 144
Silver, Pat *see* Lasky, Jesse Jnr. and Silver, Pat
Sistine Chapel 16
Skelton Castle 4, 229, 230
Smiles, Samuel 202
Smith, Adam 120
Smollett, Tobias 65, 66, 89, 111, 118
Society of the Bill of Rights 171
Society of Dilettanti 17
Stamp Act 193, 204–5
Stanhope, Sir William 26, 63, 99, 104, 241
Stapleton, Sir Thomas 62, 224, 241
Star & Garter Inn, Pall Mall 17
Stephen, Sir Leslie 6
Sterne, Laurence 4, 56, 229, 230, 231–2
Stoker, Bram 220
Stone, Dr George 124
Strawberry Hill 45, 99
Stuart, James, 'the Old Pretender' 48
Stuart, James and Revett, Nicholas 23

Sublime Society of Beefsteaks 25, 29, 46, 53, 93, 125
Sufis 33, 146, 149
Summers, Rev. Montague 7–8, 14, 106, 235
Swift, Dean 48

Talbot, Lord 68
Talbot, Mr 125–6
Tammuz 138
Tantricism 24, 45, 104, 107, 131, 132, 144–7, 165, 234, 237
Taylor, Professor E.G.R. 156
Templarism 45
Temple, Lord 99, 105–6, 116, 125, 223
Thackeray, William Makepeace 36, 54, 111, 218
Thatched Tavern 18
Theseus 135–6
'Thomas de Greys' 62
'Thomas of London' 62
Thompson, Edward 221
Thompson, Dr Thomas 62–3, 78, 241
Thomson, James 74, 75, 78, 97–8
Tolstoy, Count Leo 161
Towers, Eric 3, 5, 11, 18, 22, 41, 63, 68, 71, 76, 81, 117, 118, 130, 163, 180, 240
Trappe, La 77–8
Tree of Life 151, 152
Trollope, Anthony 43
Trophonius 100, 101, 103, 143
True Briton, The 49
Tucker, John 62, 107, 129, 177–8
Turgot 210
Turkey 18

Vane, Ann 65
Vane, Frances, Countess 88–9
Vanhattan, Henry 241
Vansittart, Arthur 63, 105, 241
Vansittart, Sir Henry 1, 24, 63, 104, 105, 144, 228, 234, 241

Vansittart, Robert 63, 105
Vansittart, Miss 109
Venice 17
Venus 101, 104, 106, 136, 143, 187, 188, 221
Vergennes, Count of 209
Viatta, Auguste 167
Virbius 138
Vishnu 145, 146
Voisine, La 166
Voltaire, François 41, 72, 161, 209

Walcott, Mary 88
Walker, Dr Benjamin 145
Wallace, Sir Richard 218
Walpole, George *see* Orford, Earl of
Walpole, Horace 6, 7, 14, 17, 18, 19, 22, 28, 29, 45, 77, 85, 86, 87, 90, 99, 101–2, 105, 106, 110, 112, 114, 128–9, 184, 217, 235, 239
Walpole, Sir Robert 37, 38, 39, 67, 72, 74, 114
Warburton, Dr William 124
Ward, Ned 5, 46
Washington, George 167, 168, 200, 210
Weber, Max 202
Weishaupt, Adam 166, 167, 168, 208, 235
Westmorland, John Fane, Earl of 16, 241
West Wycombe House 3, 12, 13, 17, 69, 98, 103, 128–31, 135, 136, 141, 200, 227, 235
West Wycombe Park 2, 12, 20, 23, 24, 53, 78, 107, 129–133, 179, 194, 195
    Caves 11, 12, 52, 90, 131–2, 137, 140–1, 143, 153–4, 165, 168, 183–5, 186, 227, 228, 234, 236
    Church of St Lawrence 12, 15, 24, 121, 131, 143, 182, 185–6, 187, 221, 222, 224
    Mausoleum 57, 78, 81, 131, 186–7, 227

Whaley, 'Burn-Chapel' 232
Whaley, Thomas 'Buck' 232
Wharton, Philip, Duke of 26, 44, 45, 47–51, 72, 73, 76, 87, 97, 110, 159
Wharton, Thomas, Marquis of 48
White, T.H. 217–20
Whitehead, Paul 3, 12, 63, 78–82, 83, 90, 106, 110, 111, 142, 177, 178, 179, 196, 221–2, 229, 239
White's Club 18, 25, 41, 53, 86
Wilkes, John 1, 2, 3, 4, 5, 6, 14, 21, 23, 26, 27, 29, 33, 49, 52, 62, 63, 80, 81, 82, 83, 84, 90, 94, 100, 101, 102, 104, 105, 106, 112, 113, 114, 115–21, 122–7, 128–9, 131, 132, 142, 163, 168, 170–6, 177,

190, 206, 207, 208, 212–6, 229, 230, 239
Willermooz, Jean Baptiste 161
Wilson, Colin 10
Windsor, Lady Elizabeth 15
Wood, Ernest 145
Woodfall, Henry 82
Woodforde, Parson 44, 102
Woodruffe, Sir John 144
Wordsworth, William 227
Wraxall, Sir Nathaniel 5

Yarmouth, Lord 218
Yates, Dame Frances 149, 150, 155, 156, 163
Young, Edward 48, 50, 73, 75, 78, 97
York, Duke of 77